W9-AOP-832

LEGACY OF DISCORD

Also by Gil Dorland

Profiles in Democracy: A New Generation of Latin American Leaders

Duty, Honor, Company: West Point Fundamentals for Business Success

The Business Idea: From Birth to Profitable Company

From Idea to Maturity

Path of Terror (novel)

LEGACY OF DISCORD

Voices of the Vietnam War Era

GIL DORLAND

BRASSEY'S
Washington, D.C.

Library of Congress Cataloging-in-Publication Data

Dorland, Gilbert N.
  Legacy of discord : voices of the Vietnam war era / Gil Dorland.
    p. cm.
  Includes index.
  ISBN 1-57488-215-5
    1. Vietnamese Conflict, 1961–1975—United States. 2. Vietnamese Conflict, 1961–1975—Influence. 3. United States—Foreign relations—1945–1989. I. Title.

  DS558 .D63 2001
  959.704'3373—dc21   00-049793

ISBN 1-57488-215-5   (alk. paper)

Printed in the United States of America on acid-free paper that meets the American National Standards Institute Z39-48 Standard.

Brassey's, Inc.
22841 Quicksilver Drive
Dulles, Virginia 20166

First Edition

10 9 8 7 6 5 4 3 2 1

DEDICATION

To my brothers John, Peter, and Richard who
fought in Vietnam—and to our father, Colonel Gil,
who instilled in us the importance of service to country.

And to Isabel

CONTENTS

PREFACE

My war began in late 1963, when Vietnam was a sideshow to the Civil Rights movement in the South and the Cold War against the Soviets. I was a young Army captain barely four years out of the U. S. Military Academy at West Point, the first of four sons in the Dorland family to go to Vietnam, two of us twice. It was little wonder that, by the time all four of us were finally back for good, my mother's hair had turned prematurely gray.

I volunteered for Vietnam for reasons that had nothing to do with falling dominos or the geopolitical rhetoric being slung around Washington. As bizarre as it might seem to today's dot-com generation, I was moved by the adventure of combat. I wanted to know how I would respond when real bullets were fired at me. And, in some very quixotic sense, Vietnam represented a rite of passage to manhood. My first step into the waist-deep rice paddies, however, abruptly ended any romantic notion that I had of war.

My assignment was to advise a fifty-year-old Chinese mercenary who had been fighting since he was ten years old; first against Chinese warlords in southern China, during World War II against the Japanese invaders, with the French colonialists against the Vietminh, and then with the South Vietnamese army against the Viet Cong (VC). His was a personal war; the communists had killed his wife and only son when he migrated south from China. Unable to speak a common language, we communicated by some inexplicable form of telepathy; but it really didn't make any difference. There wasn't a damn thing I could tell him about hunting guerrillas. I was half his age.

It quickly became clear to me that the communists controlled the countryside. When we entered villages, VC flags were lowered and hidden only to be raised minutes after our departure. In the few places that were pacified, we found peasants dying of cholera. The serum sat on the docks in Saigon while government officials waited for payoffs before releasing it. Corruption was pervasive, even when it came to saving their own people. In contrast, in VC-controlled areas, villagers had been vaccinated with serum hauled down the long Ho Chi Minh Trail on the backs of communist soldiers who had set out to win hearts and minds.

As the days grew into weeks, the frustration of chasing a ubiquitous enemy who seemed to vanish just before we appeared gnawed at my patience. The enemy that I had envisioned to be wearing black pajamas and wielding AK47s became swarming insects, sultry heat, and a relentless case of dysentery. I ached for contact with "Charlie," any action to break up the monotony.

To keep my sanity, I became a student of psychology of sorts as I observed my Chinese mentor at work. I was fascinated with the mind behind his inscrutable smile and amazed at his uncanny ability to motivate his men and to terrorize the enemy. I must have brought a bit of comic relief to the old warrior as we sat by the campfire at night, drank pig's blood, and munched on unhatched chicks and bat meat. On occasion, I went to Saigon for a weekend of R&R. The bright lights and bars and prostitutes were the other Vietnam. I read in the newspapers about the war that Secretary Robert S. McNamara said we were winning, but it was not the same war that I saw out in the bush.

My first Vietnam experience ended in late 1964 when I was critically wounded and evacuated by chopper to a makeshift hospital in Saigon. I awoke with a tube inserted through a hole in my trachea and dangling hoses everywhere. General Westmoreland's wife, Kitsy, who was a hospital Gray Lady, sat at my bedside. While I was in the operating room, she had telephoned my parents to tell them that I might not make it. For the next two months, I fought a different kind of war—a war inside myself—until I was healthy enough to return home.

Back in the United States, I watched on television picture after picture of human carnage from strange sounding places, such as Ap Loc and Ia Drang. At some point I had seen enough, and, in 1967, I signed up for a second go at Vietnam. This time I wasn't moved by some abstract romantic illusion; I believed that good leadership could save American lives. A month later, I was standing in line at a processing center outside of Saigon. Somewhere in flight, I had been promoted to the rank of major. I was assigned to the 196th Light Infantry Brigade, a no-frills, tough bunch of soldiers who went about their jobs without media fanfare.

Three months later, on Thanksgiving Day 1967, while commanding a task force in a fierce battle against the 3d North Vietnamese Army (NVA) Regiment in the Que Son Valley, an enemy antitank round hit the armored personnel carrier on which I rode and killed the track commander. The blast threw me into a rice paddy, and 12 tons of steel backed over me. There was no panic, no repentance, and no prayers. My life didn't flash before me. As the tracks climbed up my legs and over my back, all I thought was, "What a fuckin' way to go." Buried under the muck, this time I was sure I was dead.

I was air evacuated to the States and saw another war through the window of a speeding ambulance carrying me through the nation's capital to Walter Reed Hospital—a war uglier than the one from which I had just come. National Guard soldiers in full battle gear patrolled Washington's streets. In the distance, black smoke curled from burning buildings. I knew then that Vietnam had reached the streets of America; no longer was it some far-off spot on a map about which most Americans didn't give a damn.

Strapped to a hospital bed in a ward filled with mangled bodies and minds, the tentativeness of life hit home. Career and financial security lost all significance when they were pitted against such basics as breathing and walking and laughing and making love. I figured that I was on borrowed time and the hell with what others wanted of me. By then, the Tet Offensive had shaken Americans' confidence in their government. McNamara had quietly moved to the World Bank; General Westmoreland had been kicked upstairs to the Pentagon.

In 1968, while on convalescent leave in Nashville, Tennessee, I witnessed one of the most egregious acts that I had ever seen before or experienced since. In front of a packed auditorium at Vanderbilt University, the antiwar activist and Yale University chaplain, Dr. William Sloane Coffin, verbally dismembered a young veteran for voicing that he was proud to have fought for his country in Vietnam. The audience of intelligent Americans was on its feet, hooting and jeering the soldier. I thought that they were going to lynch him. Then, I saw his legs. They were cut off at the thighs—blown off by a VC land mine. I was sick and angry; I ran outside and vomited.

I left the Army shortly thereafter and purchased a one-way ticket to Greece in the hope of decompressing and putting Vietnam behind me. On a tiny isle in the middle of the Aegean Sea, I dove for sponges and sold my catches to the local markets. For a year I yielded to the whims of nature, and my mind broke from marching lockstep within the straight and narrow. Vietnam became a closed book seldom opened—until last year when I started writing about it. Suddenly, the smells and sounds and sights that formed my perspective of that tragic war came rushing back.

The idea of this book was born in a note to me from Gen. Barry McCaffrey about the Vietnam War. "Those were painful years. Our young soldiers deserved better," he wrote. It was the first time I gave thought to writing about the war. But I did not wish to write just another book; the subject had been beaten to death. As I pondered the prospect, I wondered how America's "best and brightest" military, political, and antiwar leaders and journalists of the Vietnam era viewed the war back then, and what do they think now, twenty-five years later? I knew of no single book containing a collection of such divergent, high-powered perspectives.

I began thinking that the most honest way to record their viewpoints would be in interview form. I was very aware, however, that access to controversial, high-profile figures is a formidable task, and unquestionably a primary obstacle for writing a book of direct testimonies. In 1994, I had experienced the trials of maneuvering past gatekeepers to interview all of the presidents of South and Central America, and later, other world leaders. Although most subjects will talk at press conferences and on live television where their comments cannot be misquoted, only a few will speak one on one into a tape recorder. They know the risk of having their responses distorted and manufactured into lies or being confronted with an Oriana Fallaci type, the famous Italian journalist who imposed her own persona during interviews.

I asked Don McKeon at Brassey's, one of the world's oldest military book publishers, if the concept made sense to him. We had been talking off and on for a couple of years about doing a book together. McKeon said that he liked the idea, and would publish the book.

I jotted down a list of obvious people who had played major roles during the war and with whom I would want to meet. Some of the candidates were in their late seventies and eighties, and, most probably, their conversations would be their last published words on the subject. But before I fully committed to the project, I wanted to bounce the idea off of Gen. Alexander Haig. Certainly he would have other names to add to my list, and could open the door to former Secretary of State Henry Kissinger.

I felt relatively confident that I could reach military leaders. In addition to Haig, I knew General Westmoreland from my first tour in Vietnam; my father had been his classmate at the U.S. Military Academy. Gen. Michael Davison, who had commanded the 1970 Cambodian incursion that further ignited the antiwar movement in the United States, had been my regimental tactical officer when I was a cadet at West Point. Gen. Norman Schwarzkopf, also a "West Pointer," along with McCaffrey, had taken the lessons that they had learned in Vietnam to lead Allied forces in Desert Storm.

A number of Washington politicians had served in Vietnam. At the top of my list were Senator John McCain, a Navy fighter pilot and prisoner of war (POW), and Senator John Forbes Kerry, a thrice-wounded Navy lieutenant who had resigned from the military to lead the militant Vietnam Veterans against the War. Any chance of recruiting them for interviews, however, appeared grim. McCain was running for the Republican presidential nomination, and Kerry, reputedly did not talk about his Vietnam experience.

As for journalists, I targeted David Halberstam, the former *New York Times* war correspondent and author of *The Best and the Brightest*, and the Associated Press's Peter Arnett, who had reported from Vietnam from 1962 to after the fall of Saigon in 1975. Both had been maligned by the Kennedy and Johnson administrations for their dispatches that contradicted Washington's optimistic claims of winning the war.

James Webb, a Marine platoon and company commander in Vietnam and later Secretary of the Navy, was a quick call because of his novel *Fields of Fire*, considered one of the best of the Vietnam genre, as was Thomas Polgar, the Central Intelligence Agency (CIA) station chief at the fall of Saigon, and Roger Hilsman, whom President John F. Kennedy had charged with keeping Vietnam from becoming an American war. And, of course, there was former Defense Secretary Robert S. McNamara, who unwittingly lent his name to the term "McNamara's War."

Because of my military background, my major concern was accessing antiwar activists. Clearly, I would be viewed as having a strong bias against them. Of the many activists, two names stood out, Daniel Ellsberg, the former McNamara "whiz kid" who later leaked the Pentagon Papers, and California Senator Thomas Hayden, the founder of the Students for a Democratic Society (SDS) and one of the Chicago Seven. Both of them were indicted by the U.S. Justice Department.

To my surprise, all of the individuals on my initial interview list agreed to sit down with me with the exception of McNamara. After communicating back and forth for over a year, he finally agreed to answer questions but only by extracting responses directly from his books, *In Retrospect* and *Argument Without End*. This I chose not to do. General Westmoreland, who was then eighty-six years old, and

I agreed to talk by telephone. Understandably, he had some difficulty in recalling specific events that occurred thirty-five years ago.

H. R. McMaster, a lieutenant colonel in the U.S. Army and a military historian, was the only person interviewed who did not participate in the war. He was not on my early lists, but several subjects mentioned his book, *Dereliction of Duty*. I contacted him at the 4th U.S. Cavalry in Germany. Because of his distant location, we agreed to conduct the interview via e-mail.

Le Ly Hayslip and Col. Cau Le are the only Vietnamese whom I interviewed, but neither one was on my initial list. As I approached the end of the interviews, however, it became apparent to me that the book needed a South Vietnamese soldier to speak for the unsung heroes of the Army of the Republic of Vietnam (ARVN), and a female Vietnamese villager to talk for the saddest victims of the war, the women and children of Vietnam. Some critics might question my judgment for selecting Hayslip, a former VC whose life story Oliver Stone portrayed in a movie *Heaven and Earth*. My response is that the great majority of the Vietnamese villagers were sympathetic to the VC, whereas most American soldiers, myself included, saw the villagers merely as a backdrop to the fighting. Cau Le, an ARVN regimental commander, was captured at the end of the war and incarcerated in a communist reeducation camp for thirteen years, five of them in solitary confinement.

A last minute pick was Anthony Lake, a former special assistant to Henry Kissinger at the NSC and, two decades later, President Bill Clinton's first national security adviser. I was particularly interested in Lake's perspective of Nixon's secret plan to end the war quickly and whether it entailed threatening Hanoi with nuclear weapons as several books allege.

The lengths of the interviews ranged from forty minutes with Kissinger to eight hours with Arnett. Some of the subjects talked in seamless streams of consciousness; others were precise and wasted few words. I felt that all of the subjects were forthright in their responses and as accurate as their memories could recall.

In editing interviews, I tried to ensure that I did not taint the answers with my own impressions and biases. I want readers to form their own opinions based on the responses alone. To do otherwise would be a distraction and also betray the trust of the individuals who invited me into their confidence. For simplicity's sake, the interviews are arranged in alphabetical order.

Throughout the interviews, I tried to wrap my arms around the question of why the United States, with its massive intellectual re-

sources, neglected to heed the lessons of history. Fundamental decision-making assumptions were gravely flawed because of this failure.
The greatest war machine in the world had its hands tied behind its
back because of the assumption that China would intervene if the
United States took the war north, or, if at the outset, it invaded the
communist sanctuaries in Cambodia and Laos. Was it "triumphism,"
as Kissinger suggested, or hubris, Cold War mentality, or sheer arrogance?

Hollywood, Florida
August 29, 2000

ACKNOWLEDGMENTS

My very special thanks go to Don McKeon, publisher of Brassey's, for covering my flank throughout the mission; to Lt. Col. Julian M. Olejniczak, U.S. Army (Ret.) for guiding me through editorial minefields; to a small circle of compadres for sounding ideas—Terry and Carolyn Anderson; Lt. Col. Clifton Berry, U.S. Army (Ret.); Maj. Gen. Joseph Franklin, U.S. Army (Ret.); June Pulcini; William Raiford; and Fred Rustmann; to the distinguished subjects who agreed to be interviewed; and to my wife, Isabel, for her critical eye and loving support.

PETER ARNETT

*In thirteen years of covering the Vietnam War I never dreamed
it would end the way it did at noon today.*

PETER ARNETT, *Live from the Battlefield*

Peter Arnett picked up the telephone. Within minutes, we were talking as though we had known each other for years. I told him that it would be a friendly interview. He laughed. He knew all too well about friendly interviews; before the subject knows it, he's spilling his guts.

Arnett covered the Vietnam War from 1962 to after the fall of Saigon in 1975. He witnessed America's entry into the conflict and its disgraceful departure. During those thirteen years, as he wrote some four thousand stories describing what he saw, he knew that they had to be unquestionably accurate to pass the scrutiny of the administration and the Pentagon. Too often, his reports were not in sync with Washington's spin about winning the war. His controversial coverage of Vietnam's hinterland falling to communism incurred the fury of President Lyndon B. Johnson and General Westmoreland. John Hohenberg, in his book *The Pulitzer Diaries*, writes of Arnett, "He was spied upon, attacked in the most scurrilous terms by the embassy's men, and treated as if he had been an enemy agent." But, to many of his colleagues, Arnett was and still is considered the quintessential war correspondent of his generation.

His unmistakable voice, transmitting from Baghdad to the world in early 1991 during the Allied bombing siege of the Persian Gulf War, still resonates in my ear. It was a voice that the administration reputedly took as eyewitness to the effectiveness of America's smart bombs on that city and the voice of a man whom his critics called a stooge of Saddam Hussein.

Meeting me at the door to his McLean, Virginia, townhouse, Arnett looks like a one-time welterweight pugilist with a flattened nose. He shows me his home filled with souvenirs from his travels about the globe and a second-floor library lined with floor-to-ceiling shelves crammed with books on Vietnam. Undoubtedly, it's the most exten-

1

sive collection that I've ever seen. We adjourn to the kitchen, a full pot of coffee, and a pumpkin cake.

Arnett was born in a small, old whaling town in southern New Zealand. His first job after high school was at the local newspaper, the *Southland Times*. In 1956, he immigrated to Australia and then caught a tramp steamer destined for England. He disembarked in Thailand and worked three years for an English-speaking newspaper before starting up a weekly newspaper in Laos for the Western community, many of whom were undercover CIA officials and U.S. military personnel in civilian clothes. From Laos, Arnett took a job in Indonesia as an Associated Press (AP) stringer until President Sukarno expelled him for reporting against his regime.

On June 26, 1962, Arnett arrived in Saigon as a full-time AP reporter under the bureau's chief, Malcolm Browne. There he met David Halberstam of the *New York Times* and Neil Sheehan of United Press International (UPI). These four men would form part of a journalistic cabal that the Oval Office later would condemn. At first, they wrote mostly about American policy, but, in late 1962, the Viet Cong rout of the ARVN at Ap Bac changed the focus of the conflict and the nature of their reporting. Until then, the war in Vietnam had consisted of small counterinsurgency operations of minor consequence.

Arnett and the other young reporters took their lead from Col. John Paul Vann, a senior American advisor who, out of frustration, spilled his guts about the ineptitude of the South Vietnamese military. Sheehan would later write *A Bright Shining Lie*, a biography about Vann and a story of the Vietnam War. Vann was a beacon of truth to Arnett, but his main source of material was his own two eyes. Arnett says that he spent a good seventy-five percent of his time out of Saigon in the boonies with the troops, a firsthand witness to the war.

It takes only a couple of words from me to spring him loose. The inexhaustible flow of words over the kitchen table leaves little doubt in my mind about his doggedness and competitive zeal. The first pot of coffee is dry. He asks if I want more. I glance at my watch; it's noon and we've been at it for four hours and haven't reached the 1968 Tet Offensive yet. There's still seven more years to cover. Four hours later, he finally wraps up his Vietnam experience. I ask him about "Operation Tailwind," a recent television piece that he narrated on CNN and that cost him his job. His voice ratchets up an octave; the subject hits a raw chord.

"CNN has a special unit that does investigative, magazine-type journalism," Arnett says. "I narrated a segment about a Special Forces team in 1970 that allegedly went into Laos and used nerve gas at a village where there were known American defectors. The CNN producers were convinced that what seemed to be unimpeachable secret sources were accurate. I just narrated the piece. It went on the air; the story got a lot of publicity. The Pentagon denied it and put out a whole volume of documents to support their denial. So what do I do, fall on my sword? No. I'm not going to have forty years of reporting washed down the drain. The point of my whole career is that I only report what I see. That's been the history of my life. If I see something and report it, it's probably true. This one I didn't see, and I narrated it. But on my tombstone, it'll say: He should have practiced what he preached."

He laughs, but there's a note of regret. After eight hours of listening and two full pots of coffee, I say goodbye. As I open the door to the rental car parked at the curb, Peter smiles and shouts from his front porch, "I don't envy your transcribing all that."

General Westmoreland accused the reporters in Vietnam as being too young and inexperienced to cover the war.

That criticism was first voiced by the Kennedy people. This was long before Westy [Westmoreland] got there. In 1962, when President Kennedy called the *New York Times* to get David Halberstam the hell out of Vietnam, the argument was that David was too young and inexperienced. Critics like Joseph Alsop said that Malcolm Browne, Neal Sheehan, and I were also too young and inexperienced. Christ, the reporters who landed with American troops at Iwo Jima and Normandy in World War II were all our age. The reporters who covered the beginning of World War II were kids. You had to be young and virile and bold enough to go out in the field and get your ass shot at. What we lacked in overall knowledge of military warfare, we asked the commanders. We lived the war day and night for the entire time we were there. That's how we got our expertise. An experienced journalist in his forties didn't want to hump through the boonies with a bunch of eighteen-year-old soldiers. I wouldn't do it today at my age. That was the thing that always irritated me about Joe Alsop. He flew by helicopter all over. He never walked.

So you felt that you and your colleagues were adequately prepared?

Absolutely. Not only did Halberstam graduate from Harvard, he covered the Civil Rights movement in the South and the Congo War

before he went to Vietnam. He had been around. Malcolm Browne
had graduated from Brown University, covered the Cuban campaign,
and had been in Vietnam four years before Westy arrived. When
Westy took command in 1964, I was thirty years of age. I had been
in Southeast Asia for eight years, and had been all over Vietnam. I was
married to a Vietnamese woman. My brother-in-law was a colonel in
the Vietnamese army. I knew John Paul Vann and most of the American advisors. What did he mean that we were too young and didn't
know anything? Westy was wrong.

**How vulnerable was the press to its own bias and to reporting
inaccurate information?**

In the case of the Vietnam press corps, it very quickly removed
itself from national security sort of issues or issues of patriotism.
Certainly Halberstam, Browne, and Sheehan and myself were very
pragmatic about what we saw and insisted on getting to the bottom
of the issues to understand what was happening. If we were talking
about corruption, who was corrupt? If we were talking about incompetence, where was it happening? An almost driving compulsion to
flesh out the whole picture in a professional journalistic way charac-
terized all of the reporting. You have to look at covering the Vietnam
War as sort of covering the U.S. political scene. It had never been
that way before because up to the time of the Vietnam War, there
had either been government censorship, as there was in World War
II and for a time in Korea, or self-censorship. The vast majority of
reporting in World War II was aimed at building up national pride
and enthusiasm.

Vietnam was different?

I think Vietnam was covered from a much more professional viewpoint. When General Westmoreland told us to get on the team, we
didn't understand what that meant. In World War II, it was clear that
the team meant Team America. But how could we when American
advisers in the field were telling us that the [President Ngo Dinh]
Diem regime had no chance of winning? Why the hell were we there?
The Diem regime was corrupt and undemocratic. Was that the team
we were supposed to support? Vietnam was run by a bunch of venal
dictators lining their pockets. We didn't feel that we had any interest
in sustaining the Vietnamese cause as it was at that time. Appeals
to patriotism flat didn't work. U.S. Ambassador Frederick Nolting
and President Kennedy claimed to have a bigger view that involved

anticommunism. But we didn't seen any anticommunism in the South Vietnamese government.

Did you believe from the outset that American effort in Vietnam was for a lost cause?

In the early stages of American involvement, I thought that we could whip the communists. But when Westmoreland took command, hubris set in, and I and other reporters changed our minds. Westy was the guy who was given the task of essentially managing the American ground effort. While Johnson called the shots, it was Westy's search-and-destroy tactics that were being instituted. As far as the Pentagon was concerned, Westy was the guy who was writing the budget and beating the drum.

Why did you go to Vietnam?

It had nothing to do with ideology; I went there to cover the story. At that time, I was sympathetic with what the U.S. was doing to stop the communists. But that changed. My wife was a hardened anticommunist. She would criticize me when I said anything against Westmoreland. I hid my apprehensions in covering Vietnam as a story. I took the same risks as the GIs. My mission was to go out on military operations and report back to two thousand AP-subscriber newspapers about their hometown guys. What were they doing? What was happening to them? We put as many names in our reports as we could. We wrote about American GIs going into action and about their bravery.

Did the press make up stories at hotel bars in Saigon?

You have to look at the media in different levels. If the *New York Times* printed a story that was different, all the rest of us would go out to see what was going on. If I did a story like "The Company That Didn't Want to Fight," all the other media like *Time* magazine and UPI would check it out for accuracy. So the mainstream media checked each other out. We couldn't write a story in a bar. If you wrote a story in a bar, you would be fired. We were under so much pressure in the mainstream media that we couldn't get away with lying. There were feature service reporters who invented heroic incidents that didn't happen. And there were a couple of column writers who invented accounts about Special Forces that never occurred. But overall, we simply reported what we saw and were told, and then assessed its truth. We did this for years. I think, in retrospect, most of what we wrote has held up.

You were in Vietnam off and on for thirteen years?

I started in 1962 as part of the AP bureau, and won a Pulitzer Prize in 1965 for which I felt very privileged. It was such an enormous honor to win an award that seemed totally outside the frame of possibilities. I felt I had to give something back in return for it. It was a dangerous war to cover. We had members in the AP bureau who were killed, and seventeen got wounded. But people like Pulitzer-winning AP photographer Horst Faas and myself went out because it was our commitment to the soldiers to document their efforts to win the war. Any doubts I had about what I saw, I tried to analyze them in terms of reality and run them by people like John Paul Vann. Anything that I wrote, I took great care to make sure it was accurate. I had a commitment to myself to be accurate.

Did you, as a reporter, question the underlying reason for the United States being in Vietnam, the domino theory?

I had been to Cambodia, Thailand, and Malaysia. I had lived in Indonesia. I didn't buy into the domino mindset because, in Thailand, they had contained the guerrilla insurrection in the north. The Thais were clearly not going to accept communist exploitation. I don't think for a minute that America's efforts in Vietnam saved Indonesia from communism. However, these were for editorials written by our analysts in Washington and New York. We were field reporters who wrote about what we observed. We didn't write about the overall big picture.

McNamara and Westmoreland wrote in their books that America's strategy was restrained by the assumption that the Chinese would intervene if we took the war north.

It's all right for McNamara or Westmoreland to make an issue of that now, but China was not an issue then. North Vietnam didn't need Chinese advisers; they needed Chinese weapons. There was no indication that Hanoi would have asked for China's ground force help. They certainly didn't during the French War. There was no action in Laos or Cambodia, or even in North Vietnam, that would have brought China into the war. That was a lot of rubbish. Don't forget, when China invaded Vietnam in 1979, the Vietnamese whipped their butts. I think the NVA would have whipped our butts had we ventured deep into North Vietnam.

Was Vietnam McNamara's War?

At a press conference I covered in 1964, McNamara said that he was proud that it was McNamara's War. As far as we were concerned, he was the war's greatest promoter; he was the architect of the war. McNamara came to Vietnam often. I covered almost every press conference he ever gave. He praised the war effort and denied that there were reverses. He was unconscionable. He would infuriate us. Military officers, who, two hours earlier, had briefed him on negative appraisals, would later hear him say the exact opposite when he was leaving country. We knew that because we knew the briefing officers.

Did you report this?

There was a disconnect in what we personally felt about McNamara and what we could say as reporters. We were limited on how critical we could be because there were no high-ranking officers directly criticizing McNamara. They would tell us off the record that McNamara sucks. Those who did express negative opinions, like John Paul Vann, saw their careers go down the tubes. It was very difficult for us as reporters on the scene to counter McNamara. It was impossible to say we were losing when McNamara could argue that the statistics showed that we were winning. It was like Westmoreland, through his aides, complaining that I wrote all my analyses without Westmoreland's viewpoint. Why should I? The viewpoint of Westmoreland was given nightly at the 5 o'clock follies briefing. I was an independent observer who reported what I saw. I didn't want Westmoreland's opinion that we were winning. I wanted to see proof. I wanted my pieces to be totally factual and based on reasoned analyses that I trotted by everyone that I knew in country. If Westmoreland wanted me to see him, I would have done it. But he never asked me. I often thought it was a pity that I never had a chance to sit down and talk with the guy. I believe Westmoreland to this day is convinced that I did all my reports sitting at a bar in the Constellation Hotel.

Didn't the press have an obligation to confront McNamara when he claimed we were winning the war?

Our colleagues in Washington should have confronted him. But the Washington press basically took the side of the administration. We in the field were considered mavericks—discontented, disillusioned, and uncontrollable reporters who weren't tuned into the real picture. That was McNamara's and LBJ's [Lyndon B. Johnson's] view of us because they had all the facts at hand. We couldn't call McNamara a liar. We could question his judgment, cover the battles, and prove that the war wasn't going bloody well. Who was going to listen to Peter Arnett? Hell, Bob McNamara had run Ford Motor Company. That was one of the great frustrations of the war for us. We knew that the war was going badly but couldn't do anything about it.

Lyndon Johnson also said that the war was going well.

Exactly. How can a reporter in the field compete with a presidential dictate? We couldn't. We were left in the field witnessing the downturn, the stalemate, and eventually the total chaos of the American effort. It wasn't until the Tet Offensive that the truth started to seep into the consciousness of the American people. The Tet Offensive was a godsend. We were able in one moment to explain that we weren't winning the war. The VC were inside the U.S. Embassy in Saigon and in the front yards of reporters that had never gone out into the fields. Suddenly, the war was in their faces.

Westmoreland claimed we won the Tet Offensive. He said that the propaganda from the press was the reason why the American people perceived we had lost.

How do you write it any other way? There's gunfire all over the city. Parts of Saigon were burning. Gen. Fred Weyand [Commander, II Field Force] said he blew half of Cholon away; killed hundreds of innocent people. How the hell do you not write about it? The only way to do it was to hit it hard. The media suddenly was a factor for Washington to deal with. The communists were smart enough to figure out the media. Johnson and McNamara never did. They criticized us but never really read what we were writing—what John Paul Vann and others in the thick of combat were saying.

The Tet Offensive showed America's vulnerability?

And how powerful the communists really were. Like the piece I did on Ben Tre in February 1968, a provincial capital in the Mekong Delta of about thirty-five thousand people. I went to Ben Tre with half a dozen other reporters. I had the advantage over the others because I had been there several times before the Tet Offensive, and I knew all the advisers. The other reporters wrote about a great victory for the Americans. But the whole town was obliterated; at least five hundred civilians were killed. How? We had to blow away the city to defend a small American compound and the province chief. Americans had spent millions of dollars on Ben Tre since 1961. We had trained Vietnamese militia, and, in the end, we killed five hundred people in the city to prevent the communists from taking it over. It was ludicrous. I reported, "We had to destroy the town to save it." That summed it all up. For years, I was told that I had invented that story. I didn't invent it. If I could invent something like that, I wouldn't be in the news business. I would be a prominent fiction writer.

Did you ever suggest in any of your dispatches that Westmoreland step down?

No, I didn't have the temerity. In the AP, you couldn't do that. Mainstream American media at the time was very tame. If you look at David Halberstam's writings, they were relatively tame for most of the war effort until he started writing *The Best and the Brightest*. By 1967, my articles challenged mainstream media's version of events. I knew then that it would be difficult for me to be heard above the White House spin, and the spin from Westmoreland and reporters who supported the war effort.

So what did you do?

I waited for a story that would reflect my assessment of the war. Hill 875 in the Dak To Valley in November 1967 was one of them. We had heard that a battalion was trapped on Hill 875. I managed to get in with the relief force. I found most of the officers and soldiers killed or badly wounded. That was a hell of a story, a really dramatic, gut-wrenching report. It received headlines all over the world. The piece opened by saying that the living and the dead were the same gray color on Hill 875; the only way you could tell the difference was when the rockets came in. Those living would scramble for the bunkers, and the dead didn't move. That was a way for me to explain what was really happening and how difficult it was to win.

You wrote in 1969 about American units that didn't want to fight?

Many of my colleagues in Saigon said that was rubbish. I would never write a report based on hearsay. On this one occasion, we lost a photographer and a battalion commander when a helicopter crashed in the jungles. An American infantry company was ordered to go into the jungles and find the downed helicopter. The company commander flat refused to obey the order. I was there and wrote about this incident. It was an important story because it really gave a sense of what was happening within the military and how it was coming apart at the seams. I named everyone involved to give concrete evidence. These were the stories that made an impact about how the war was disintegrating. These were the examples that could break through the administration's spin about the war.

Did you cover the My Lai incident?

The My Lai massacre was something that had nothing to do with the media. The press totally missed the story; we didn't know about it. That whole episode came out in the military court-martial. The press covered the trial.

In Michael Lind's book, *Vietnam: The Necessary War*, he criticizes you for being antiwar?

I am antiwar. I covered eighteen wars and I don't like them. They're dramatic journalism, but I don't pray each morning for a war. And when I go to a war, I want it over. I wished Vietnam had been over much sooner than it was. When they criticize me as being antiwar, do they think that I'm some sort of an idiot? Talk with [Gen.] Norm Schwarzkopf and [Gen.] Colin Powell; they're antiwar, too. Who the hell wants to be pro war?

Did you ever lose your objectivity in reporting?

I couldn't contain my anger during the Cambodian incursion in 1970. I rode on a tank with the 11th Cavalry into a village in the middle of a rubber plantation called Snuol. There were dead bodies of women and kids all over the place from air strikes. I didn't see any NVA bodies. American GIs went crazy looting stores before torching them. I really felt disgusted. I thought that I had had it; my objectivity was in shambles. The communists didn't loot; they didn't steal from the peasants. They wanted their support. The ARVN troops looted, and then the Americans did. I sent the story home. Two days later, I was informed that the AP home office had killed the story because it didn't characterize American forces favorably. UPI and *Newsweek* ran the story. Two months later, I left Saigon with my family for the United States.

You returned to Vietnam?

In 1971, I returned to write a story about the drug situation and the degree to which GIs were involved. Vendors were selling heroin powder outside of U.S. bases. It was a dollar a shot. The heroin was flown in on Vietnamese Air Force aircraft from Laos. The CIA was flying it in from mountainous areas where the Maoist-resistance forces were fighting the communists because it was the only thing that the anti-Maoists could sell for money. It was madness. I stayed in Vietnam for about four months. I went back in 1973 to write a series on the deterioration of the war and the buildup of North Vietnamese involvement. The Ho Chi Minh Trail was a four-lane highway. There was no U.S. bombing. I forecasted then that it was just a matter of time before the country fell to the communists.

You returned again in 1975?

The day the central highland's province capital of Ban Me Thuot collapsed, I went on record then that Saigon would fall by the end of April, which was picked up by several of the media. I helped get my wife's parents out of Vietnam, but I decided to cover the bloody takeover. I really didn't give much thought about what would happen to me.

Why did you stay in Vietnam?

I stayed in Saigon for the same reason I kept going back. I felt I owed it to the AP to stay. I had covered the war from the beginning and wanted to be there at the end. In my heart of hearts, I thought that it was my duty to stay as a reporter.

What happened during those last days of Saigon?

On the night of April 29, there were only twenty or thirty mixed nationality media left. I could see the city disintegrating. By early morning of the 30th, the final hope of leaving was gone because the last helicopters had left the embassy's rooftop. It was over. On that early morning, there was gunfire and renegade groups of South Vietnamese troops smashing windows, looting, and throwing their uniforms away. There were a few dead civilians in the streets who had been freshly killed. I put two grenades in each pocket and grabbed a pistol and thought, "Fuck it." I wasn't going to let the mob get me. I wouldn't let some crazy ARVN soldier shoot me. I would dump the grenades and pistol if the North Vietnamese showed up. I stopped by the American Embassy. It was being looted by a mob.

By midmorning, the streets were empty; the place was dead quiet. We all had a real sense that the takeover was coming.

Then the Viet Cong entered the city first?
Yeah, wearing black-uniforms and carrying VC flags. The NVA followed shortly afterwards. I was standing on Tudo Street in the middle of downtown Saigon watching big Russian trucks filled with NVA soldiers. They all wore pith helmets and carried communist flags. They were just sitting there gawking at the big buildings. By that time, people came out of their homes and watched. I ran from there to my office, sent a quick bulletin, and then ran to the presidential palace. A few minutes earlier, the tanks had crashed through the wall. I was very relaxed. I climbed on a tank, took pictures, and introduced myself to NVA officers. It was obvious that they had orders to get along with everyone. I was absolutely amazed. After all these years, the war was finally over.

What was going through your mind?
I thought about all the sacrifices, the over two billion dollars in cost, the sixty thousand Americans dead, and over a million Vietnamese dead. And for what, an uncontested, methodical, and highly disciplined takeover? I felt like weeping. I drove out to the airport and stood at the McNamara Bridge where a Viet Cong kid had attempted to kill McNamara. I saw a battalion-sized unit jogging toward me with all their gear. Jog, jog, jog. They carried mortars and machine guns, right past me. That was how they went through the jungle; that was how they got to Saigon. Jog, jog, jog in the hundred degree heat with all their gear. What a sight. That really brought it home to me.

Did the communists detain you?
They didn't touch me; they didn't touch anyone for a while. They let us send our dispatches to the States, then one day they closed down our communications. Eight days later, they opened up our lines, but this time they censored our cables. Within three weeks, they started to pick up South Vietnamese military officers and political types and sent them to reeducation camps.

No bloodbaths?
That was very interesting because Washington promoted the idea that there would be bloodbaths. From what I could see, there were

no bloodbaths, no mass executions. One particular official I had known for years claimed that he had evidence of mass executions. He was trying to tell that to all the journalists in a last desperate effort. It wasn't a classic communist takeover. Had Joseph Stalin been running it, they would have killed millions. They basically pushed people out of society and put them in reeducation camps. That was what I reported. That was the end of my Vietnam career.

MIKE DAVISON

Almost universally the troops wanted to know why we hadn't invaded Cambodia sooner. And they couldn't understand why the newspapers and magazines at home weren't more appreciative to the danger and sacrifice that they were making in the jungles of Cambodia.

—INTERVIEW WITH *The Hurricane*, SEPTEMBER 1970

On April 30, 1970, thirty thousand Allied forces under the command of Lt. Gen. Michael S. Davison crossed the border into the Fishhook of Cambodia in reprisal to increased attacks by the NVA against the pro-Western government of Lon Nol. In vintage Nixon style, the two-pronged attack had been shrouded in secrecy. Even Defense Secretary Melvin Laird and Secretary of State William Rogers, who had opposed a Cambodian incursion, were unaware of the plan until the last minute.

The political maneuverings and tangled relationships in Washington that led to the president's decision to commit U.S. troops in Cambodia were bizarre. In his book, *The White House Years*, Kissinger described Nixon as being consumed at times by "maniacal eruptions of irrationality." But, with all the secret discussions weighing the pros and cons of an invasion, the White House underestimated the reaction of participants in the antiwar movement, who had been relatively quiet since Nixon had started pulling troops out of Vietnam.

General Davison, who had taken command of Field Force II in mid-April 1970, was given seventy-two hours' notice by Gen. Creighton W. ("Abe") Abrams, commander of the Military Assistance Command, Vietnam (MACV), to plan for and assemble a joint force of U.S. and ARVN troops to destroy NVA supply depots along the Vietnamese border in Cambodia and to knock out the Central Office for South Vietnam (COSVN), the mobile headquarters for enemy activity in Vietnam. Abrams himself, just hours earlier, had received a back-channel communication from Kissinger to initiate the crossover operation.

Despite all the political turmoil in Washington, Davison's fighting force cleaned out the Cambodian sanctuaries and set back NVA offensive capabilities for months. It was a remarkable feat under the short-notice conditions, yet it was played out in the United States as a broadening of the war after the president had promised to pull out.

Four days after Nixon's April 30 television announcement of the Cambodian incursion, National Guardsmen fired rifles into an unarmed crowd of students at Kent State University and killed four youths. Five days later, one hundred thousand demonstrators marched on the White House to unleash an antiwar uproar that would eventually lead to Congress cutting off aid to South Vietnam and to America's first military defeat.

On a positive note, had the incursion not occurred, the communists would have had a lot more guns and bullets to shoot at American soldiers. Captured enemy material amounted to almost 23,000 individual weapons, enough to equip seventy-four NVA infantry battalions, and 143,000 rockets, mortars, and recoilless rifle rounds, equivalent to fourteen months of firepower. The count might have been even greater had the Allied forces not been forced to withdraw because of political pressure from Washington.

I first laid eyes on Mike Davison forty years ago. A West Pointer, class of 1939, he was my cadet regimental tactical officer at the Military Academy, a bird colonel then—tall, lean, and ruggedly handsome. Unfortunately, the occasion of our brief encounter was not pleasant for me, a young cadet. I had been caught AWOL from an 0545-hours reveille formation, the wee morning hour when the academy starts its day. After being found guilty and levied a punishment of two months' confinement to my room and forty-four hours of walking the concrete area in front of Central Barracks, I saluted, about faced, and started to leave when Davison asked me a question that has stuck with me ever since.

"And how many reveilles did you miss, Mister Dorland?" I turned around. "One hundred two, sir," I replied, braced for the worst. A grin crept onto his face, one of the types that tell you that he had been there too.

Instantly, I recognized the grin and the tall, lean, soft-spoken retired four-star general, remarkably fit for eighty-four, on the steps of his Arlington home. We adjourn to his study. I mention our first encounter at West Point, but he doesn't recall it. Mrs. Davison sticks her head in the doorway and says that she's going out to a book-reading club meeting. He smiles and tells her to enjoy herself. I turn the recorder on. I'm interested not only in the Cambodian incursion but also his perspectives on the Vietnam War from his perch at the Pentagon during the McNamara years and from his position as chief of staff to Adm. John ("Jack") S. McCain, Jr., Senator John McCain's father, at Pacific Command in Hawaii.

You were closely involved in the buildup of American forces in Vietnam?

In 1966, I was on the staff at the Pentagon responsible for organizing and shipping units to Vietnam. Gen. Harold K. Johnson, the Army's Chief of Staff for whom I worked, thought that we should call up the National Guard and Reserves. We were beginning to run out of people to send to Vietnam, and he believed that the call-up would get the American people involved in the war because there was a lack of public understanding about what was going on in Vietnam. I can recall late one Saturday night General Johnson being very upset, which was unusual for him. He had just returned from a White House briefing with President Johnson, where he again had requested that the National Guard and Reserves be activated. He said that President Johnson refused to consider such an act, even though the president thought it was vital to succeeding in Vietnam. General Johnson told me that he thought he should resign from the service. I told him that I understood his feelings, but, speaking from the point of view of the Army, we didn't want him to leave because he provided the leadership the Army needed.

Yet General Johnson went to his grave regretting that he didn't resign.

I know. In hindsight, I wouldn't have recommended that he not resign. I think that his resignation might have carried a strong message to the White House. But, at that time, I was just thinking about the well-being of the Army. General Johnson was a wonderful chief of staff.

Should the chiefs of staff have resigned en masse when McNamara and President Johnson refused to heed their advice?

The president is the commander-in-chief of the armed forces. Under the Constitution, the chiefs are subordinate to him and must obey his orders. In my opinion, resignation is an alternative to be exercised only in the most serious and justifiable circumstances. I do not know the content of "their advice" to the president, so I cannot make a judgment other than my comment on Gen. Harold K. Johnson's decision when viewed in retrospect.

McNamara and his "whiz kids" were reputed to be difficult for professionals in uniform to work for?

Most of my colleagues and I saw the "whiz kids" [young Defense Department civilian intellectuals] as very smart and energetic but lacking in basic knowledge of the armed services and matters affecting operational and tactical doctrine and training. On occasion, their decisions were inappropriate or disruptive. As a consequence, it got to be pretty damn difficult. For example, in carrying out my responsibilities as acting assistant chief of staff for force development, it was apparent that we needed to expand the use of helicopters, which necessitated opening up a second aviation school to train more pilots. We badly needed helicopter pilots. Yet McNamara rejected our proposal because his "whiz kids" had recommended against it. His making these kind of absurd decisions irritated the hell out of us.

Did you believe McNamara's claims in 1966 that we were winning the war?

As the acting assistant chief of staff for force development, I was actively engaged in organizing the units to be sent to Vietnam. I was reasonably up to date on operations being conducted there by our forces. At that time, it seemed clear that we were making progress but that we yet had quite a way to go before we could say we were winning the war. The North Vietnamese attacks in Tet 1968 were illustrative of this.

From your viewpoint at the Pentagon, did you buy Washington's rationale for sending American soldiers to Vietnam?

In the context of a national security policy to prevent the expansion of communism in Asia and to preserve the freedom of South Vietnam, I favored sending our forces there. But, I believed it necessary to send adequate forces to get the job done. Adequate forces should include activating the National Guard and Army Reserves, not only to enhance the early availability of forces but also to communicate clearly to the public in local areas across the country the seriousness of our commitment.

Did you support General Westmoreland's recommendations to build up the number of American troops to over five hundred thousand?

Yes, I did. Westmoreland was the person charged with the mission of defeating the North Vietnamese and preserving South Vietnam. His estimate of the forces needed was, I presumed, based on his estimate of the enemy situation confronting him. I had no reason to contradict him. He was the man on the ground, not me.

Did you believe then that ARVN could win the war without American soldiers on the ground?

In 1966, based on what I knew about ARVN through various reports, I did not think ARVN could succeed without U.S. forces being present. However, every effort should be made to enhance ARVN's combat capability and availability of forces so that the role of U.S. forces could be diminished and eventually withdrawn.

While you were at the Pentagon, did you believe we could win the war under the territorial and political restrictions imposed by the Oval Office on the military?

I didn't know all the details of the restrictions, but it did seem to me, as I understood them, that they made the task of winning much tougher and perhaps unattainable.

Apparently, we didn't learn our lesson in Vietnam. Recently, there has been much discussion about the president micromanaging the war in Kosovo from the Oval Office.

I agree. President Clinton had established a "no casualties policy" in Kosovo, whereas the military wanted to conduct the operation another way. By having a "no casualties policy," we were in effect limiting the application of military force. This meant that the Air Force was restricted from going below 14,000 feet, which was not a very effective altitude to support ground forces. Clinton said he did this to save American lives, but, at the same time, it prevented us from achieving the objective—which was to stop ethnic cleansing. The net effect of the "no casualties policy" allowed the Serbs to escalate ethnic cleansing prior to when the bombing started. Gen. Wes [Wesley K.] Clark strongly objected, but was overruled by President Clinton.

Did you assume in 1966 that China would intervene if we invaded North Vietnam with American troops, as McNamara and many others did?

We had talked about the possibility of China. I was of the opinion that, to succeed, we should apply the forces necessary to get the job done, which meant taking the war north and invading the Cambodian and Laotian sanctuaries. I thought there was a possibility that China might intervene. But if we could clear the North Vietnamese out of the sanctuaries, push their forces north of the border, and seek a peace agreement, there might not be an intervention. This would not be an effort to invade North Vietnam and take Hanoi but to contain North Vietnamese forces within their own territory.

Prior to your taking command of the Cambodian incursion in 1970, you were at Pacific Command in Hawaii?

I was chief of staff to Adm. Jack McCain, who was the CINCPAC [Commander-in-Chief, Pacific]. I was responsible for coordinating the staff activities within the headquarters.

The Oval Office reputably kept the Cambodian operation under tight wraps. Not even the Secretary of State knew about the invasion until after it was launched. Were you aware of plans for an American-led incursion into Cambodia while you were at Pacific Command?

No. I can't even recall any messages or conversations concerning a Cambodia operation. When I say any messages, there were a lot of back-channel messages that went directly from the White House or the Pentagon to Abrams in Vietnam. Admiral McCain didn't necessarily hear about them.

Did the Oval Office typically bypass the military chain of command and micromanage the war from Washington?

I wouldn't say that the Oval Office typically bypassed the military chain of command, but I know, from my time as CINCPAC's chief of staff, that this frequently occurred. Usually, the commanding general of MACV would inform CINCPAC of the messages that came directly to him.

Besides the Pacific Command, there were also MACV and the Pentagon, not to mention the Oval Office, directing operations in Vietnam. Were there too many chefs in the kitchen?

Yes, there were too many chefs in the kitchen. This condition could, as you might imagine, create contradiction, confusion, and cause actions not necessarily in accord with the local tactical situation. But, McCain and Abrams had an excellent relationship and could deal effectively with any major problems that came up.

When did you take command of Field Force II in Vietnam?
I reported to Vietnam in late March 1970 and assumed command of Field Force II in mid-April. At the time, Field Force II was comprised of two American divisions and a cavalry regiment, an Australian and New Zealand task force, and a Thai division. It was strictly an operational command, elastic in size and configuration depending on the mission. Shortly after taking command, Gen. Creighton Abrams gave me 72 hours' notice to clean out NVA supply depots in the Cambodian sanctuaries.

Surely President Nixon must have known that a Cambodian incursion would stir up the antiwar movement? Up until then it was relatively quiet.
I really can't address that.

As commander, you must have been aware that the operation would send a signal to the American people that we were expanding the war?
I had no thoughts about expanding the war. My thoughts were all about the benefit that we could derive from cleaning out the supply dumps and preventing the NVA from using the sanctuaries as rest areas before sending units into South Vietnam.

Did your troops question why the people back in the United States were violently opposed to the Cambodian operation?
They asked why the people back home didn't understand what they were doing. That was the common question.

How did you answer that?
I told them that I didn't know. I had no way of knowing.

Did the antiwar demonstrations affect your soldiers' morale?
One should understand that when we crossed over into Cambodia, at the platoon level, the squad sergeants were all "shake and bake" noncommissioned officers (NCOs). They were guys who were drafted and, in basic training, picked out as having the potential for being an NCO. The only people with two or more years of service

were the company commanders, the first sergeants, and maybe one or two of the platoon sergeants. Because of that, there had been some degree of morale problems. But at the infantry company level, the soldiers were more concerned about their buddies in the foxholes next to them. Morale could have been higher if the media had focused on positive aspects of their accomplishments rather than on the negatives. The press loved to jump on the few exceptions and magnify them. And, too often, the media took examples of people back in the rear areas with a lot of free time and applied them to fighting soldiers.

Most of those soldiers were sons of blue-collar workers.

You're right. That was one of the great tragedies of the Vietnam War. College students should not have been excused from service because he or she had achieved more academically than kids with only high school diplomas. It should have been mandatory that all citizens be equally treated as far as service was concerned. Selective service should have drawn on everybody without exception and eventually did include college students.

Did you have a drug problem with your troops?

There was drug usage amongst the troops in Vietnam. It was a much more prevalent condition among the rear area troops than those in the combat units. However, I did start a drug suppression program in Field Force II to include a rehabilitation center at my headquarters, in which soldiers who had become addicted to heroin would be treated and hopefully relieved of their addiction.

[Davison pulls out a February 8, 1971, letter that he wrote to then retired Gen. Hamilton H. Howze eight months after Davison's withdrawal from Cambodia and hands it to me. The letter was in response to an article Howze had written in the *Army* magazine of January 1971. Davison says that this was how he felt at the time about the morale of U.S. troops. I read it aloud.]

"Recently there has been a spate of press stories about deteriorating morale and discipline. I am pleased to note that you don't believe much of what you read in the press. I think that it is safe to say that the press is distorting the situation to suit its editorial purposes. Certainly no soldier in his right mind enjoys getting shot at or, indeed, relishes fifteen days at a time humping in the jungle. Certainly he gripes about the "lifers." So what else is new? Well, the facts are that this "sloppy, surly, undisciplined" soldier continues to go out in the jungle, follow orders, and seek out the NVA. He does not go with eagerness nor enthusiasm that marked the performance of our soldiers in 1965–66, but he goes. And it is amazing that he is still a good soldier considering all those who are on the sidelines telling him what a poor soldier he is."

Your orders were clear as to how long Field Force II would remain in Cambodia and how deep you could penetrate?
Initially, there was no time restriction. But, about the first of June, I was told to withdraw by June 30. As for penetration, we were limited to 15 kilometers, which was later expanded to 30 kilometers. However, if a tactical situation arose where my troops were threatened, I sure as hell would go in deeper than 30 kilometers.

Did you request to go deeper into Cambodia?
Yes. I discussed this with Abe [Abrams]. But 30 kilometers was it.

This was a political decision?
Yes, I believe so.

At any time did you ask to extend the time limitation?
By the first of June, the number of caches uncovered was starting to decline. By the end of June, the number had dropped appreciably to where it raised the question whether it was worth staying there. The answer was probably no. We had captured enough supplies to prevent three NVA divisions from operating for a year.

Did you know where the supply dumps were prior to crossing into Cambodia?
We knew the location of COSVN headquarters. It was easily identifiable. However, the supply dumps were heavily concealed in the jungles. Our guys were damn good at uncovering them as attested to by the vast amounts of supplies that we found.

Had there been any discussion of keeping American troops in the sanctuaries to prevent the NVA from returning after Field Force II withdrew?
No. I presumed that the political feeling back in Washington was not to occupy another country.

Why didn't we hit the sanctuaries earlier in the war?

My soldiers asked the same question. I assumed Washington was against sending American soldiers into Cambodia. The administration's orders were for the military to use minimal force to establish the Vietnamese government as a self-sufficient and developing democratic republic. There also was great concern about China intervening.

But, from a military point of view, couldn't we have stopped the flow of NVA troops and equipment into South Vietnam by eliminating the sanctuaries?

Cleaning out the sanctuaries during our operation in Cambodia demonstrated the effectiveness of eliminating this support for NVA troops. As a result, the NVA was unable to perform any effective operations in the provinces within the Field Force II area. The Viet Cong also lost its effectiveness. Economic activity in the area increased considerably. Agricultural production increased and the lumber industry reemerged. A similar action was needed in Laos to include a permanent blocking of the supply road inside Laos running south from North Vietnam to support communist forces in South Vietnam. Such a blocking would have had, in my opinion, a dramatic effect in creating conditions that would lead to a peace agreement.

Had General Abrams taken command in 1964 instead of Westmoreland, do you think we would have invaded the Cambodian sanctuaries earlier?

That's a difficult question to answer because presumably the attitudes in Washington, and in particular the White House, would not have changed—so he would have had to face the same political conditions that Westmoreland did. But Abe was a better tactician than Westy. This was the second time I served under Abe. He was a terrific soldier, outstanding, one of the best leaders I've ever known.

You said that you had only seventy-two hours from the time Abrams gave you the orders to invade Cambodia. Was there any political announcement from Washington prior to your crossing the line of departure into Cambodia?

I can't answer that in detail. But I know that we kicked off early in the morning of April 29 and Nixon made a public announcement sometime that afternoon.

Were you able to surprise the NVA?

We surprised the enemy in most of the areas; however, we didn't surprise them at their field Pentagon, COSVN. It wasn't underground like the supply caches. COSVN was a mobile headquarters to the extent that it had trucks and other forms of transportation. We later found out that there was a leak in the B-52s' communication system. COSVN knew twenty-four hours in advance that B-52s were going to strike and warned its ground forces that we were coming.

COSVN had the capability of intercepting radio messages?

I assumed that they had electronic capabilities to pick up our communications.

Did you make contact with large NVA forces?

There were a few contacts initially with battalion-sized units, but, for the most part, contacts were at the company or platoon level at the various supply dumps where we took over and evacuated the supplies.

Was the operation successful?

Absolutely. We took out more enemy weapons and supplies than we had anticipated finding. This severely limited the ability of the NVA to operate and damaged the internal structure of the Viet Cong in the provinces around Saigon. The presence of the VC became almost nonexistent. We could drive most anywhere, whereas before we couldn't. Rice production sprang alive in the delta, and the lumber industry started up again because the workers could get into the jungles, cut down hardwood trees, and float them down the river to Saigon. This turned out to be a substantial benefit to the Vietnamese economy and to the Vietnamization of the country. In addition, we uncovered intelligence regarding the number of NVA troops in Cambodia. U.S. intelligence had estimated that there were about thirty thousand. As it turned out, COSVN records revealed that there were more than sixty thousand.

When you were on the ground in Cambodia, did you think we could win the war?

From my narrow point of view, I believed that we could win militarily if we had called up the National Guard and the Reserves and had the Air Force been permitted to attack North Vietnam's infrastructure in terms of bridges, factories, and power facilities. On the political side, our foreign policy people would have had to deal with the Chinese.

DANIEL ELLSBERG

*For myself, to read, through our own official documents, about the
origins of the conflict and of our participation in it, is to see our
involvement—and the killing we do—naked of any shred of legitimacy.*

—Daniel Ellsberg, *Papers On The War*

Who was this Harvard summa cum laude that leaked the Pentagon Papers to the *New York Times* and contributed to the chain of events that led to the downfall of the president of the United States and halted America's involvement in Vietnam? Was he a traitor as the Nixon administration tarred him, or was he a patriot?

Ellsberg was not a typical antiwar activist. He was a Marine during the Suez crisis in the mid-fifties, and then one of McNamara's whiz kids during the early years of the Vietnam War. He went to South Vietnam in 1965 with Maj. General Edward G. Lansdale, a counterinsurgency expert who had helped the Philippine government crush the communist-led Hukbalahap rebels. Graham Greene used Lansdale as the model for his protagonist who tried to capture the hearts and minds of the people in his novel, *The Quiet American.* A fervent advocate of the war, Ellsberg spent much of his tour in the bush with American combat units implementing his pacification programs until he contracted hepatitis in March 1967.

Peter Arnett describes in his book, *Live from the Battlefield,* bumping into Ellsberg out in the boonies. "We found Ellsberg in combat uniform and a floppy khaki hat, waist deep in a rice paddy, pulling himself through the muck, a submachine gun in his left fist. . . . " I asked Ellsberg if it wasn't a bit unusual for an armed civilian to be out in the bush with the troops. He replied, "What better way to find out whether the pacification was working than at the place where it was happening."

This firsthand experience, coupled with his analytical skills, made Ellsberg a natural choice by McNamara to participate in the writing of a history of the U.S. decision making in Vietnam from 1945 to 1968, later to be known as the Pentagon Papers.

From his experience in Vietnam, Ellsberg reached the conclusion that the Vietnam War, at best, was an inevitable stalemate with no victory possible. The Pentagon Papers did not prove this, but they did show that Vietnam had been an American war since the conclusion of World War II. The senseless killing of American and Vietnamese, as well as his face-to-face encounters with American youth being sent to prison because of their refusal to participate in an unjust war, converted Ellsberg from hawk to dove. Ellsberg wrote in his book, *Papers on the War*, "I found them [draft evaders] to be sober, intelligent, principled; they showed, in fact, the dedication I had respected in many officials I had known in Vietnam. But they were acting on different premises, which I now shared. These personal acts of 'witness' gave me what reading alone could not."

In October 1969, Ellsberg sent the *New York Times* a letter that called for the unilateral withdrawal of U.S. forces from Vietnam. At the same time, he revealed the Pentagon Papers to Senator J. William Fullbright of the Foreign Relations Committee. By 1971, as he described in his book, " . . . two more invasions had taken place; another million tons of bombs had fallen; nearly ten thousand more Americans had died, as well as hundreds of thousands of Indochinese. It had become painfully clear that much of Congress, too, was part of the problem; so I acted, as well, to inform the sovereign public through the 'fourth branch of government,' the press." All hell broke loose with the publication of the Papers in 1971 by the *New York Times*. Kissinger, who had consulted Ellsberg prior to Nixon taking office, aspersed him to Nixon as a "fanatic" and "drug abuser."

I first met Ellsberg, then sixty eights year old, at a deli in Washington, D.C. Over sandwiches, we chatted about my book and about a book he was writing, and he agreed to an interview during my next visit to Washington.

Three weeks later, I am sitting at a dining table in Ellsberg's small apartment off Connecticut Avenue. Words gush from him in a stream of consciousness as he unfolds the critical events that drew the United States into war. For two hours, he talks without interruption; his voice passionate, on a subject he has nurtured since his first trip to Vietnam forty years ago. There is a pedantic intensity about him that urges me, as if I were a student, to heed the lessons that he knows so well. Then, he drops Nixon's threat of using "nukes" to force Hanoi to pull out of South Vietnam. Earlier, President Dwight D. Eisenhower's rattling of nuclear weapons had brought a halt to the Korean War. Ellsberg says that Richard Nixon was then Eisenhower's vice president and remembered how effective the threat had been.

Ellsberg was very aware of nuclear weapons as an instrument of foreign policy. In 1959, he had studied game theory and risk in nuclear warfare as a systems analyst and long-range military planner at the The RAND Corporation. Later, in 1968, he said that he had drafted a list of options for Henry Kissinger, then President Nixon's national security adviser. He is quick to point out that he deliberately did not include the use of nuclear weapons in North Vietnam.

Ellsberg excuses himself and disappears into a bedroom. He returns with a 1967 photograph of himself in full battle gear in Vietnam. Clearly, he is proud of his involvement with the military in the bush. I note the lean body and face; except for his full head of white hair, he hasn't changed much physically.

Smeared by the Nixon administration, Ellsberg is well aware that he is still perceived by some as a traitor. I wonder what I would have done had I read the draft Papers as Ellsberg had in 1969. Would I have turned my head as did his RAND colleagues and moved on to the next stop in life rather than risk going to prison?

You worked for Robert McNamara at the Pentagon?

I started working for John McNaughton [assistant secretary of defense for international security] on August 4, 1964. McNaughton was directly under McNamara. When I say directly, he had a private line to NcNamara, and when McNamara called, McNaughton would run down the hall. He never left the building until McNamara left, and I never left before him. I was involved in the planning for the escalation of the war in Vietnam.

You're referring to the build up of American troops?

Correct. In July 1965, I wrote a speech for McNamara announcing the addition of one-hundred thousand troops to the seventy-five thousand that were already there and the mobilization of the reserves. But Lyndon Johnson—who had run for president on the notion that he would keep the U.S. out of a war in Southeast Asia—decided to announce his policy himself. So McNamara didn't give his speech. Johnson said he was sending fifty thousand more men. He lied to the American public. He told them fifty thousand when he had already committed one hundred thousand. And Westmoreland already had requested another one hundred thousand to be in Vietnam by early 1966, and that wasn't going to be the end. The public was totally misled. I knew that then.

Did President Johnson plan to escalate the war in late 1963 and early 1964, after Kennedy's assassination?

On election day 1964, I represented the civilian side of the Defense Department, along with a representative from the Joint Chief of Staff, at an interagency meeting to discuss the State Department's alternative policies for Vietnam. Basically, all of the options involved various ways to escalate the war. I wanted to avoid escalation and get out. Planning for the bombing had been in the works throughout the election campaign with the full expectation that we would be bombing soon after the election. Oddly, there wasn't much talk of sending troops. I now know that there were plans going on in the Pentagon and at General Westmoreland's headquarters in Saigon. But the expression of it was inhibited by the election campaign, particularly by General Maxwell Taylor, who wanted to keep a lid on troop planning. I think in Lyndon Johnson's mind, he thought he would send troops in 1965. It was a crazy idea because it was almost certain not to succeed.

You were against sending troops?

Not after Johnson started bombing in 1965. I spent a lot [of] time addressing strategies to cause the Viet Cong to lay down their weapons, or force Hanoi to accept indefinitely two Vietnams with the South being run by an anticommunist government. I had already concluded that we couldn't win. I also thought that Hanoi would pursue its goal at any cost to unify Vietnam under communist control. I don't say that with admiration, because we're talking about a leadership that was willing to risk everything, including having its people hit with nuclear weapons. But once we had committed and started bombing, I believed we should at least do what it took not to lose.

How did you get involved in the writing of the Pentagon Papers?

I volunteered in July 1965 to go to Vietnam with General Edward Lansdale's team in the hope that he had some magical, political way of dealing with the war. Lansdale was going to work on political aspects as he had successfully done in the Philippines. I thought that this might at least help us avoid defeat or stalemate. I arrived in Saigon in September 1965, and, for the next two years, I evaluated pacification projects from the Mekong delta to the DMZ [Demilitarized Zone]. During the last six months, I was a special assistant to the deputy ambassador in charge of pacification, William Porter.

While there, I recommended to McNamara that a study be made of the history of decision making behind the United States involvement in Vietnam. McNamara regarded that as a significant influence on his decision to start the Pentagon Papers. I was one of the first to be asked to be on the study. Most of my colleagues were military officers who had served in Vietnam.

When did the actual work begin on the Papers?

The study got underway in September 1967 and was completed in early 1969. The study's content covered the period from World War II up to March 1968. In November and December 1968, I was at The RAND Corporation in charge of a study on alternative strategies and approaches for Vietnam. This included writing a paper for Henry Kissinger's first presentation to the NSC [National Security Council] in January 1969. I ruled out the use of nuclear weapons. I would not be associated with a study that considered the possibility of using them. As it turned out, I was out of sync with President Nixon on this point. He entered office intending to end the Vietnam War the way Eisenhower had ended the Korean War while he was vice president—by threatening the use of nuclear weapons. I didn't know about nuclear threats at the time. I discovered this later. To threaten nukes is to use nuclear weapons. If you can get your way without having to pull the trigger—as when you point a gun—they can be very effective. Of course, if you don't get your way—and you do pull the trigger—the results can be catastrophic.

Was Nixon bluffing, or did he intend to use nuclear weapons against the North Vietnamese if his threats didn't work?

I think there was a real possibility that he would carry his threats out if there hadn't been an antiwar movement. I learned later that he had specific nuclear targets as early as 1969. My study of the Pentagon Papers covering a twenty-three-year period convinced me that this was the kind of stupidity that presidents will do.

What was your source of nuclear targets?

Roger Morris, an aide to Kissinger on the NSC staff, worked on escalation plans supporting Nixon's nuclear threats. In October 1969, Morris told me he had seen folders containing nuclear targets with photographs that included a railway junction a mile and a half from the Chinese border.

Was the threat to use nuclear weapons part of Nixon's secret plan that he touted in his 1968 presidential campaign to quickly end U.S. involvement in Vietnam?

Nixon believed nuclear threats would quickly win the war. That was almost inconceivably stupid, unrealistic, foolish, unwise, ignorant, and naïve. There's no single word for a foreign policy analyst that could adequately express such incompetence. To think that Hanoi would back down really took a moron. It absolutely wipes out my opinion that Nixon and Kissinger were worthy of any kind of respect as foreign policy makers. Whatever they did in any other field, that error in 1969 was totally discrediting. To carry out that policy of threats, Nixon had to keep it secret from his own defense secretary, Melvin Laird, and his secretary of state, William Rogers. Both of them had their feet on the ground to the extent that they didn't share this idiotic belief. So Nixon essentially kept it from them. [H. R.] Bob Haldeman [White House chief of staff] said that Nixon was really quite certain that he could win the war during his first six months in office. If not, then certainly in the second six months. But having failed to get the North Vietnamese to back down, he convinced himself that it was because the antiwar movement had encouraged Hanoi to continue fighting. So he had to pacify the antiwar movement in a variety of ways while carrying on with his threats.

Did Nixon plan to invade North Vietnam?

A limited invasion of southern North Vietnam was among his contingency plans. He did, once he realized that the intervention of China was unlikely. But he didn't heed the lessons from the French. During the first eight years of the French war, Ho Chi Minh carried on the battle while the French occupied Hanoi and Haiphong. I didn't see how even seizing Hanoi and Haiphong would give us a better position than the French had had. Had the U.S. occupied North Vietnam with hundreds of thousands of troops, the NVA could cross into Laos, Cambodia, and China and fight from there. And I never thought a massive-shock attack of bombing would be effective. The CIA didn't believe bombing would work either. We tried it enough to convince me that these were not people to break under bombing. In short, there was no military way to win the war. Winning was an illusion. However, we could have avoided defeat and communist takeover of Saigon. To put it in simplest terms, we could have reached a stalemate if we were willing to pay the price with American troops. In some wars, there is no substitute for defeat.

Did the possibility of an extended war and more American casualties lead to your decision to copy the Pentagon Papers?

It did. I believed there should be a coalition government, or the U.S. should withdraw unilaterally and let the politics sort it out. I did think that the communists would take over the government fairly quickly. This was preferable to our continuing the war and the unconscionable loss of American and South Vietnamese lives. By the end of the summer of 1969, I became aware that it was Nixon's secret intention to pursue mutual withdrawal indefinitely by threats of escalation. I felt that these threats would be defied like all of the earlier ones. Almost nobody else could imagine that Nixon would expand the war in order to avoid "losing" Vietnam.

Nixon was reelected in 1972 despite his deceptions.

Astonishingly, the public was apparently willing to accept a prolonged war if the number of troops and casualties steadily decreased. That meant the burden of the war was going to be bombing. In 1969, I wanted to stop that from happening. From my calculation, I felt that had the public known about Nixon's plans for expanding the war, congress and the public would have stopped him. They would have averted thousands of deaths on both sides. Had I documents then that proved what Nixon was planning to do, I would have revealed them.

Even if it meant going to prison?

If I was willing to risk having my legs blown off in Vietnam, I certainly could risk going to prison for my country. A lot of people who didn't feel responsible for the war came to feel that they should be willing to go to prison to help end it. Five thousand young men were incarcerated. In short, I believed a citizen should be willing to take the same risks for his country that we routinely expect of soldiers in the military. We shouldn't just be risk-takers only when we're wearing a uniform. Those officials who took part in getting us into Vietnam should have felt they owed something to their country to end it.

When did you start copying the Pentagon Papers?

I started in early October 1969. At that time, I still hoped that the threat of releasing the Pentagon Papers might encourage Nixon to avoid escalation. But, within a month, he announced his plan to step up the war. On November 15, the largest demonstration in U.S.

history took place simultaneously in San Francisco and Washington. This, after the Moratorium demonstration of October 15 across the nation, stopped Nixon from initiating his plan. About two weeks earlier, I had given the first batch of Pentagon Papers to Senator William Fulbright. Twenty months went by. Two more invasions took place, Cambodia and Laos. The bombing of North Vietnam had started again. Fulbright told me he would release the Papers, but he didn't. As a rule, people in the executive branch and Congress will not jeopardize their status, their prestige, and their careers. Fulbright wasn't prepared to go that far to defy the administration.

You knew that by leaking the Pentagon Papers you would be called a traitor?

I extremely dislike being called a traitor as I am by a lot of people. I object when people say that I was charged with treason. It is not true. People who knew me considered me a patriot. Maybe a misguided patriot, but they would not think of me working for some foreign power—or wanting to hurt the United States. In fact, they knew I was trying to stop the meaningless killing of American soldiers. I was not legally charged with treason. I didn't even come close to it. I didn't give secret documents to a foreign power. I wasn't committing espionage. I was doing something that to some lesser degree is done every day of the week. Secrets are leaked to the press. It makes executive officials extremely angry, but it doesn't lead to charges of treason.

There were allegations of a conspiracy.

The White House did believe that I was part of a conspiracy of dovish officials. When it came to anyone with access to the Papers, I was the only one. When it came to actually distributing them, I had to have help. These were people outside the system, people who were against the war. I didn't let any of my colleagues at the Pentagon know what I was doing. I thought their careers would be in jeopardy from just knowing me. I wanted to protect them from any suspicion of helping me. I wanted them to be able to say in lie-detector tests that they had no knowledge or suspicion of what I was doing. Apparently, before I considered copying the Papers, I told a few of my colleagues that McNamara should release them to the public. But once I got serious, I gave absolutely no indication as to what I was doing.

So you thought the information you were copying would force the Washington to negotiate an end to the war?

In 1969, the Pentagon Papers did not constitute documents of this degree of dynamite. They revealed a quarter century of presidential deceptions and broken treaties and lies that President Johnson made three years earlier—but not Nixon's lies. Had I had the documents that could prove the war was expanding, I would not have bothered with seven thousand pages of history. But I didn't have them. So, all I could do was show what had happened in the past was happening again, implausible as it was. Nixon's policy was so foolish and reckless that no one would believe a man smart enough to be elected president of the United States could do such a stupid thing. How could Nixon believe that threatening to reescalate the bombing would win the war after we had already dumped 50 percent more tons of bombs on Vietnam than we used in all of World War II? The U.S. dropped 3.2 million tons of bombs by 1968, compared to 2 million tons in World War II, with no effect whatsoever.

Did Nixon try to quiet you?

Not at first. The Papers didn't prove what Nixon was doing, so he had no reason to be frightened of them as Johnson would have been in 1964. Had I exposed these same documents in 1964 and '65, I think I could have averted the war.

You were sympathetic to the antiwar movement?

When I came back from Vietnam in 1967, I thought we should get out, as did most of the people who worked on the Pentagon Papers. Remember, most of them had served as officers in Vietnam and later became high Reagan administration officials. Up until then, I personally had never met any antiwar people. I had no direct contact with them, but I was sympathetic to what they were saying. I don't know where they got their knowledge, but they were on the right side. They were prepared to give up their careers, even to go to prison for what they believed. Later, when I had met some of these young people who went to prison, I realized that they weren't fanatics, crazies, and wild kids. They were very committed and very conscientious. They gave a different impression than Jane Fonda being photographed in a North Vietnamese antiaircraft battery. That was very injudicious on her part. By the way, when I finally did meet Jane Fonda, I was quite impressed with her. I did think her public statement deprecating the American pilots was stupid and very ill advised.

But in terms of her commitment against the war, I thought she was very serious.

Didn't some of these activists support the National Liberation Front?

Some did. Incidentally, I respected the NLF's [National Liberation Front's] fighting ability, but I didn't respect their Stalinist regime. So I was never one who was enthusiastic about the NLF, nor could I identify with the NLF.

What was your feeling about those activists who went to Hanoi?

I had no problem with the people who went to Hanoi seeking ways to negotiate an end to the war. I was well aware that the U.S. government wasn't seriously pursuing negotiations.

What was Nixon's reaction when you gave the Papers to the *New York Times*.

Nixon wasn't concerned about the Pentagon Papers being published. In fact, he liked the idea because the Papers incriminated the Democrats. In particular, he was happy to have the *New York Times* inculpate John Kennedy for the assassination of Ngo Dinh Diem because he was still facing Teddy [Senator Edward] Kennedy as his most worrisome opponent—despite Chappaquiddick. He wanted to put Democrat lies and crimes on record. Nixon actually encouraged Charles Colson and Howard Hunt to forge documents showing that Kennedy had directly ordered the assassination of Diem. Hunt forged cables to that effect and tried to peddle them to *Life* magazine. By the end of my trial, I had possession of the forged cables. That was one of the little time bombs that Nixon was worried about.

Nixon must have loved you.

Yeah. Nixon said that what we need is our own Daniel Ellsberg. Somebody who really knows the documents, knows the history, and can put this all together.

But you were indicted.

John Ehrlichman, the president's counsel, had strongly urged that I not be charged because it would give me a platform to speak out against the war. It was good advice. Nixon wanted to destroy me outside of the courtroom, not inside. But the Justice Department indicted me even though it didn't have a valid law to charge me because of the First Amendment. The U.S. didn't have an official secret's act. That is why no one had ever been indicted before for leaking top secrets to the press. There had been no prior prosecution, no conviction. Instead, they charged me with theft and violation of sections of the Espionage Act. The Act had never been used against leaks. But, in my case, they decided to go ahead.

Did you spend any time in prison?

No. I was released on $50,000 bond. Meanwhile, Nixon thought that I had copied documents other than the Pentagon Papers, some of which came out of his National Security Council. I actually worked on NSC documents after Nixon's election in 1968 and in the White House in February and March 1969. I had given copies of the documents that I had worked on to Senator Charles Mathias, who wanted to end the war. When the *New York Times* began publishing the Papers, Mathias immediately called John Mitchell. Nixon knew right away that I had NSC documents. He assumed that someone at the NSC had given them to me, which was not true. They were documents I had worked on. Five people on the NSC had resigned in 1970, which was after I began copying the Pentagon Papers and a year before they came out. They had resigned in protest of the Cambodian incursion. Nixon assumed that those people gave me documents, and he could not afford to have them revealed. He hadn't yet bombed Haiphong and the dikes. He hadn't invaded North Vietnam. He hadn't sent B-52s over North Vietnam. But he threatened all of them.

So Nixon had to stop you?

Nixon had to stop me from revealing the NSC documents that he assumed I had. Not only would his Vietnam strategies have been blocked, he also would have faced impeachment. He couldn't dissuade me by threatening jail because I was already looking at 115 years in prison for twelve felony counts. He could only blackmail me or kill me. So he tried both. First, blackmail. He sent some Cuban-Americans from Miami to break into my psychoanalyst's office to dig up information to blackmail the psychoanalyst into telling what I had told him. They were all CIA assets on the payroll as contract employees. They even looked at my doctor's tax records to see if he reported all of his income. Incidentally, one of the people who broke in happened to an accountant. But they didn't find the information they were looking for.

You were seeing the psychoanalyst because of pressure from the White House?

No, I wanted to understand myself better; what had gone wrong in my marriage, and why I had trouble publishing. I didn't have a writing problem, but I did have a publishing problem.

We all do.

(laughter) I wouldn't recommend a psychoanalyst for that reason. Nine months later, I released an NSC memorandum with the intent of letting Nixon know that I was unloading information that I had. Nixon sent the same guys who had broken into my doctor's office to incapacitate me, totally.

"To incapacitate you"?

Right. They don't talk in the Agency about killing and assassinating. They talk about "neutralizing" or "incapacitating with extreme prejudice." But, some of the eleven Cuban-Americans sent to do the deed realized that they had been given a false cover—they were meant to be caught. So they staged a fistfight in a crowded area where they would be arrested. They were locked up. Someone showing government credentials vouched for them and had them released. That night, the same guys reconnoitered the Watergate. About a month later, they were caught inside the Watergate on their second break-in. They had the goods on Nixon. So Nixon paid Hunt to keep quiet about the attempted assault and about the break-in at my doctor's office. Nixon obstructed justice to hide his own personal involvement in efforts against me. It had nothing to [do] with his political campaign. It had nothing to do with politics directly. It had everything to do with protecting his Vietnam policy. Nixon had to keep his policy from the American public because Congress would have stopped him. He wanted the right to make foreign policy secretly, unilaterally, and personally. In short, Nixon wanted king-like powers.

You were indicted on June 28, 1971, by the federal government?

I was indicted on two counts of converting government property to personal use and of illegally possessing government documents. Later there were twelve criminal charges added, including violation of the Espionage Act. On May 11, 1973, after four months in court, the judge dismissed all charges before they went to the jury on grounds of government misconduct against me.

It would have been easier for you do keep quiet and do nothing.

I know. But it seemed quite logical, reasonable, and responsible for me to speak out because I had taken a part in the escalation of the war. I had a responsibility to try and correct that mistake once I thought it was the wrong course. As far as I can tell, I was one of the few out of many officials who had worked on the Vietnam War and turned against it, who felt that sense of responsibility. Others in the know went on to other pursuits. For example, after McNamara left the Defense Department, he openly said in his book that he felt no responsibility to take action to end the war. He left in 1968; the war went on for seven years more. He had known for at least two years that the war was hopeless and should be ended. To me, that was a peculiar way to think. It seemed very logical to do something about it.

What are your feelings about McNamara keeping quiet?

McNamara is no different than his colleagues or superiors. To single him out for being reprehensible is unfair. Understandably, he's culpable for all his failings, all his omissions, all his lies, and all his arrogance. But he's exactly like everybody else in the system. Do you think McNamara was the only one to realize that the war was a hopeless venture? Bull. He was the one that admitted he knew— that's where he differs. The war was pursued from top to bottom by a nearly unanimous core of civilians and military who knew the war was hopeless.

Throughout all this—and the smearing of your name—did you consider yourself a patriot?

I always considered myself a patriot from my earliest days to the present. In 1956, I turned down a prestigious fellowship to Harvard to extend my term in the Marine Corps because my battalion was going to the Middle East because of the Suez crisis. I didn't want my battalion going into fighting without me. That's the kind of conventional patriotism I had. In 1969, I asked myself whether I was willing to go to prison. That was easy for me to answer. When I believed in the war, I volunteered to be on the front line in Vietnam. When I thought the country was heading in the wrong direction, I could not follow blindly. I had to tell the American public what I knew to help change the country's course.

ALEXANDER HAIG

The Army realized that the war could not be fought and won under the terms laid down by the doctrine of incrementalism, but no senior general, to my knowledge, was telling the civilian leadership this.
—ALEXANDER HAIG, *Inner Circles*

As early as 1962, while President Kennedy was still weighing the prospects of upping the ante in Vietnam, then Lt. Col. Alexander Haig watched the impending Asian war from the office of the Army's deputy chief of staff at the Pentagon and, in 1964, as military assistant to the Secretary of the Army Cyrus Vance and later as deputy secretary of defense under Secretary Robert McNamara. In 1966 and 1967, his perspective shifted to ground zero in the jungles of South Vietnam as a combat battalion commander with the "Big Red One," America's 1st Infantry Division. In late 1968, Kissinger tapped him to be his military advisor on the National Security Council. Eighteen months later, Haig made fourteen trips to Southeast Asia as the personal emissary of the president to negotiate a cease-fire and the return of American prisoners of war. In 1972, he traveled to China as head of the advance party for Nixon's historic visit.

A West Point graduate, class of 1947, Nixon had promoted Haig from two-star to four-star rank in 1972 over 240 generals senior to him, which had further fueled the controversy swirling about his meteoric career and proximity to the presidential throne. Having been at the political epicenter during some of the country's most trying moments, Haig was at Nixon's side as chief of staff when the Watergate crisis signaled America's first loss ever in war. At the time, his celebrity was so widespread that White House Council John Dean falsely accused him of being the mysterious informant, "Deep Throat," with whom *The Washington Post*'s Bob Woodward and Carl Bernstein secretly met about the Watergate break-in. Nine years later, in 1981, Haig would become the self-described "vicar" of foreign policy as secretary of state in Reagan's first administration.

I meet with the general at his Palm Beach, Florida, home, a spacious residence on the Intracoastal Waterway. He is the first subject to be interviewed. Although he was dressed in slacks and a polo shirt, I can still envision him at seventy-five years of age in his Army green uniform with his chest full of ribbons. I show him a proposed list of interviewees for the book. Mrs. Haig enters the study with a tray of ham and cheese sandwiches. We dig in while tinkering with the names on the list. One by one, General Haig gives me his impressions and suggests one or two more individuals who can bring other viewpoints to the party. He says that he will call Herr Kissinger on my behalf.

Lunch finished, we launch the interview process that will take a year to complete. With sweeping and provocative swaths of caveats and candor mixed with whimsical humor, he points out the Kennedy and Johnson administrations' failure to heed the lessons of history. His blue eyes dance as he talks with multisyllabic words that, three decades earlier, journalists had termed "Haigspeak."

General, could we have won the war in Vietnam?

Absolutely, had we taken the war to Hanoi, and I mean both airpower and at least demonstrated credibly that we were prepared to use ground troops. In the spring of 1965, Gen. Harold K. Johnson, the Army's chief of staff, came to me and Lt. Col. DeWitt Smith, "Cy" Vance's military assistant. Vance was then deputy secretary of defense. I was also a lieutenant colonel serving as deputy special assistant to both Secretary of Defense McNamara and his newly appointed deputy Cyrus Vance. This was just before General Johnson's 1965 trip to Vietnam following the Gulf of Tonkin incident and terrorism against U.S. forces. General Johnson said that President Johnson wanted a military appraisal of possible actions open to him in Vietnam based on General Johnson's detailed assessment as to "what the traffic would bear."

That sounds very political.

Right. So Smith and I agreed to give him a list of actions we considered correct for the country, not simply what was politically correct. We put together a list of some thirty actions in ascending order, starting with the easiest politically down to really substantial steps, such as making it clear to the Russians [Soviets] that we were going to take the war to the North and also making it clear that if the Russians stepped up their involvement, we would deal with that as well. It was our conviction that if we took the necessary steps, to include mobilization, the Russians would not let Hanoi's actions provoke a potential showdown between Washington and Moscow. I was convinced then, as I am convinced now, that the Russians never would have allowed it because at the time they had other far more important axes to grind.

Are you suggesting that the Vietnam conflict might never have expanded had we told the Russians that we were going to take the war to Hanoi?

Yes, provided we also made it clear that if their client continued to violate the 1954 Settlement, we would be prepared and would indeed undertake credible steps in that direction. Too often during the Cold War, we recoiled from hard-nosed assessments of what was necessary. If clear-headed assessments suggested the risks were too high or the impact too costly to our interests, then, of course, we should not have become militarily involved in the first place. I was serving in Europe during the earlier crisis in Vietnam. It occurred during the Eisenhower Administration. Gen. Matthew Ridgway was the Army's chief of staff. I had observed him earlier in Korea and admired him immensely. He was one of those soldiers who stood up for his convictions, whatever the personal cost. He told the White House not to get into a ground war in Southeast Asia. As a result, I had concerns about our being in Vietnam at all. But I also knew that we were being tested by Moscow. It was testing by Moscow that made Vietnam of strategic importance in terms of national interest. Had we shown the Russians that we were really serious, including mobilization, there probably would never have been a war. When our political leaders try to have it both ways, they frequently bring about the very outcomes they wish most to avoid.

What did you base your conclusion on?

Russia's history throughout the Cold War. So long as they had other people dying for them in the so-called "wars of liberation"— and as long as we were foolish enough to confine our reactions to the so-called liberators instead of confronting the source of the problem, which was Moscow—we were operating at risk and creating no-win situations. In my experience, the only way to treat the Russians was to be firm, to mean what you say, and only say what you mean. When you don't, you confuse them. A Russian general once told me jokingly that Russians "never believe you penurious capitalists until you actually spend your money." Then they know we are serious. So I always believed we had to let actions, not words, speak for us.

Steps like mobilization before risking the lives of our young men would have been convincing.

Was Hanoi a stooge of Moscow?

Not really. They were dedicated revolutionaries with minds and interests of their own. But everything North Vietnam did couldn't have been done without the logistics, political support, and counsel provided by Moscow, as well as the umbrella of deterrence provided by Moscow against a clear-headed United States response. Our misreading of China inhibited our thinking at the time.

How did General Johnson respond to your recommendations to take the war to Hanoi?

When General Johnson returned from his trip to Vietnam, he submitted less than half of our list, excluding all the more vigorous steps. That's the list that went to President Johnson as the professional military's viewpoint. And that set the tone and scope for the subsequent introduction of American ground troops into the South. In Vietnam, it was the implementation of what I call the "flexible response" mentality. This approach blossomed during the Kennedy/Johnson years. President Johnson told me shortly before his death that he greatly regretted this approach.

Why did General Johnson cut out half of the list?

I can't answer that. All I can say is that he may have thought that what he submitted was all that the traffic would bear. But conceding to the politically expedient path is not the role of a military adviser. Generals have a sacred obligation to speak the truth to their political leaders. But we have produced on occasion, since World War II, a breed of military leader unwilling to stand up if doing so would risk his career. If one is not willing to jeopardize his or her career by telling the truth to his political superiors—who are generally not trained or steeped in the art of warfare—then you invite the worst outcome. There is nothing in a military career more important than integrity and a sense of political obligation. Nothing. This is what the American people expect of their professionals.

Did you subscribe to Washington's concern that China would intervene if we pushed the war north?

That's what I have come to call the "Korean Syndrome," which itself was a product of a profound diplomatic failure. Earlier during the Korean War, we had had no communication with China since the revolution of '49 that resulted in the evacuation of Chiang Kai-shek and the Kuomintang to Taiwan. We obtained most of our intelligence on the mainland from Taiwan, so it was secondhand, with a self-serving spin. In Korea, when we crossed the 38th Parallel and penetrated to the Yalu River, nobody explained to the Chinese that we weren't going into China and that our moves were designed to counter Soviet imperialism. Because of an absence of any communication with the Chinese and their misreading of our intentions, they entered the war to prevent what we did not want in the first place. The same problem developed in Vietnam because Washington failed to communicate with and understand China's true interest in Southeast Asia. We never grasped the fact that in many respects they were as concerned about the Soviets as we were—probably more so. We didn't learn otherwise until Richard Nixon opened communications with China. I recall my own discussions in Beijing with Premier Chou En-lai when I led the advance team for Nixon's visit in 1972. He made it very clear to me, without actually saying so, that the Chinese didn't want us to withdraw from Southeast Asia because of their concerns about Russia. They saw the Vietnam conflict as an encirclement of Mainland China by Moscow. Our fear of Chinese intervention was a reflection of a total lack of strategic intelligence and an unwillingness on the part of our political leaders to establish contact with our perceived enemies so, at least, we might learn something about Chinese thinking and they about ours.

And, of course, the Chinese invaded North Vietnam three years after the fall of Saigon.

When I was the NATO Commander in 1979, a Chinese official told me that they were going to have to punish North Vietnam because of Hanoi's implementation of the discredited "domino theory." The NVA was in Cambodia and Laos and was threatening Thailand. So, in 1979, China invaded across the northern border of Vietnam, even though they were not militarily prepared to do so. It cost them fifty thousand lives, but they stopped Hanoi and thereby frustrated Moscow's proxy expansion in the region.

In preparing your list for General Johnson, did you consider using nuclear weapons?

No, it wasn't necessary or appropriate.

Should we have threatened the use of nuclear weapons in North Vietnam, and would the American people have accepted this?

I think the people would have supported President Johnson early in his term, but this does not mean he should have done so. By the mid-sixties, the balance between the U.S. and the Soviet Union in nuclear terms had begun to approach equilibrium; not like during the Cuban missile crisis when the U.S. was so superior in nuclear capability that no rational Soviet leader would have considered a nuclear exchange. At that early date, missile rattling was more feasible, as it had proved to be for President Eisenhower in his successful efforts in 1953 to end the Korean conflict. The main problem in the Vietnam War for the U.S. was incrementalism.

So instead of going for a quick kill, we did piecemeal commitment?

This thinking came out of the perversion of the military strategy during the Kennedy years. Early on, it was part of the Berlin contingency planning. This was before Vietnam. To cope with Russian pressure on the enclave of West Berlin, strategies were developed on the third floor of the Pentagon, and, unfortunately, some in the military went along with incremental escalation. When there was a blockade of trains or road convoys into West Berlin, we exercised what, at the time, we sarcastically called the "poodle blanket"—a tit-for-tat strategy that assumed the enemy would be stopped at the lowest level of combat intensity. Therefore, if the Russians did something provocative, we responded with a proportionate counter. For example, if the Russians used a platoon to block the road, we countered with a platoon to open up the road, and then, if necessary, a company, and then a reinforced battalion. No one seemed to recognize that this kind of incrementalism usually invites escalation. There was another dimension to this naïve thinking. It involved winning the hearts and minds of the people. President Kennedy conceived the Army Special Forces as somewhat of a substitute for conventional fighting forces. The Army, in order to get money—which is frequently the key motivation in the Pentagon—became overeager advocates of this concept. It was a serious perversion of military reality. The Pentagon thought that they could put enlightened young soldiers in Special Forces configurations, which could turn the hearts and minds of the population away from the evil communist into model democrats. In hindsight, it was a ludicrous approach, a total misreading of reality. And it made it easier for us to get involved in Vietnam under the illusion that our values would overwhelm evil at the local level. The problem was not values but how to convince the Russians to keep their wards in Hanoi from violating international law and pursuing the rule of the bayonet.

But the military was restrained by the political assumption that China would intervene if we took the war to Hanoi. Who was responsible for this assumption?

It was the Kennedy core group, but they had many conservative allies as well. It was conventional logic in Washington and among the press.

You weren't a Kennedy fan?

It wasn't a subjective issue for me, but rather wrongheaded and unprofessional strategic thinking that concerned me. President Kennedy attracted many very bright and very capable people, but some also had certain shortcomings. It's always been my view that it takes one kind of person to get you elected and another type of person to help you govern. Very few presidents that I have known have had the wisdom to bring in the very best that our country can offer to help them govern once they are in office. Instead, there is a tendency to reward those who helped get you elected or who share your worldview. It is always risky to reward political operatives with highly substantive jobs unless they have demonstrated excellence in the field. This is especially true at State, Defense, and Treasury. President Johnson said he should have listened to his gut feelings instead of listening to his advisers, many of whom had been with Kennedy and were part of the perversion of sound strategic thinking. President Johnson personally said this to me.

And Robert McNamara, was he the right choice for Secretary of Defense?

I'm not a McNamara hater. He was a brilliant man who knew how to translate facts and figures into convincing visual depictions better than anyone I know. He was dedicated and patriotic, but like all of us, he was sometimes wrong. Take, for example, U.S. intelligence. When McNamara came in, he thought the CIA and the service intelligence agencies had inflated the Soviet threat terribly. He believed that the establishment always painted the Soviets 10 feet tall. History confirms McNamara was right. The CIA did that because hard questions weren't being asked. McNamara then went about correcting the problem but went too far. Under his policies, high technology was introduced and sometimes was given greater weight than human judgment. This downgraded the human side of intelligence—including judgment, experience, and intuition—replacing them with technological assets. Everything had to have technological confirmation. A fact was not a fact unless you had a photo or a confirming electronic intercept. Therefore, there was a growing lack of tolerance for human judgment in the analytical side of the intelligence process and less and less emphasis and resources were given to the human side of intelligence. The result ultimately was to underrate Soviet capabilities, especially in the changing nuclear equation.

Are you suggesting that faulty intelligence was behind the escalation of the number of American troops in Vietnam?

No, I don't think it was a question of bean counting. It was really a question of raising the cost to our enemies to the point where their interests were in such jeopardy that they would be inclined to cease and desist from their violations of international law. If you can't do that because of conflicting interests that are of more importance to you, then don't get involved. Vital interests must be at the center of the calculus. Had we taken the steps necessary to convince Moscow and Hanoi that we were prepared to take actions that would jeopardize their interest, it is probable there never would have been a Vietnam War as we know it today. Certainly, the history of the Cold War from Harry S. Truman to Reagan suggests that to be true.

Why did you volunteer to go to Vietnam if you thought the war was being conducted incorrectly?

I was a professional soldier, and it was my duty. Also, it was my conviction that you had no credibility unless you had been there and seen the battle firsthand. I was convinced that I could help to remove some of the sophistry from our strategic thinking. I left Vietnam even more convinced because I never witnessed a battle with the Viet Cong or the North Vietnamese that we didn't win decisively. We squandered over fifty thousand lives by not employing our overwhelming power. I could not then and cannot now understand why. We seemed to think we could have good relations with the Soviets while they were supporting actions that cost the lives of fifty thousand plus young Americans. When we launched actions against Hanoi in a less restrained way and it risked the Moscow Summit, they agreed to settle and went right along with the summit as well. Unfortunately, it was historically too late, and our legislature proceeded to throw away this modest victory by voting to prohibit future air actions against the North and by all but eliminating our assistance to the South.

When you were a battalion and brigade commander in Vietnam, having already seen the folly in Washington, did you ask yourself why you were there?

Of course. Regularly. But it didn't change my conviction that we could win the war quickly if we wanted to, and I mean moving our full airpower to include, if necessary, ground power against Hanoi.

Why didn't we communicate with the Chinese?

Because we erroneously thought they were the enemy, and one should not communicate with the enemy. We see that same attitude resurfacing in some circles today.

And we didn't talk with the enemy?

That's right. Remember that there was a hotbed of anti-Chinese sentiment in America after the collapse of the Chinese Nationalist regime on the mainland. The mainland regime under Mao was considered bloody-minded communists. They violated human rights and were brutal to their own people. But did they represent a clash of interests with the United States that made them mortal enemies? I think we should have asked the same questions that Nixon did later. We might have been surprised by some of the answers. This is not to suggest that we should not promote our values. We do this best by contact and example, not pedantic threat and bluster or, above all, military power.

Did you buy into the domino theory? *Page 45*

Probably, in the sense that the North Vietnamese wanted to spread Marxist-Leninist ideology as though it were a religion and Moscow was their mentor and logistician. They weren't nice guys either. But that wasn't the issue. The issue was how to preserve the vital interest of the American people? You don't needlessly throw away young American lives while failing to utilize your assets. If, for good or bad reasons, you are unwilling to do that, you should avoid conflict in the first place. Today, as we assess our experiences in Vietnam, we forget that but for China in 1979, we would have witnessed the domino theory in action. Too many contemporary politicians overlook this. That is why Churchill once said "read history if you wish to master the secrets of statecraft."

What was the national interest of the United States then?

To contain Marxist-Leninism from spreading, which was being attempted primarily by a calculated Soviet strategy focused on the developing world because the Soviet Union didn't want to risk a European confrontation with the major powers. Because of NATO, we were too strong there. And we still had too many nuclear weapons for them to risk nuclear war. So they attacked through "the soft underbelly" of the developing world. They sponsored wars of liberation in Africa, Southeast Asia, and Latin America, and frequently harnessed our sensitivity to social injustice to their cause. Most assaults were replete with ambiguities that frequently confused the Free World. Look at Chechnya today, where post–Soviet Russia is again brutally violating international law and our government is legitimizing genocide by comparing the conflict to our civil war.

Besides the domino mindset, was the military-industrial complex behind the perpetuation of the war?

I don't think so. I have seldom seen any evidence of that. Basically, most of our industrial leaders are patriots and are more dedicated to the success of America than their own personal or corporate successes. That warning from Eisenhower about a "military-industrial complex" was extracted out of context and ran directly contrary to his own lifetime of experience and demonstrated wisdom.

Who then can we point to?

There's a lot of blame that can be spread in a lot of circles. But I would sometimes point to the professional military. Many of the most courageous and patriotic men I have ever known are military. This was my chosen profession. But, on occasion, individuals in uniform have failed to stand up and challenge the politically motivated Washington bureaucrats. Also, I would worry about a military advancement system that rewards conformism. You have to start out with a sense of confidence that your officer corps is imbued with integrity, straight talk, and a sense of duty with the courage of their convictions. That's why there is no substitute for our service academies. What I am saying is, the academies must prepare student officers to speak their minds and prepare young professionals who aren't afraid to risk their careers on behalf of key issues of substance.

This is especially relevant as one rises in rank and responsibilities expand.

Should members of the Joint Chiefs resign when the Washington bureaucrats refuse to heed their advice?

If the issue is of grave consequence to the interests of the American people, of course. On occasion men and women reach high positions and become willing to compromise and do what's expedient and politically advantageous rather than follow the dictates of their own consciences. Such individuals neither serve their political leaders well nor the interests of American people.

Did you consider resigning because of disagreement with Washington's handling of the Vietnam War?

Not until I reached a higher level of responsibility, where I was much closer to unfolding events. Still later, I resigned twice from two separate administrations on issues of principle, which I have never regretted doing.

Was Westmoreland also guilty?

In my view, Westy was an honest and courageous general. He offered advice the best he could as commander of the troops on the ground. Sometimes, it was welcomed. Increasingly, it was unwelcomed, such as after the 1968 Tet Offensive when he requested more troops to finish the job and was relieved for doing so.

You mentioned earlier the needless loss of American lives. Are you referring to sons of blue-collar workers?

This hits a sore point with me. When I came back from Korea in the early '50s, few in America seemed to know or care that there was a war going on. It was an unbelievable situation with high employment, a booming economy, and the new technology of television just being introduced. The young people drafted for the war came largely from families that had little or no influence. That is where the corruption in the military draft really began. In World War II, it wasn't that way. They put your number in a fishbowl, and, if it came out, you went. Mostly it didn't matter who you were, or who your father was, because we believed we were fighting for the survival of our country. Korea was somewhat confused, and Vietnam was even more so. But, the draft became more and more perverted, so we were drafting and losing young men largely from the inner cities and the farms whose parents had little political influence. Anyone who could afford higher education could get a deferment. Many of these deferred students entered the antiwar efforts. This was understandable since the war went on and on without results and with only mounting casualties to show. Because most of the casualties came from families of those who had little influence, a responsible political opposition to the manner in which the war was conducted never really developed in a way that would have altered our policies constructively. It is not as simple as it might appear. I, for one, would revisit the question of conscription and universal service.

During Nixon's 1968 bid for the presidency, he told the American public that he had a secret peace plan that would quickly end U.S. involvement in Vietnam. What was secret about the plan, and why didn't it work?

I was asked to join the Nixon administration after he was elected. While assistant to Henry Kissinger and then as deputy national security adviser, I usually urged more vigorous pursuit of the war. But I am convinced that President Nixon did believe that through a combination of carrots and sticks he could bring the war to an honorable conclusion. Actually, he did that after the bombing and mining of Hanoi and Haiphong, but it was too late because our legislature and the people had lost their stomach for the effort.

When you were with Nixon and Kissinger in the White House, did you believe that we could still win the war?

Absolutely. I was convinced that we could end the war in a matter of months—and on favorable terms. For example, in early 1969, when a C-131 was shot down over international waters adjacent to North Korea, I told Kissinger that this was our chance. This meant mobilization, vigorous action against Pyongyang, and informing the Russians that Hanoi would be next unless the North Vietnamese pulled their troops out of South Vietnam. Speeches were prepared for the president for this reaction, but the president decided to turn the other cheek.

Why?

The secretaries of defense and state were vehemently opposed to this action, as were many of the president's closest advisors. President Nixon told me years later that his failure to act early in his presidency was the biggest mistake of his presidency. Later, in Christmas of '72,

I advised Nixon that we were going to have to bomb Hanoi, no holds barred on military targets to include the ports. Nixon agreed. B-52s were used in what are now called the "Christmas bombings." The B-52 losses were very high in the first two raids. What we didn't know was that the Russians were running much of Hanoi's air defense systems. Actually, the tactics that we used were wrong. The targets were not properly prepared or approached. The U.S. media, of course, went ballistic. It was really a difficult period. Our senior military commander in the Pacific sent a message to the Joint Chiefs to stop the attacks immediately. But the chairman of the Joint Chiefs and the strategic air commander urged that the raids continue. Tactics were changed, and the losses stopped. Nevertheless, Congress threatened to impeach the president if the attacks continued. There was serious discord in the president's cabinet. The only supporter was John Connolly [Treasury Secretary], but he, too, eventually caved in. The president, with my full support, continued to bomb. By shortly after Christmas, we got a message from Hanoi that they were ready to settle. I advised President Nixon that if we continued the bombing for another month, we could probably insist that the North withdraw from the South. But Nixon had to consider the political consequences, so he settled for the terms previously negotiated by his national security advisor. From the day they signed the Paris [Peace] Accords, Hanoi started to violate the terms. In the meantime, Watergate started to unravel the president's authority, and little could be done to sanction Hanoi's violations of the Paris Accords.

Any lessons to be learned?

First, we must decide that it is in the vital interest of the American people before risking American lives. We must decide if the issue is worth shedding the blood of our sons and daughters. If so, then the struggle should be conducted with all of our assets. Should the situation not appear to be sufficiently in our national interest, we should avoid military conflict and seek other solutions if at all possible. Furthermore we should rethink on an urgent basis whether armed forces are the appropriate or practical way to promote our values.

DAVID HALBERSTAM

The only thing wrong was that the war was not being won; it was, in fact, not being fought.

—DAVID HALBERSTAM, *The Best and the Brightest*

Denounced by the Kennedy and Johnson administrations as a radical-left winger out to undermine America's efforts in Southeast Asia, David Halberstam was the first U.S. newspaper correspondent to stake out Vietnam full time. Arriving in Saigon in July 1962 fresh from the war in the Congo, he saw the conflict at its grass roots by accompanying American advisers and their South Vietnamese units in the bush. It quickly became apparent to him that the ARVN didn't have the stomach to fight the hit-and-run Viet Cong guerrillas, and he wrote about this.

His firsthand reports in the *New York Times* sharply contradicted Washington's positive take on the progress of the war. He accused Washington of refusing to pay heed to history—that America was making the same mistakes as France. He contended that America's involvement was driven by domestic politics; Kennedy sent eighteen thousand military advisers to Vietnam because he did not want to appear soft on communism in the upcoming 1964 presidential election.

The Harvard-educated Halberstam was one of a handful of war correspondents who formed the early Saigon press corps that consisted of Malcolm Browne, Peter Arnett, and photographer Horst Faas of the Associated Press and Neil Sheehan of United Press International. The Kennedy administration and the military hierarchy in Saigon and at the Pentagon charged that they were inaccurate in their reporting and sought sensationalism. Westmoreland said that they were too young and irresponsible. All five would go on to win Pulitzer Prizes for their reporting in Vietnam; Faas won two.

Unlike Arnett, who spent thirteen years in and out of South Vietnam, Halberstam was there for only fifteen months and departed before the American troop buildup in 1964. And yet, to this day, the sixty-five year old best-selling author is associated with the Vietnam War. In his book, *The Best and the Brightest,* he indicts the Kennedy and Johnson administrations for the deplorable manner in which they plunged America into an unwinnable war. He calls McNamara the most egregious of the lot and spares the former secretary of defense no mercy as he slashes and burns McNamara's statistics and his fatal underestimation of the will of the North Vietnamese to fight.

Halberstam describes McNamara in *The Best and the Brightest*: "If the body was tense and driven, the mind was mathematical, analytical, bringing order and reason out of chaos. Always reason supported by facts, by statistics—he could prove his rationality with facts, intimidate others. He was marvelous with charts and statistics. Once, sitting at CINCPAC for eight hours watching hundreds and hundreds of slides flashed across the screen showing what was in the pipe line to Vietnam and what was already there, he finally said, after seven hours, 'Stop the projector. This slide, number 869, contradicts slide 11.' Slide 11 was flashed back and he was right, they did contradict each other. Everyone was impressed, and many a little frightened. No wonder his reputation grew; others were in awe. For it was a mind that could continue to summon its own mathematical kind of sanity into bureaucratic battle, long after the others, the good liberal social scientists who had never gone beyond their original logarithms, had trailed off into the dust, though finally, when the mathematical version of sanity did not work out, when it turned out that the computer had not fed back the right answers and had underestimated those funny little far-off men in their raggedy pajamas, he would be stricken with a profound sense of failure, and he would be, at least briefly, a shattered man."

Why does David Halberstam's name stand out above the literally hundreds of correspondents who passed through Vietnam, when he departed before the real war began? Why does Arnett call Halberstam "The Man?"

At his spacious West Side Manhattan apartment, he towers over me at 6 feet, 3 inches. We move into the kitchen because, as he says, the acoustics are better for recording our conversation. Sitting at a narrow breakfast table with cappuccino, he launches into a long preamble about how Johnson and McNamara lied to Congress and to the American people.

Luckily, I am able to flip on my recorder before he is too deep into his soliloquy. His words gush out with a thumping cadence like pistons in a steam engine, often shifting directions at midsentence, not once sputtering. I'm getting a whiff of the relentless energy that drove the top brass in Saigon, the Pentagon, and the Oval Office nuts some thirty-eight years ago. It's no wonder that President Kennedy told the publisher of the *New York Times* to call off his dog.

Finally, Halberstam pauses and, for a brief moment, the burrowing reporter becomes the interviewee: "Now, what can I do for you?" he asks. There's a twinkle in his eyes; he is having fun.

You were the first American newspaper reporter to be permanently assigned full time in Vietnam?

In June 1961, I was working for the *New York Times* in the Congo. At the time, the Congo was a much bigger story than Vietnam. I found out that I was good enough to be a war correspondent. I also found out that I could control my fears, which was a great test for me. It became clear by mid-1962 that Vietnam was going to be a major confrontation. I was young and single and started writing letters asking the *Times* to send me there. I wanted to go badly. I was the first person to volunteer for Vietnam and arrived there in July 1962. There was one other distinction that I'm very proud of. I was the first person that had his name [Halberstam, New York Times] imprinted on his fatigues because I never wanted to hear later that someone whom I interviewed didn't know who I was.

What part of the country did you cover?

At first, I traveled the whole country. The capitals never have anything to report, plus an eccentric dateline was more likely to get a good play in the newspaper. The Mekong Delta was the place where it was all happening, so I concentrated on My Tho, a small provincial capital just south of Saigon. Col. John Paul Vann was there. He was considered the hottest dog in country and a great teacher to us kid reporters. In a war that was scattered like Vietnam, you have to pick out one or two places and keep going back to them. The more you go back, the more the people there will trust you. If you are a distant guy in for a quickie, they won't tell you a damn thing. I was young and naïve, but I knew that much.

Did you then buy into Washington's reasons for being in Vietnam?

U.S. policy was all about public relations to make the U.S. look like it was winning as Kennedy got ready for a tough political year. The big game was in Europe. It was Berlin; Kennedy meeting

Kruschev; the Cuban missile crisis. Vietnam was this peripheral little thing that Washington didn't care about. Kennedy would say that he didn't want to get into a Third World War because some captain woke up in the morning and had a hangover. To answer your question, I initially believed most of the stories that Washington was putting out. I thought we ought to be in Vietnam at least for a while to help the people help themselves. We owed the South Vietnamese the right to fail. But we were dealing through a feudal-archaic elite that had no connection to the ordinary people. So I was getting more and more pessimistic by the minute and began to think that all the domino stuff was wrong. But I never thought that a half a million Americans would be sent there to repeat the French experience.

You didn't buy into the domino mindset and that the Chinese would intervene if we took the war north?

My instinct was that there were dominoes but of different sizes, shapes, and colors. Had we not been thinking that all communists were bad, there would have been a case for an Asian Tito. We could have worked through Ho Chi Minh and had an outpost based on nationalism against the Chinese. The North Vietnamese were more concerned about their historic enemy, the Chinese, than about the U.S. or the French. There's a great phrase of Ho Chi Minh's: "It is better to fight the French for ten years than to eat Chinese dung for another thousand." But, Washington was selling a monolith-communist block for domestic-political reasons. Communist countries were all one color on the map. By 1962, '63, and '64, when decisions to escalate U.S. involvement in Vietnam were made, Washington had considerable knowledge of Sino-Soviet tensions. We had intercepts of Russian and Chinese troops clashing on the borders, but Washington didn't want to accept gradations in the communist world. Vietnam was premised not just on dominoes but on a monotheistic block. The administration kept CIA intercepts and recommendations about the Sino-Soviet split hidden from the public. They weren't ready to deal with the political consequences of admitting that there was major tension in the communist world.

When did you first realize that Vietnam was a lost cause?

Very early on. Vann's people were very candid with us about the capacity of the Viet Cong to replenish. I also could sense Vann's frustrations. By late 1962, I had done enough recon of my own to know that America's official optimism was a living lie. No matter how hard I tried to be absolutely objective, the evidence coming in—the undertow—was enormous. The ARVN was only pillow punching. ARVN commanders wouldn't listen to American advisers on how to hit the VC. Diem didn't want to take casualties because of loss of face and, more important, he wanted his own troops close to Saigon in case of a coup. Diem's top commanders weren't there because they were great soldiers but because they were politically loyal. I kept getting these ingredients.

This was when there were only American advisers in Vietnam?

Only a few thousand advisers. The Army was sending really good people to Vietnam in those days. It was the best ticket in town. They were wonderful men. I really loved them. They reminded me, by and large, of high school principals in a small midwestern town. Horst Faas, an Associated Press photographer, and I rented a villa in Saigon. American advisers would come in from the fields and stay with us on their weekends off. They kept telling us about how the ARVN was losing, while their superiors in Saigon claimed that they were winning. You can imagine their frustration. It was like push-pull. If the official channel pushed down and suppressed the truth, the truth would come out in unofficial channels. Think of your average light or bird colonel. Those guys were feisty, independent guys. They weren't ass kissers. They weren't bureaucrats.

So you thought it wasn't in the cards for the South Vietnamese to defeat the Viet Cong?

It became clear that it wasn't going to happen. It just wasn't about Diem. He wasn't the cause of the problem; he was a reflection of it. I remember talking with Dave Hudson, a civilian strategies adviser in the delta. He was a strange guy who later took his own life. He told me early on that the problem with Vietnam was that the ARVN commanders and province chiefs were usually from the North, usually Catholic in a predominantly Buddhist country, almost always from the upper class, and put as much distance between themselves and the peasants as they could. In our nice Western way, we told them to go out and touch the people, but they wanted nothing of it. While on the other side, the local VC commissars were of peasant origin from the same region they operated, spoke the local dialect, were every day doing something with the peasants, and had been fighting the revolutionary war for twenty years—always on the winning side.

I thought bingo! There it was. Everything about the problem in Vietnam tacked together with that.

That was your wake-up call?

It brought everything together for me. The communists had a dynamic that worked. They promoted people based entirely on merit. The VC were very good soldiers. They never wasted men. They moved at night. You could never encircle them. They were used to fighting armies that had more air power, technology, tanks, and artillery. Their officers were very good. They couldn't afford political officers like the ARVN. There was a dynamic that drove them and made them meritocratic. Some of my American adviser friends told me that they would have much preferred to work with the Viet Cong.

When did you become aware that McNamara didn't want to hear the truth about what was really happening?

We were at first slow to pick up on this. We were innocent kids, and everybody was saying how brilliant the Kennedy people were. We assumed that these terrific guys wanted the truth; but then I realized that General [Paul D.] Harkins [head of MACV] was part of a lying machine. Harkins was a Max [Gen. Maxwell] Taylor plant. He was like a paralyzed rabbit who had just seen a snake about to strike him. He did what Taylor told him to do, which was to lie. And Taylor reported to McNamara. It's amazing the lying that went on. And now all these lies are coming out in books confirming how mendacious they were, all for political reasons. It just never ends. They wanted to protect Kennedy in the upcoming election year. They didn't care about Vietnam.

You observed this firsthand?

Yeah. When McNamara visited Vietnam on one of his many fact-finding trips, Ambassador Henry Cabot Lodge asked Neil Sheehan and myself to attend a briefing with the Secretary. Incidentally, Lodge also thought the war was a lost cause. Just prior to the briefing, we were told that we couldn't talk about the military situation, which allowed McNamara to go back to Washington and say that he hadn't heard anything that would make him think that we weren't winning the war. It was brilliantly done.

Did you report this in your dispatches?

We did. And the U.S. government tried to shut us up. The stuff aimed against us got real ugly and very personal, politically and sexually. I mean it was really nasty stuff. Five kid reporters were the major obstacles to Washington's political charade. There was Mal Browne, Peter Arnett, Horst Faas, Neil Sheehan, and myself—virtually the entire press corps at the time. We didn't have reputations then, but all five of us went on to win the Pulitzer Prize for our work in Vietnam. In those days, George Allen, who was one of the CIA's top people and a stellar figure in Westmoreland's group, told me that the only way that the CIA could find out what was going on was to read Neil Sheehan's and my dispatches. Everything else was doctored and sanitized. We showed that the war was not being won; it wasn't even being fought. I'm very proud of that reporting; it stands up very well today. I didn't have any great knowledge of Asia and of the world. The geopolitical stuff I learned in the last thirty years. But about what was happening on the ground, we were way ahead of the curve. The administration's response was to try and destroy our credibility—to diminish us personally. They said that we were radical left-wingers, that we were gay. Kennedy asked the publisher of the *New York Times* to pull me out of Vietnam. Johnson later referred to Neil Sheehan and me as traitors to our country and to our colleagues. There was a systematic attempt at briefings and at Washington social gatherings to undermine us. The damn bureaucrats living in the lap of luxury in Washington said that we never left the Hotel Cavavelle's bar. Bullshit. I went out on fifty to sixty missions with the ARVN, risking my life.

You were a target of character assassination?

Character assassination and public relations. It was very ugly stuff. Very mean. When [Senator] Mike Mansfield came over in 1963, we were asked to have lunch with him. By then, we were really weary of Washington politicians; one more high official to piss on us. Lunch went on for four hours. Mike was wonderful, and when he got back to Washington, he stood up on the Senate floor and defended us. It was the first time anybody had publicly spoken out for us. He said that the executive branch had more important things to worry about than some young American reporters overseas. We sent him a telegram saying that he made us all wish we were voting residents of Montana. I've had this affection for him ever since.

Was Vietnam McNamara's War?

It was in the sense that he made it in his vainglory and in his arrogance. I really disliked Robert McNamara. He saw Vietnam as an issue he could grab and dominate in order to look good to the Kennedys. He was a world-class brown nose, always upwardly mobile. His loyalty was to the president and not to the country. He was the guy who whacked anybody who tried to tell the truth. I mean there's just story after story about McNamara being the hit man. He was ferocious. This was very much the way he operated at Ford. I did a book on Ford Motor Company and got to know him fairly well. He was incredibly ambitious and ruthless in his assumptions of what he thought Henry Ford wanted. He would devastate the arguments of those people who contradicted his. In the Kennedy administration, George Ball [deputy undersecretary of state] told me that he went to meetings where McNamara would flail away at him about information that McNamara made up. He made stuff up on the spot to devastate people making contradictory claims. It was McNamara's egregiousness for power. It was his demented ambition. He disguised it in his own mind as loyalty to the man who held the office.

You weren't a McNamara fan?
   You're damn right. He was a pathological liar. He's still lying in his new book. He's still not telling the truth about why he made such egregious mistakes. He's got to know; he's not stupid. But he won't deal with that. He was lying when he said that we could never get accurate intelligence. He was on guard with a quad 50 trying to keep the information from coming in. All he had to do was put up a green light, and the stuff would come roaring in.

What were Kennedy's marching orders to McNamara?
   I think Kennedy's signals to McNamara were that he wanted Vietnam tamped down, to keep it on the back burner. That was his only marching order. Kennedy didn't want Vietnam to become an issue. He had more important stuff on his mind.

Kennedy needed McNamara?
   McNamara was important to Kennedy because he knew the numbers. He was the symbol of what technology could do in this little peasant country. But Washington made the same mistake that the French did. I just came back from Dienbienphu. It was the forty-fifth anniversary of that battle. I was the managing editor of the *Harvard Crimson* when it happened in the spring of 1954. You can't believe the arrogance of the French and how they overestimated their

own strength and underestimated that of the Vietminh. The Vietminh were very good, very tough, and not to be taken lightly. Then, after the French were annihilated, the Americans underestimated them. The arrogance of McNamara believing that technology would over- whelm them, that they would buckle when they saw the first American soldiers and fighter bombers. It was a total misreading of their ability to adapt to us—and disrespect for history. McNamara didn't study the French war. He didn't care about it. There was a real kind of racial arrogance to it. America paid a terrible price for that arrogance. I can remember John Vann telling me in 1967 that the NVA learned to fight us in the battle of the Ia Drang Valley in November 1965. Westy said we won because we killed 1,100 of their people and only lost 100 of our own. It wasn't a victory; it was exactly what they wanted. They virtually lifted layers for us to come in. Vann said they learned to fight within 30 meters to neutralize our air and artillery. If the Americans brought in air and artillery, they'd bring it in on their own people. We underestimated the willingness of these peasants to pay the price. We won every set piece battle. Westy still believes that he never lost a battle. We had absolute military superiority, and they had absolute political superiority, which meant that we would kill 200 and they would replenish them the next day. We were fighting the birth rate of a nation.

Did Kennedy intend to pull out of Vietnam after the 1964 election?

Kennedy was a cool piece of work and very pragmatic. He wanted to get through the 1964 election. The last thing he wanted to do was to use his second term in the rice paddies of Vietnam. We lost something when we got Lyndon Johnson. Kennedy was much more modern, much more sophisticated, and much better read. He knew that nationalism was the issue, not pure communism. He made this distinction when he visited Vietnam in the 1950s as a junior congressman. I don't think Johnson ever understood that. He saw Vietnam as the spreading of communism. I wrote about that in *The Best and the Brightest*. Given the macho way people like Joe Alsop played on Johnson's ego, there was no doubt about which way John- son would go. I feel sorry for him. It was a tragic presidency. Would Kennedy have pulled out? Kennedy was a very good politician. He would have figured out a scenario that would have allowed us to get out. He also knew peace was becoming an issue with the American people. He gave a bunch of speeches right before he was killed about peace and a new era and received huge responses. But, having said that, he also deepened U.S. commitment from six hundred to eighteen thousand advisers. He gave us the McNamara team, McGeorge Bundy [NSC adviser], and all those other guys. And he gave us Max Taylor, who wasn't another Matthew Bunker Ridgway.

You liked Ridgway?

Ridgway was one of my great personal heroes. He's arguably the greatest American soldier of the century. Ridgway's loyalty was always to the men who served under him, and Taylor's was always to the people that were above him. Taylor was a most political general.

And General Westmoreland? Was he the right man for the job?

I've never been very hard on Westmoreland. He looked like a general—great for the cover of *Time* magazine. But he had no feel for that war. Everything in his experience was conventional. He was the most conventional-thinking man in a war that was completely unconventional. He would have been wonderful fighting on the plains of Europe, but he wouldn't have been a star because he wasn't original enough. The civilians sent him over to Vietnam, and then, when it didn't work out, they tied the can to him. Bundy and McNamara walked away and left him holding the bag. Kitsy Westmoreland can probably tell you more about this. She essentially was his chief of staff. She had to be smart enough to know that the war wasn't going anywhere. She had to know that her husband was going down with the war and that he was probably in over his head. She was a wonderful woman and very heroic. There's a great novel in her.

You believed then that the U.S. buildup in 1964 was futile?

I did increasingly so. The war was essentially over by mid-1964. The Viet Cong had the ARVN pinned down. The ARVN was afraid to go out and fight, particularly at night. I was really stunned when we started sending American soldiers over. I remember sitting in a bar at the American Embassy in Poland. There were a bunch of guys from the embassy who were upbeat because they thought American troops would bring a quick end to the war. I told them that a lot of Americans were going to come back in wooden boxes. The Viet Cong and NVA were tougher than they thought, and they had a dynamic that would be very hard to penetrate.

Was there any time during your stay in Vietnam that you thought we could have won the war?

No. The disease was in the very nature of the country. There was a reason why the South Vietnamese didn't have good leadership. It was a feudal society. They didn't want it. Probably the last chance to do the right thing would have been around 1950 to 1954. By the time of Dienbienphu, it was a done deal. The North Vietnamese won the country fair and square. That gave them their historic legitimacy. Then we stole half of it from them at Geneva. This little country that had driven out the French, defeated the ARVN with all the American firepower, Hueys, fighter bombers, and American advisers. Then, they stalemated the mightiest army in the history of mankind. We sent a very good army there. We didn't get back a good army. So you have to have enormous respect for the North Vietnamese. Why were they willing to do the things that the ARVN were unwilling to do? It was about leadership and about political dynamics. I was learning that all the time. It was on-the-job learning.

Did you ever see any evidence of an industrial-military conspiracy perpetuating the war?

Never. In fact, the Vietnam War probably damaged the industrial-military complex. They liked big-ticket things, and canvas jungle boots weren't a big-ticket item. The driving impulse of Vietnam was political and the shadow of the Democratic Party having lost China in the late 1940s and early '50s.

You later returned to Vietnam?

I went back in 1967 for three months for *Harvard Magazine* and went around to all the places I knew from earlier. John Vann was very good at opening doors for me. Vann was pessimistic about our chances of winning but liked that his own career was on the rise. The more the war went down and lost legitimacy at home, the more his career went up. He had become some kind of a power junkie, sort of like Lawrence of Arabia—Vann of Vietnam. He didn't want to come home and be just another guy. I was profoundly depressed with what I saw. To use a phrase that Bernard Fall said so brilliantly: "We were fighting in the same footsteps as the French, although dreaming different dreams," because we didn't think of ourselves as a colonial power.

You didn't believe that we could win?

I thought we had lost. In fact, within a year, I started writing *The Best and the Brightest* because nothing was working, and I sensed the U.S. was going to pull back. The political equation at home was not going to tolerate our staying in Vietnam. The war was tearing America apart.

It is difficult to realize that over thirty-five years have passed since you worked the rice paddies of Vietnam.

I know. I was twenty-eight years old when I went there, and I'm sixty-five years old now. I mean, I'm all gray-haired, and yet Vietnam is still my identity. It never goes away. It's still the dominant story of my life.

TOM HAYDEN

*Time has proved me overly romantic about the Vietnamese
revolution. . . . The other side of that romanticism was a numbed
sensitivity to any anguish or confusion I was causing to U.S. soldiers
or to their families—the very people I was trying to save from
death and deception.*

—TOM HAYDEN, *In Reunion*

As I ride the rickety elevator cage to the California Senator's
second floor office in an old bank building on Pico Boulevard,
I think about the young radical who marched in the Civil Rights
movement in the South, violated the State Department's ban on travel
by twice visiting Hanoi, and disrupted the 1968 Chicago Democratic
Convention. What gave Tom Hayden the temerity, the presumption,
to take on the U.S. government?

While a junior at the University of Michigan in Ann Arbor, Hayden
met with leaders of student demonstrations against House Un-American Activities Committee (HUAC) and of southern sit-in movements
by black students and became a committed reformer. In late 1961,
he cofounded the Students for a Democratic Society (SDS) and, for
the next two years, was the organization's president. In 1964, he
moved to an all-black ghetto of Newark, New Jersey, and sponsored
rent strikes and welfare demonstrations. In 1965, his focus shifted
to the antiwar movement, and he flew to Hanoi to establish contact
between the American peace movement and the North Vietnamese
government.

Hayden's secretary informs me that he is stuck in traffic and will
be a few minutes late. He has just returned from Seattle, Washington,
where he led a demonstration against the World Trade Organization.
I'm amazed at his persistence, at his stamina. Four decades, and
he's still involved in causes. Activism is in his blood.

The door opens, and Hayden enters. Two assistants converge on
him with documents and checks to be signed. He hasn't been in his
Los Angeles office for more than a month. He glances over at me,
apologizes for being late, scratches his signature on checks and docu-

ments, barks a few commands, and then ushers me into his office. He pulls off his rumpled suit jacket and tosses it on a chair. He loosens his tie and fidgets with the top button of his wrinkled dress shirt until it finally releases.

Sporting a grayish-white goatee and a full head of gray hair, he slumps into his chair and kicks his feet up on the desk. His nose is unusually large, his skin scarred from acne during adolescence; he's an unlikely candidate to have been married to the glamorous actress, Jane Fonda. As he depicts in his book, "I was a famous radical who was morally and politically skeptical about fame; she was an actress whose career itself depended on public acclaim. We must have appeared like a remake of the beauty and the beast." He's a bit tense but soon relaxes as we share our common appetite for Albert Camus and how the French existentialist has impacted both of our lives.

You were against American involvement in Vietnam from the beginning?

In the early 1960s, I was deeply involved in the Civil Rights movement in the South. The country had been lulled into a certain confidence because Lyndon Johnson had campaigned on a slogan of not sending American military to Vietnam, so I didn't take the prospect of war seriously up until then. I really didn't think about Vietnam. But with the movement of American troops in 1964, I began to see Vietnam as an unexplainable diversion back into Cold War politics and militarism and away from civil rights and poverty at home. I wanted military spending to be shifted from the arms race to domestic-poverty programs. Johnson lied. The Democratic Party as a whole was behind the war and lied to the American people.

That's when you became involved with Vietnam?

Vietnam became a preoccupation of mine. I plunged into everything that had been written during the conflicts with the French. It was clear to me that Vietnam was a national independence war and not an expansion of communism based in Peking and Moscow, as Washington wanted us to believe. My concern was how were we going to fight poverty in the United States if the country was going to divert its resources to a war in Vietnam?

When did the FBI start making a file on you?

I guess that I came to the FBI's attention in 1960 or '61. I had been hitchhiking around the country as a student journalist and wrote about some students who had been beaten and hosed on the steps of a government building in San Francisco. They had been protesting J. Edgar Hoover's pet institution, the House Un-American Activities Committee. My focus was on the bravery of the students who were willing to be hosed and beaten for what they believed in. I knew something about HUAC from the [Senator Joseph] McCarthyism period in the 1950s, when dissenters were muzzled or tormented because they were communists—or allegedly communists. So in my mind, the effect of the Cold War was to escalate the arms race, while keeping people quiet at home. In other words, unite the country against a foreign enemy, which meant there was no official recognition that we had problems in the United States. All of our problems were seen as arising from conspiracies abroad. This policy came across to me as outrageous paternalism. We were supposed to be quiet, obedient, and keep our places. If we got out of line, we were seen as troublemakers and, worse than that, as pawns of a conspiracy abroad. The FBI dutifully reported to Hoover that I had written an editorial criticizing HUAC, which was really an editorial praising the students. That may have started an FBI file on me, but I'm not sure there was one then.

You were deferred from the draft?

I remember arguments with my draft board as to whether I was nonviolent. Basically, I said that I hadn't thought it all the way through, but that I was nonviolent particularly toward the Vietnam War. I was classified 1Y because of a lifetime allergic reaction to dust.

Would you have served if you had been physically accepted?

It's hard to predict what I would have done. I didn't know if there was a way to go into service without engaging in killing. I knew nothing about the road to Canada. It wasn't clear how much time I would serve in prison, nor did I know if I even would be sent to Vietnam.

You were involved with the Students for a Democratic Society at the time. Was this a genuine movement to protest the war, or was it a way for students to avoid going to Vietnam?

SDS was on many campuses around the country long before Vietnam. It grew out of the overall birth of student idealism in the 1960s. It could have been the atmosphere of the time, or the civil rights movement in the South, or the election of a young new president.

But, it was definitely a generational rebellion against the perceived failures and apathies of the country. It had nothing to do with Vietnam. From 1965 to 1970, it was a big tent under which hundreds of thousands of people with twenty or thirty causes paraded—everything from trying to reform the Democratic Party to trying to burn down the government.

There have been charges that the SDS was a communist front?
The SDS was homegrown radicalism; populist in spirit. The American Communist Party was fairly feeble. It didn't play any kind of leading, guiding, or central role in the organization, not only because it was weak but also because the SDS was a youth rebellion. There weren't a lot of youths in the communist movement. There was a flirtation with more revolutionary figures like Fidel Castro and Che Guevara, but that was more of a romantic identification.

Were you a communist or a member of the Communist Party?
No. I think Herbert Aptheker, with whom I traveled to North Vietnam, was the only communist that I ever knew well. I primarily saw him as an intelligent, obviously doctrinaire, very well-meaning, older Jewish guy from New York who had written history books.

You must have gone through hell in making a decision to go to Hanoi in 1965?
Today, we would say that I was "freaking out." I was twenty five years old; I had never been outside of the United States, except once to Tijuana [Mexico]. I was completely naïve about what I was getting into. I was born and raised in a totally apolitical family. There was no talk in my house about politics or protests. For whatever reason, I was a strangely curious kid. I thought the world was sort of crazy and absurd. My father didn't talk to me for fifteen years after I told him that I was going to Hanoi. He already thought I had lost it by wasting my college education when I decided to work with poor people in a Newark ghetto. My mother went into total trepidation as if something was going to happen to her, but at least we continued to talk. There were two primary things in my mind—and I'm just being perfectly frank about this. One was the romantic adventure of going to North Vietnam. The other involved Staughton Lynd, a very dear and personal friend of mine, who asked me to go with him. He was a Quaker who worked with me in the Civil Rights movement in the south. He was a little older than me and a lot wiser.

Were you aware of the consequences for going? Vietnam was off-limits to American citizens.

Yeah. Discrediting the work I was doing in civil rights was a very worrisome factor. And there was the little matter of breaking the law because what we were doing was civil disobedience on an international scale. We were taking the risk of being prosecuted for traveling to a country that was classified as a "no-go" area for Americans. The prospect of prison didn't bother me. Accusations of being an enemy of my own country were my greatest worry.

Why then did you?

The United States was bombing North Vietnam, but no one was allowed to see it. We were rendering these people as faceless objects and dehumanizing them. I thought maybe I could help uncover information about whether we were bombing civilians. Staughton had a utopian idea that we were going to sit down with the North Vietnamese leaders and negotiate a peace proposal that would end the war. I was too young to even imagine that role.

Of all the millions of people in the United States who could have gone to North Vietnam, did it ever cross your mind back then, "Why me?"

I don't have an explanation because it would mean that I am either extraordinarily special or extraordinarily egotistical. I don't know, but it was an attitude that people like me had at the beginning of the sixties. It was a confidence that we could do it, even though it had never been done before.

You flew directly to Hanoi?

No. We flew to Czechoslovakia and East Europe and then spent five days in China before arriving in Hanoi.

U.S. policy at that time was based on the assumption that China would intervene if the United States pushed the war north.

I heard some rhetoric in China about that, but I was not able to measure it. The McNamara model at the time was that Vietnam would be like Korea. In other words, if we went north, the Chinese would intervene. I got no sense of that. China was preoccupied with its Cultural Revolution and the allegation that the Soviet Union was becoming too soft. They saw Vietnam in terms of Russia, but I definitely came away with the view that the main issue for China was the Soviet Union. China didn't want a Soviet ally on their southern border. They were thinking first and foremost from their own standpoint, not that of the Vietnamese. I don't have an opinion on whether the Chinese would have intervened if the United States had invaded the North in 1966. It's a scary scenario, and since it didn't play out, you can judge for yourself.

Obviously, you didn't broker a peace agreement during your visit to North Vietnam?

Obviously. A representative of the communist Peace Committee met us at the airport in Hanoi and escorted us to the usual factories and museums. Perhaps what struck me the most was the country's historic revolutionary nationalism and how uninformed Americans were about it. To me, it was clearly a fight for the unification of one Vietnam. After the collapse of the French, the United States violated the 1954 Geneva Accords that called for a national election in 1956. Instead of going ahead with a secret ballot election, the United States broke its word and backed a Republic of South Vietnam. It was clear to Washington that Ho Chi Minh would win overwhelmingly.

You were called a traitor when you returned from Hanoi.

I know, but I thought going was an American thing to do. The best way that I could support the American soldiers was to stop the killing.

Why did you return to North Vietnam two years later in November 1967?

I had a far-fetched hope that there could be a bridge to dialogue and peace talks. There were six or seven of us. But, it turned out to be the same sort of visit as in 1965, when we witnessed the war through the North Vietnamese eyes. There was also further discussion of prisoner releases. That was one of the real reasons that I went. The North Vietnamese wouldn't turn the prisoners over to the United States government; they wanted to release them to an American in Cambodia. So they called me. I was twenty seven years old then.

Was that a propaganda move on the part of Hanoi to release the American captors to an antiwar activist?

Everything about the conflict on both sides was political and jockeying for position and getting their message out.

Did the U.S. government attempt to stop you from going to Hanoi?

No. I told the State Department that I was going and that I would tell them what I learned, but it became complex when I had these POWs on my hands. The State Department must have had some interesting internal conversations about me—that the prisoner release would be botched if the POWs weren't allowed to leave with an antiwar activist. I don't remember whose commercial airliner we boarded in Cambodia. We flew to India, then to someplace in the Middle East. There were U.S. intelligence people in the plane. On the last leg to the States, it was very moving to watch the three former POWs looking at the lights of New York after having been prisoners on the Cambodian-Vietnamese border three days earlier. It was very emotional. When we hit the ground, I went one way and they went another.

Did you sense that Washington was using you?

I was resigned to being used by everyone for a good end.

Did Hanoi think, at this point, that the war could be won on the streets of America rather than on the military battlefield?

I think they thought the war would be primarily won in Vietnam. But had the United States been winning the war, they absolutely believed that there would be no antiwar movement. The antiwar movement could develop only if the United States was strategically stalemated or defeated. There was a role for public opinion, but they didn't expect that people marching on the streets of America would win the war for them.

So you didn't think that you were part of Hanoi's grand strategy in 1967 to help build an antiwar sentiment in the United States?

I think that they hoped the war could be resolved in 1968 by a combination of the Tet Offensive and the effect it would have in the United States. The first battlefield was South Vietnam. The first political theater was the South; the second political theater was in the United States.

Were you debriefed when you returned to the United States?

I had a meeting sometime shortly after returning at the State Department in Washington. I told them my opinion about the war.

I didn't have any special insights from the trip. They thanked me. It was all very odd.

Shortly afterward, Nixon came into power with his secret plan to end the war. Were you aware of U.S. threats to use nuclear weapons on the North?

Yes. Nixon's secret plan was a deceitful scheme to escalate the war. I have seen documents in which the North Vietnamese estimated potential nuclear weapon damages. I believed that the American effort would escalate to tactical nuclear weapons if it was unsuccessful conventionally. The United States would never tolerate defeat. I also learned about this when I was in Hanoi from North Vietnamese strategists. They were considering what their options were in terms of a nuclear attack.

They were creating plans in case of a nuke attack?

Yeah. They definitely considered America's use of nukes a possibility. They were very aware that a nuke attack would kill millions of their people, and that it would be moral suicide for the United States.

You were one of the Chicago Seven at the Democratic Convention in Chicago in August 1968?

By that time, I had radicalized quite a bit. At the beginning of 1968, I believed that it was possible that Robert Kennedy could win the nomination and the presidency and end the war. I had met with him on a few occasions on this subject. When he and Martin Luther King were killed, I shifted to a more implacable stance.

To the point that you were willing to risk going to prison?

I expected to be arrested and jailed.

What was the purpose of disrupting the convention?

Our strategy was to show that the Democratic Party would lose all credibility if it didn't promise to end the war. It was our last card to play. I don't think that the full history has been revealed or understood about whether the party considered ending the war or what went on behind the scenes. We wanted to make the price of the war so heavy to continue that they'd end it. Reason had never worked; moral persuasion had never worked. We didn't have forever to reason or moralize because people were getting killed in increasing numbers. At that point, we had come to an existential turning point that to continue the war, it would have to be over our dead bodies. We were prepared to go to jail and, if necessary, die. I say existential because very often the peace movement was misunderstood because it had so many elements. I had an increasingly obsessed feeling that death was everywhere. Death was on television, in body bags, and children napalmed in Vietnam. How could we protest from the sidelines? It required getting as close to risking your life as possible, or we weren't really serious.

Did you consider yourself a patriot?

Patriot is a very abused term. I was brought up a certain way in this country under certain expectations, ideals, and values. I would go into a rage because those values that I thought were American were being betrayed. If I were in a foreign country that didn't have the same values or traditions, or criminal justice system, I'd have different expectations. If the government was oppressive, I'd react differently. But in that sense, yeah, I fashioned myself a patriot.

And yet you were once again called a traitor by your government.

They called us traitors and subversives. There was an overtone of "We know what is best for you" and "You are being misled," or "You didn't get properly raised by your parents," as if they thought we were rebelling against our parents and authority.

Or manipulated by the communists.

I felt a certain admiration and respect for the valor of the Viet Cong. I think many American soldiers did as well. That is different from being manipulated. It just added to the misery of why we were slaughtering these people. The insulting concept in the U.S. was that the Viet Cong kept coming because they were Asian; they didn't care about human life. It was our government that was taking their lives by the thousands. No, I don't think that there was any manipulation. You must remember that, at that time, it was widely believed in this country that youthful disturbances were always manipulated by outside agitators on behalf of foreign powers. It is harder to make that argument now that the Cold War is over and there is no Soviet Union. It was really insulting then to students because it was precisely adult authority from which they were feeling alienated. The war was fought intensely around dinner tables. I wasn't alone when my father wouldn't speak to me for fifteen years. There were thousands of similar cases across the country. On the other side, there were fathers who coerced, manipulated, if you will, and pressured their sons to go to Vietnam—and their sons were killed or wounded or came back drug-addicted. Those fathers had something to work out that was almost irresolvable as well.

You were indicted at the Democratic Convention along with other members known as the Chicago Seven?
We were indicted in March 1969 by the incoming Nixon administration. John Mitchell was the attorney general. The trial began in September 1969. We were charged with two counts. First was conspiracy to cross interstate lines with the intent to incite or cause disturbance. Everybody was acquitted on that. The second charge involved a specific act for each person. Mine was confrontation with the police. That charge carried five years. We were all found guilty. Every day, the courtroom was rocking and rolling with arguments and bizarre witnesses and outbursts by the judge. It turned out that all the legal arguments, all the rhetoric, all the witnesses didn't fundamentally matter. Two-thirds of the jurors thought we were all guilty and should be put in jail. The other four jurors thought that no matter what we had done, the war was wrong so we shouldn't be blamed. They could have hung the jury. Instead, they compromised. For me, that was a metaphor for what was wrong with adult America. There were people who absolutely felt that we were innocent, but, despite the Constitution and the instructions to the jury, they consciously voted for a guilty verdict for seven individuals whom they thought were innocent in order to get the other jurors to acquit on the first verdict. So they made a political compromise to give us five years instead of ten because they couldn't agree with each other.

Did you serve time in prison?
No, none of us did. We were granted bail and were retried in late 1973 on contempt charges. By then, the atmosphere in the country had changed. I was cleared of all charges.

When did you meet Jane Fonda?
A year after the trial in 1971.

Why do Vietnam vets still harbor such disdain for her?
Was it because she was a famous woman, a beautiful movie star? She touched something in the GIs that I certainly didn't.

What about the allegations of her standing on an antiaircraft emplacement in Hanoi and talking about shooting down American pilots?

I wasn't there, but I don't believe she said that. I do know what Jane told me. Jane was taken on a tour. She was a very smart but exploitable person. She was a movie actress who was used to being led around and having her picture taken. Her motivation in going to Hanoi was entirely understandable. She had been led to believe that the bombing was so severe that dikes might be destroyed, and that only by having an internationally known personality go there would attention be drawn to this issue. That was why she went. Before that, despite whatever they said about her, she was consistently pro-GI in a friendly and subversive way. She went to military bases and put on alternative performances to the Bob Hope show. She believed the American GIs were being misled, and she wasn't going to be censored or prevented from trying to reach them. When she was in Hanoi, you have to remember that there were antiaircraft installations everywhere from small antiaircraft guns to big SAM missiles. At one of these installations, the North Vietnamese wanted her to say hello to the antiaircraft crew. Somebody asked her to sing an American song and then a Vietnamese song. And then a French photographer asked her to pose with the conscripts from the village. She climbed onto the artillery installation and looked through a scope, and click. She knew the minute the guy took the picture that she was in trouble, and the rest is history. But how this happened was fascinating to me. It's a version of what you call war stories. They get bigger, and, at a certain point, you don't know what is true or what is elaboration.

In 1974, you lobbied in Congress to cut off money for Vietnam?

Right. We organized a group called the Indochina Peace Campaign and lobbied in key states with the largest electoral votes. We opened an office in Washington because the tide of opinion about the Vietnam War had changed, and it was then possible to influence congressional votes to cut off funding or to make funding conditional on peace gestures.

Did your campaign's efforts help bring an end to the war?

It certainly felt like we helped end the war. The people that we were opposing never gave us any indication that they were planning to end the war on their own. That was never communicated. There were votes cast in Congress that terminated funding. Those votes were cast because of the stalemate on the battlefield and the increasing skepticism in Congress brought on by the public who felt the administration had lied to them. But, yes, we influenced legislatures to cut the funding.

Many claim that the antiwar movement prolonged the war by encouraging the North to hang tough.

I've never seen evidence that the war would have been shortened if there had been no antiwar movement.

In hindsight, would you have done anything different?

In 1969 and '70, I was angry most of the time. It was a terrible state of mind. I grew up in a time when drugs were seen as controversial, and I did no drugs. But I wonder how much living on the edge and drinking and feeling that I was going to jail affected my ability to have compassion or to think clearly. I know that there were a lot of people who probably experienced the same feelings. For example, I was furious when Nixon brought the POWs home and used them to justify the continuing of the war. I regret that I didn't show more respectful compassion for the POWs.

What about the spitting on vets?

I heard that antiwar protesters spit on returning vets, which I internalized as the truth. I was ashamed and upset about it. But then, I realized that spitting was being turned into a manipulative myth that discredited the antiwar movement when the vets had been really abused by political policies and not by the opponents of the policies. It didn't make any sense to me that antiwar protesters were hanging around airports and spitting on returning vets. I never could document one incident.

Looking back, did you think that your antiwar activities might have had a negative effect on the soldiers fighting in Vietnam?

Yes, absolutely. I didn't want the soldiers to get killed, and I didn't want them to be dishonorably discharged. I wanted the soldiers to help end the war by communicating to the press, their commanders, and the folks back home. I can understand that if you were a soldier and believed that we should be fighting the war, you would be aggravated by some guy saying the war is wrong. On the other hand, there were a lot of soldiers who thought the war was wrong and who thought maybe the people who were opposing it could shorten it before they got their heads blown off. As with everything else in this conversation, there were many spectrums.

And most certainly the GIs in Vietnam?

The ones that I felt the worst for were the soldiers who knew they were the last ones to die. Think of the guys who were dragged over there in 1969 and '70. They knew half the country was totally against the war. They knew their chances of getting wounded or killed were significant. They got into drugs. They got into undisclosed levels of mutiny. They were dishonorably discharged by the thousands, and, through all of that, some of them were going to be the unlucky guys to die for a cause that they didn't believe in. The soldiers from 1969 to 1971 have to be considered the ones who did the dog's duty and suffered the most. I don't know what comfort you could give them. Didn't they know that they were risking their lives for a government that wasn't telling the truth about a war that they weren't going to win? Those guys' stories really haven't been told.

LE LY HAYSLIP

Western culture meant bars, brothels, black markets, a
minh—bewildering machines—most of them des
—LE LY HAYSLIP, *When Heaven and Earth Changed Places*

The first thought to strike me when I first heard about Le Ly Hayslip was the odds. What were the odds that a twelve-year-old peasant girl in a remote South Vietnamese village could make it out of the rice paddies and later have her story told on Hollywood's big screen—in Oliver Stone's *Heaven and Earth*? The odds were infinitesimally higher that she never would have made it past her fifteenth birthday. And Le Ly wasn't just a poor peasant girl—she was a Viet Cong.

At the risk of being called blasphemous names by Vietnam vets that still write her hate mail because of her VC past, I asked her on the phone to talk about the women and children who were caught up in the Vietnam tragedy—the war's real victims. Countless numbers of women and children were killed and maimed by bullets and mines and napalm and raped by marauding soldiers who saw them as mere spoils of war. Countless more were uprooted from their land and their ancestors and their dreams and hopes. Many were taken to torture chambers and stripped of all dignity to divulge a brother's or uncle's location. They watched in horror when American bulldozers plowed open their ancestors' sacred graves and leveled whole villages within an hour. Most of us never once felt their pain or even understood their anguish and terror. They were faceless, inanimate objects who came to life only when they pulled out a grenade from beneath their skirts and killed one of our own.

I recall seeing young girls like Le Ly, perched on top of water buffalo and carrying their infant siblings on their hips, as I trudged through nameless villages. Had I only then been able to see us Americans through these children's eyes with the unfathomable terror of some and curiosity of others. None of this crossed my mind. I also remember their mothers and grandmothers prematurely aged by the sun. They are images of who Le Ly would have grown up to be had it not been for the war.

.neet Le Ly at her five-bedroom home a block from the golf .urse in La Costa, California. She is just under 5 feet in high heels. I can almost envision her wearing a flowing silk *ao dai,* the traditional dress of Vietnamese women. She escorts me into her office. Placed about the room are mementos for her humanitarian efforts from world leaders and U.S. legislators. On the coffee table are her books, *When Heaven and Earth Changed Places* and *Child of War, Woman at Peace,* and a book about the making of *Heaven and Earth* with Oliver Stone. She shows me a loft that she built to house a Buddhist temple and shrine in honor of the ancestors whom she worships daily.

She tells me about her humanitarian projects, which involve building schools, orphanages, and medical centers in Vietnam, and about her upcoming trip for the grand opening of a vocational training center of which she is managing director. This will be her forty-seventh return visit to Vietnam. Her voice reveals her Vietnamese heritage, but her mind is that of a street-savvy, complex, and contemporary woman. As I listen to her, I find it increasingly more difficult to visualize her back in the tiny village of Xa Hoa Qui, Quang Nam Province, that she calls Ky La Village in her book.

Le Ly's life began as the sixth and last child of a rice farmer. She says that all the males in her family, except for her father, left her village for the North in 1954 to fight for the communists. One of her brothers was missing in action, and another one spent three years on the Ho Chi Minh Trail. Her father committed suicide by drinking battery acid after being tortured in her village by U.S. soldiers.

As was the case with many village girls throughout South Vietnam, Le Ly was a Viet Cong sentinel charged with warning the guerrillas— whom she refers to as liberators. I pause and wonder how many of the innocent-looking little girls whom I came across signaled my whereabouts? I believed then that I was in Vietnam to keep her people free of communist oppression, and yet she says that 85 percent of the South Vietnamese supported the VC. I am stunned; I had no idea. I wonder if she's right.

I ask her about being raped by two VC young men when she was fourteen. Did this not change her feelings about the virtues of the Viet Cong? She says dismissively that the two young men were victims of the war. She harbors no hatred for them. Her almost mystical take on life fascinates me and takes me to a side of her that I hope can shed some light on how she ended up in La Costa.

Le Ly left her village, after having been twice arrested and tortured, and moved first to Da Nang and then to Saigon with her mother when she was fifteen. There, she worked as a maid for a wealthy businessman. She was evicted from the house when she became pregnant by the owner and returned to Da Nang, where she supported herself and her son by working as a black marketer selling whiskey, laundry soap, and gum. She says that, to make more money, she sometimes sold marijuana, *Playboy* magazines, and dirty pictures to American GIs—while, all the time, she was sympathetic to the Viet Cong. She's quick to point out that she didn't sell her body, day in and day out, as did many other girls. On one occasion, however, she had sex with two American GIs to earn enough money to purchase a house for her mother and son so that they would not be homeless any longer.

It was in Da Nang that she met Ed Munro, a civilian construction worker thirty-five years her senior. They married, and she had a second child before moving to San Diego in 1970. She describes the cultural shock as catastrophic—a water buffalo girl abruptly thrust into metropolitan America.

In 1986, she returned to Vietnam. What she found disturbed her. Her village was still ravaged by the war. Land mines, homeless Amerasian children, and poverty were everywhere. She decided to do something about it and has not stopped since then. She calls herself a bridge builder between her two worlds.

You grew up in a small village outside Da Nang?

It was a small village then, of about twenty to thirty families, situated on desert sand near China Beach. We were very poor but happy. For the first twelve years of my life, my name was Phung Thi Le Ly. When the war came to my village, my father taught me how to be a man and a woman at the same time. Our history talks about the Phung Thi Chin, the Trung sisters, and other heroes that beat the Chinese, the Japanese, the French, and then the Americans. There was no difference between the invaders. They raped our women, tortured our men, burned our houses, and destroyed our villages and temples and our ancestor's graveyards.

Were you a typical Vietnamese villager?

Yes. I am a lucky typical villager. First, I was born in late 1949. That was almost the end of the war with the French that concluded in 1954. In those first years of my life, I had already witnessed what my older sisters and mothers had to do to keep from being raped by the French and Moroccan soldiers. Those were horror stories that I will never forget. There were many "My Lai" massacres that took place in my country that no one knew about. We did not ask for war; we didn't ask for anything but to be left alone. I worked in the rice paddies with our water buffalo, and when we returned home each day, I took care of our ducks and chickens. My dream was to marry a village boy, to live in a little bamboo hut, and to have five children. When I got old, my children and grandchildren would be around me, and when I died, I would be buried next to my ancestors. My children and grandchildren would burn incense and worship me every night so that I could be reborn again and take care of my karma. It was a very simple life.

When were you first aware that your country was at war?
When President Ngo Dinh Diem was assassinated in 1963. The Viet Cong warned us that the South Vietnamese army would sell out our country to foreign invaders and destroy our village. I was twelve at the time.

Did you believe the Viet Cong?
Of course; they were people from our village. I knew they told us the truth. The guerrillas from my village we called "uncle" and "brother" and "sister." They were liberators. We didn't call them Viet Cong. Viet Cong was a name the Americans invented.

They were freedom fighters?
Right. Before the Americans, our mothers and fathers fought against the French. It was the same thing. At first, we didn't know who the Americans were. We thought the French had come back because they looked the same. If strangers invaded our homes here in La Costa, California, what do you think the people here would do—just watch and do nothing? No way. They would fight just like we did in my little village in Vietnam. Even at ten years of age, we wanted to help our freedom fighters.

Did you think the NVA were also freedom fighters?
Yes, of course. There were three types of freedom fighters. There were the guerrillas from my village; the liberators south of the 17th Parallel, who moved around the country and sometimes fought with the NVA and whom the Americans called "Viet Cong"; and the NVA that came down from North Vietnam. We only saw the NVA from a distance; they never came into my village.

What was important to you and the villagers?

Most importantly, the villagers wanted to live in peace and harmony with father sky-heaven and motherland earth. We wanted to be able to work in the rice paddies without interruption. We wanted to worship our ancestors, take care of our children, and take care of our parents and grandparents. Those were our basic needs and wants. If anything destroyed that, then we had to fight.

Did you have any sense of communist ideology when you were a girl?

We believed that communists were somewhere outside of Vietnam, like in Russia. We never used the word "communists." We didn't understand who they were, where they were, or what they were.

Did you know about Ho Chi Minh?

Of course, we sang to him every night. That's another thing I did during the daytime. I sang and danced for the South Vietnamese army. I killed chickens and ducks and cooked for them, but they didn't pay. At night, we sang and danced for the Viet Cong. We sang to Uncle Ho that he would bring love to our village. So we played both roles. But our hearts and minds were at night with the freedom fighters. In the daytime, helicopters and machine guns represented horror and suffering. At night, under the beautiful moon with the people in black uniforms, it was very peaceful. We felt that something protected us in the dark. It helped us continue with our work in helping our brothers and uncles fight against the Republican soldiers.

What did you and your friends do to help fight the soldiers?

Our role was mostly to signal the freedom fighters when we saw South Vietnamese soldiers. We were sentries. If we found out when the South Vietnamese would attack, we told our parents, who would get the message to the Viet Cong. We also stole weapons, hid the Viet Cong underground, helped the wounded, cooked and sang songs for them, and buried the dead.

How did you signal to the Viet Cong that soldiers were in the area?

Sometimes we changed the color of our skirts to send signals. For example, black was a very dangerous color; white was the coast was clear; and brown meant to watch out. When I rode on my water buffalo out in the fields, if there was a white American patrol leader, I would shout, "There will be a white water buffalo crossing the rice paddy." If the patrol leader was black, I would shout, "Black water buffalo is coming." Sometimes, it would take four or five people to relay the message before it reached the Viet Cong. But we had to be careful because if an American soldier was wounded or killed in or near my village, the Americans would drop bombs or fire rockets and destroy our village. If one South Vietnamese soldier was wounded or killed, the villagers would be taken to prison camp and beaten and tortured. If one Viet Cong was killed or wounded, the VC would blame it on the villagers and lecture us on how to do a better job. We children and villagers wanted to make sure the Americans and Vietnamese were safe so that they would return to their base as soon as possible. We took the Viet Cong underground so they wouldn't get hurt or killed. Our job was not to kill the enemy. Our job was to make sure everybody was safe so we could survive.

Did you believe that you were doing an important job for your people?

We didn't know how important that was. It was fun.

Fun?

We were children. We went out at night. We were so scared. Our parents were worried to death about us. We hid like in the game of hide-and-seek. Helicopters would fly above us with machine guns in the door. For a little girl ten to twelve years old, to run from place to place and hide was fun.

What did you think when you first saw a helicopter?

An American helicopter we called "may bay chuon-chuon," the dragonfly, landed in the middle of my village. We thought that heaven sent something down from another planet. Two huge men jumped out. We just looked at them and thought, "Wow!" We hoped that they would return to visit us after they left; we were so excited. It was like we were given a special gift from this machine from the heavens like in *E.T.* movies. But our parents knew something was wrong. They thought that it was the French returning with new machines.

You didn't know they were Americans at that time?

No. Our parents told us that they were the French.

The Viet Cong didn't tell you who they were?
Most of them were villagers just like us. At first, they didn't know.

Did Americans understand the importance of your ancestors?
How many families do you know here in America that put a memorial to their ancestors in the middle of their living room? God created our "ong ba to tien," our ancestors, and our ancestors created us. Every night we talk to them. When we refer to our ancestors that means we refer to God. Our ancestors are our God. How can we turn our backs against God? They give us life and everything on earth to live with. When the Americans destroyed our ancestors' graveyards, we felt that they were evil. How dare they come into our country and dig up our ancestors' graves with their bulldozers? How dare they destroy our temples and shrines where we worshipped the souls of the dead? How dare they do such a thing when we wouldn't dare walk on our ancestors' graves?

Did you believe the fight between North and South Vietnam was a religious war between Buddhists and Catholics?
Oh, yes. When the French were in Vietnam, they interrogated my parents about their religion. My parents always answered "luong giao," which means they had no religion. If they had replied that they were "dao ong ba," or Buddhists, they would be forced to destroy their ancestors' altars and shrines and replace them with a big cross. My parents were then forced to go to the Catholic church. This mentality carried over to the American war. When the Americans came to our village, we saw them the same as we did the French and gave them the same answer. We didn't know any other religion except Catholic and Buddhist. We tried to protect our heritage, the family tradition, by practicing teachings of Taoism and Confucianism. We didn't have temples so we worshipped at home. The Americans said that was wrong; that we must go to church. Some Christians came to our village and built a church, handed out Bibles, and taught us to believe in Jesus Christ. They told us that Buddha was not the right man to worship. The more they tried to educate us about their God, the more we wanted to fight.

Did you kill any Americans?
We didn't have any guns, so we didn't kill anybody. None of the children in my village had any weapons. The best thing we could

do was to help set up bamboo booby traps. Later on, we learned that bamboo didn't do so well, so we used nails.

When you were raped by two Viet Cong, did that change your mind about freedom fighters?

The two men came from my village. I worked underground with them for days digging a tunnel. They knew that raping me was wrong. But the war was so terrible, watching people being killed every day— I think they were a little crazy. I don't know the reason why they raped me. I had nothing against them then and still don't.

Your mother taught you how to survive?

We say that "khon cung chet, dai cung chet, biet thi song," which means if you know what is going on, you die. If you don't know anything, you still die. But if you know what to do, then you survive. That meant, to survive, we had to play stupid.

Your mother took you to Da Nang when you were a child. What was your impression of the big city before the American soldiers arrived?

For a little girl, it was like going to the moon. The people looked rich. There were many beautiful things that we would have loved to have in my village, like electricity and running water. There were cars and motorcycles, women with makeup and beautiful clothes, and the marketplace filled with good food. But, in one or two days, I cried and cried. I wanted to go back to my water buffalo, dogs, cats, and ducks in my village.

What did you see when you moved to Da Nang after the Americans had come?

I was fifteen then. Everything changed. There were a lot of bars, nightclubs, and girls in miniskirts and high heels. The American GIs were everywhere. There were so many trucks, jeeps, and tanks in convoy. Almost everyone carried a weapon.

What did you think, as a young Vietnamese woman, of the prostitutes?

When I was growing up in the village and worked with my mother and sister in the rice paddy, I overheard them talk about Vietnamese women selling their bodies to the French and Moroccan soldiers. They asked how these women could sleep with men who killed their people. Even as a child, I hated those women who slept with the enemy. So when the Americans arrived and my sister had an American boyfriend, it was very hard for me to accept. At first, when the American boyfriend was inside her home in Da Nang, I stayed outside until he left. I wondered how my sister, my own blood, could destroy our family name.

But you married an American?

My first husband was a civilian contractor. He built roads for the Americans. My second husband was in the military, but in the Korean War, not in Vietnam. I did not marry or become involved with anyone who fought against the Viet Cong until I fell in love with the U.S. Army major who helped me and my children get out of Vietnam by helicopter.

Did you know then that the prostitutes spied for the Viet Cong?

Of course, many of them. Do you know why women became prostitutes? Because Americans burned their homes and villages, and they became homeless. Everything was turned upside down. So they went to the cities for work. They were war refugees. The Americans called them stupid "gooks." Also, many young girls left their villages to find work in the cities. Government officials hired them to work in their homes. Some worked in American compounds. When they returned to their villages to see their families, they talked about what they heard and saw in their jobs. That information was passed on to the Viet Cong. Americans didn't understand about our desire to stop the war. The Vietnamese people said that when the war comes to our house, all women must fight. I would say that 85 percent of the Vietnamese were farmers who didn't want Americans to destroy and kill our people. What would you do if you were a Vietnamese villager? Would you fight? I think so. It was the noble thing to do.

Are you saying that 85 percent of the Vietnamese people wanted the Viet Cong to win?

Yes. Most of the people in the big cities were Viet Cong sympathizers but pretended to be in support of the South Vietnamese government. We had a saying: "An com quoc gia, tho ma cong san." Eat the rice of the Republican but worship the communist. All the jobs were in the cities, and even though many men wore the South Vietnamese uniform, they did it only for survival. That is why they were called "puppet soldiers." Almost all the workers in the big cities tried to help the VC, in the hope that the war would end so they could return to their land and villages to be with their ancestors. The networking between the city people and the VC in the villages was simply part of our citizen's duty to our fatherland and fellow country-men. As you know, in 1975, when the North made their final offen-sive, almost everyone turned their backs on the South Vietnamese government and either fled the country or became a Viet Cong. When the NVA entered the cities, almost everyone supported the victors. That is the reason the North was able to take over the South overnight.

Did America fight on the wrong side?

I am not a politician to say what was right or wrong, but mostly all of the Americans came to Vietnam without knowing anything about Vietnamese history, tradition, beliefs, and systems. They never tried to understand how the French lost the war. They never really tried to help the villagers. At night, the Viet Cong came to my village and showed us what to do to be free of the foreign invaders. The South Vietnamese army came in the daytime and told us what to do to make sure that we'd be free from the communists. The Americans came to my village and told us what to do and how to live our lives to stay free from the evil Ho Chi Minh. Every side tried to tell the villagers how to live so that they could be free from their enemy. None of them asked the villagers what they wanted. Not once did they ask about our ancestors and whether we were happy or sad. Or what we were thinking about and the feelings in our hearts. By the end of the war, in 1975, over fourteen million villagers had become refugees. Those are basic questions that no one asked. They all wanted us to be one of them. They forgot that we had feelings too. We had our own thoughts about what we wanted for our country and about what we believed from our ancestors. The Americans thought that, with money, power, and technology, they could easily win the war. They were wrong.

Why did the Americans lose the war?

Our ancestors would not allow the Americans or any foreigners to win. The French, the Chinese, the Japanese, and then the Ameri-cans all thought they could win. What could the Americans do differ-ently? Drop a nuclear bomb and kill all the Vietnamese? But the Americans got tired because they fought without a cause. Do you know why they were really in Vietnam? Most of the Vietnamese believed it wasn't to win the war. The U.S. was in Vietnam to demonstrate the effectiveness of its latest weapons as a warning to the Russians and for economic reasons. Fifteen million tons of bombs and ammunition dropped on Vietnam created a lot of jobs for the people in the business of war.

Did you hate the American soldiers then?

I didn't hate them. I was just scared of them. They were so large; some were over 200 pounds. Compared to Vietnamese men, they were giants. There was a big difference from seeing GIs in my village versus seeing them in Da Nang. The Americans in the city were friendly, more human. But in the village, they were dirty; they pointed weapons at us all the time. Our lives were in their hands. We had no idea what they said and what they were thinking. The only thing we could think of was death; it was them or us. When they rounded up innocent villagers, tied ropes around the necks of our men and blindfolded them, and took them away or killed them on the spot, wouldn't you be scared?

What did the American soldiers do in your village?

In 1966 and '67, I went to many villagers to sell goods on the black market. I witnessed a lot of cruelty. Americans kicked and beat old village men. When some children asked GIs not to walk in the rice paddies, they beat the children's heads. GIs beat fathers in front of their children. It was much easier to take a beating in a torture camp than to have their pride and inner feelings shamed. There was no way the villagers could express to the American GIs their feelings, their anger, and their hurt. They couldn't even cry. How could these villagers watch their wives raped in front of them, their husbands tortured, and their children killed or wounded? They had to deal with that day in and day out for many years. Some GIs were nice to the villagers and children, but most were racist. They hated us, not only because we were their enemy but also because we were different in color and size. Their insults and foul language were often directed at us as a race, not as an enemy. I saw the same cruelty in my village when I visited my father on his deathbed.

Are the Vietnamese men violent by nature?

When some drink, they talk a lot and become aggressive. They can't hold their liquor. But in every society there are good and bad. Of course, there are egos that will do anything for power. But in the villages, the men are more in harmony with each other. In villages, everybody knows everyone else. They live together as a community and look after everyone's interests and generally are not violent toward each other.

When did you learn to speak English?

In 1966, when I was sixteen years old on the streets of Da Nang, my very first word was "hello." My second was "You buy?" I sold things to the American GIs.

Could the Americans have won the war?

Only if they killed all the Vietnamese. Had the Americans not gotten involved, Ho Chi Minh and Ngo Dinh Diem would have signed an agreement in 1960. But the Americans didn't want that to happen. Uncle Ho and Diem had worked out a way to bring the two nations together as one. When we were supposed to have an election, everyone knew that Ho Chi Minh would win.

Because Ho was Buddhist and Diem was a Catholic?

Because Uncle Ho was the father of our country. He kicked out the French and the Japanese. He had the right to be our leader, but the Americans didn't want him to win because they thought the country would become communist. That was why the Americans offered to help the South fight against the North. It was the wrong decision.

You don't believe Vietnam would have become communist?

I don't believe Uncle Ho would become Russian or Chinese communist. Uncle Ho wanted an independently united Vietnam just like the United States did over two hundred years ago. What was wrong with that? Americans assured Uncle Ho that they would help him in his fight for independence. He had learned from American history how to become a democratic republic. He wanted Vietnam to be a democracy, but he was betrayed when American politicians broke their word and continued to support the French. He had no choice but to seek help from Russia.

But look at Vietnam today under communist rule. The people still suffer. You wouldn't want to live there, would you?

There would be more progress if there hadn't been an embargo against trading with Vietnam. After the embargo was lifted in 1994, there have been many changes. Multinational companies are setting up businesses. It's simply a matter of time before Vietnam is on its feet, but we must overcome the image that Vietnam conjures. You call it the Vietnam War. In Vietnam, we call it the American War. The war was a short period in a long history of intrusions by China, Japan, France, and America. But there are very ugly and negative images about Vietnam even after twenty-five years—images of Red Communist rule, of killing zones, of Hamburger Hill, of young prostitutes and refugees and boat people, of helicopters lifting off the American Embassy's rooftop, or Charlie [American slang for Viet Cong and NVA]. Since the fall of Saigon, the media have focused on MIAs and POWs, PTSD (posttraumatic stress disorder), and Agent Orange [toxic herbicide], all negative images. There are still unexploded land mines and ammunition left by the Americans, and over 71 million liters of toxic chemicals.

Do you believe that you were chosen for a special reason to journey from being a little water buffalo girl in a small Vietnamese village to living in La Costa, California?

Absolutely. I was chosen to come in my mother's womb, which is why I came back to this planet. This is but one life of many. My old soul tells me that in this life I must do something for other people. This keeps me young and happy, and pays back my bad karma that I created in an earlier life. When I do things for others, I know that I am not alone. Every breath I take, every word I say, is not by me but from someone up there. I am nothing but a puppet to follow what heaven wants me to do. That is why all the things that I went through, and all the good and bad karma, is part of my payback for what I did before. The question is whether I am willing to pay. The answer is "yes," I am willing to pay whatever it takes. It is very hard for the world to understand this concept because they don't understand reincarnation and karma.

As a young girl, were you aware of what you're now saying?

Yes. Every time I saw pain, I felt pain. I never wanted to hurt anybody. I always wanted to reach out to help others. When I was captured and tortured by the South Vietnamese, I knew then that my body was only a temple for my soul so that it could carry out its mission on Earth.

When you were being tortured, could you see yourself from outside your body?

I wasn't in that state at that time. I could feel the pain. I knew that my soul was still in my body. I knew that pain was a part of life.

They tortured you to find out where the Viet Cong were?

Yes. They asked me what I did for the Viet Cong; did my family support the VC; what did I do at night. All those types of questions.

Were you afraid of death?

I wasn't afraid of death, but I was very afraid that I would leave my parents behind because most children that went to torture camp were never seen again. My parents would never find my body and know what happened to me. That was more frightening to me than my own death.

ROGER HILSMAN

In guerrilla warfare, insurgents could be defeated c
their fellow countrymen, not by foreigners.
—ROGER HILSMAN, *American Guerrilla*

He is the man whom President John Kennedy ordered to keep Vietnam from becoming an American war. He is the man accused by Secretary Robert McNamara of giving the green light to a military coup that led to the assassination of President Ngo Dinh Diem.

A West Pointer, class of 1943, I first met Roger Hilsman through his book, *American Guerrilla,* an account of his three and a half years with Merrill's Marauders in the jungles of Burma during World War II. After being wounded, he joined an OSS guerrilla operation behind Japanese lines. One of his missions involved parachuting into Manchuria and rescuing Americans held in a Japanese prison camp. By great coincidence, his father, Roger Hilsman, an Army colonel captured three years earlier in the Philippines, was among the POWs. On seeing his son, his father jokingly asked, "What took you so long?"

When the war ended, Hilsman resigned from the Army and earned his Ph.D. in international politics from Yale University. After teaching at Princeton University, he joined the Congressional Research Service in Washington in 1956. In 1961, Kennedy selected him to be director of intelligence and research at the U.S. State Department, a job that entailed making immediate analyses of changing world situations for the Secretary of State. Two years later, he was appointed to the position of Assistant Secretary of State for Far-Eastern Affairs.

Having been a guerrilla fighter in Asia and an expert on counterinsurgency, Hilsman believed that guerrilla wars could be won only by gaining the popular support of the people. In Vietnam, that meant removing the unpopular Diem from the presidential palace and providing economic support to the South Vietnamese. An outspoken critic of the administration's support of Diem and of its optimistic assurances of a quick end to the conflict, Hilsman became a target of McNamara's wrath.

The eighty-year-old former Merrill's Marauder and assistant secretary of state shows few signs of slowing down when he meets me at the door to his New York apartment near Columbia University. I quickly see why McNamara could not get him to "heel," as he had intimidated other bureaucrats in the Kennedy and Johnson administrations to do.

With the death of Kennedy and Lyndon Johnson purging from his administration opposition to his U.S. expansion policy in Southeast Asia, Hilsman resigned from the government in February 1964 to become professor of government and international politics at Columbia University in New York City.

Pushing aside packing boxes from a recent move that clutter the living room, Hilsman unloads a volley of choice words from his military days against McNamara for keeping quiet after resigning in 1968 as defense secretary while the number of dead Americans in Vietnam doubled. McNamara broke his silence in 1995 with his book, *In Retrospect*. "He twisted the truth in his book, falsely blamed others, and defiled the historic record," Hilsman charges. "Everything McNamara has done has been an attempt to shape or manipulate the evidence that historians will use so that he looks good. I never fully realized the extent of his lying until I read *In Retrospect*. I was horrified. Every page I turned—things that I participated in and knew about—were misrepresented."

During the early sixties, could the South Vietnamese have held back the communists from taking over the South?

At first, I thought if President Ngo Dinh Diem would make the social and political reforms that we were suggesting, there would be a chance of resolving the crisis. I later decided that it was hopeless, mainly because of Diem. If some colonel had come forward with leadership ability and instituted the strategic hamlet plan that Sir Robert Thompson [British expert on guerrilla warfare] used in Malaya to defeat the Communist guerrillas, maybe over fifty years the South Vietnamese could have succeeded. But I never saw such a man who could replace Diem. We looked. God knows we looked.

Could massive bombing of North Vietnam have stopped the communists?

As an infantry commander in World War II, I had been bombed by the U.S. Air Force too many times to believe that bombing could win wars. Strategic bombing in my judgment doesn't work, but I am in great favor of close-in air support. The items of significance transported over the Ho Chi Minh Trail into South Vietnam were radio communication equipment and small-arms weapons. Hell, they were wheeling it down on bicycles. Bombing only showed the desperation of the United States to the Asians. Bombing has little effect in nonindustrial countries based on bartering systems. What the hell was a bomb going to hit? However, Gen. Curtis LeMay [Air Force chief of staff] wanted to bomb the North Vietnamese back into the Stone Age. He said that we were swatting flies in South Vietnam when we should have been killing larvae in North Vietnam.

You strongly opposed American involvement?

Absolutely, under any circumstances that the American public would tolerate. From the beginning, I was totally supportive of President Kennedy's plan. His intention was to stall by keeping American involvement as low as possible and then withdraw when he found an honorable opportunity. Had Kennedy lived, I think he would have found the excuse to get out within weeks after Diem's assassination.

What makes you so sure of this?

In early 1963, Kennedy called me to the Oval Office. There were only the two of us. He said that he wanted this private talk to make sure that I understood that my primary mission as assistant secretary for Far Eastern affairs was to keep the United States out of a war in Vietnam. The South Vietnam government wasn't going to make it, but that we should do everything to help them short of sending American soldiers to fight. After the Buddhist crisis in the summer of 1963, Kennedy instructed Secretary Robert McNamara to develop a withdrawal plan. In the fall of 1963, the Joint Chiefs of Staff presented a plan. The very next day, Kennedy ordered the first 1,000 of 16,500 American military advisers in Vietnam to withdraw. The plan called for a total reduction within months, but Kennedy was assassinated before it could be implemented. He also told me in that meeting to stay on top of the CIA because he didn't trust them. That lesson he learned from the Bay of Pigs.

Didn't Kennedy want to get past the elections before pulling out the remaining American advisers?

I don't think so. Most Americans at that time didn't know where Vietnam was on the map. If you asked them where Vietnam was, they wouldn't know what the hell you're talking about.

Who then wanted to send American troops into Vietnam?

Robert McNamara and Walt Rostow [head of the State Department's policy and planning staff] had recommended the introduction of an American division to be placed just below the DMZ to prevent NVA infiltration. Its mission was not to fight the Viet Cong. You must remember that all the infiltrators up until the escalation of the war and the bombing of the North were ex-southerners. The recommendation was sent in a cable to the White House. Kennedy hit the roof. He was livid at their preempting him. He was absolutely determined not to let Vietnam become an American war. Here, these guys were recommending the introduction of American troops to seal the border. That was the one thing Kennedy would never agree to.

Kennedy was that determined?

You bet. Kennedy would ask all of us what we thought, while he rarely revealed what he himself thought. Remember my job was to keep Vietnam from becoming an American war. Well, on the front page of the *New York Times* was a story about a major general that had visited Vietnam about the time of the battle at Ap Loc. My phone rang early in the morning; I was just starting to eat breakfast. Kennedy could turn the air blue when he was angry. "God damn it, what the hell are you doing?" he shouted at me. "I thought I gave you specific instructions. Why did you let this goddamn general go out to Vietnam?" When he paused for breath, I told the president that I had never heard of the general before; that he never asked my permission to go. Kennedy hung up the phone on me. That afternoon, a National Security Action Memo came out with strict orders that no officer of general or flag rank would visit Vietnam without the written permission of the assistant secretary of state for Far Eastern affairs. That tells you Kennedy's view in a nutshell.

Did the military-industrial complex want a war?

No, quite the opposite. The military-industrial complex loved having cold wars, but it hated hot wars. The only industry that benefited from the Vietnam War was the helicopter business. Corporate America supported Washington's decision but not for economic reasons. It was anticommunist by nature. The military were not warmongers. They knew what happens in war and that American soldiers would get killed.

Did Washington attempt to communicate with Hanoi?

No, not directly. There was dialogue going on through Poland where we were communicating with the Chinese, but never directly with Ho Chi Minh.

Were nuclear weapons on the table as an option to end the war quickly?

Yes and no. Nukes were never considered long enough to generate some real staff work. They got shot down for obvious reasons. What the hell would they use nukes on? The only targets where a nuclear bomb might have had an effect were the Haiphong dikes. We did consider that.

Wasn't the domino theory the primary reason for U.S. involvement in Vietnam?

The domino theory was a lot of bull. Kennedy made a terrible mistake of mentioning the domino effect in a press conference when he was being hard pressed on foreign aid to Southeast Asia. It was something out of the Eisenhower era. Nevertheless, the Walt Rostows of the world kept going through everything Kennedy said and pulled out this one phrase to justify why we got involved in Vietnam.

Did you believe China would intervene if we took the war to North Vietnam?

I did. I also knew that Ho Chi Minh wouldn't tolerate Chinese soldiers crossing its border. The last time China invaded Vietnam, it stayed a thousand years. But if American troops had gone into North Vietnam, I don't think there would be any question that China would intervene.

Why were we in Vietnam when Laos was considered a more strategic geographic position to stop the communists?

President Kennedy sent Mike Forrestal, an aide to McGeorge Bundy at the NSC, and myself to the Plaine des Jarres [Plain of Jars] in Laos to survey this possibility. When we returned to Washington, we had a meeting at the State Department about sending the 101st Airborne to the Plain of Jars—not to fight but to stabilize the situation. As I was leaving the meeting with Gen. Lyman Lemnitzer [chairman of the joint chiefs] and Secretary [of State] Dean Rusk, Rusk asked Lemnitzer if he could get the 101st into the Plain of Jars. Lemitzer said that he could get them in all right, but getting them out was the problem. That ended any talk about sending Americans into Laos.

McNamara was quite adept at using numbers and charts to depict his point of view.

First of all, you have to be damn careful dealing with McNamara, because his selective memory is such that nothing he said could be trusted. The Vietnamese generals used to joke about him, telling me that "Your secretary of defense likes statistics. Viva le statistic. If he wants them to go up, they'll go up. If he wants them to go down, they'll go down." McNamara was an arrogant bastard. He would entertain no view but his own. He made a monopoly of the truth.

McNamara instituted body count.

McNamara blamed the military for the idea. Can you believe that? It was another of his statistical measures to show that we were winning.

Didn't Secretary Rusk back up the State Department's view-points and confront McNamara?

Let me tell you what happened. I would go to the NSC meeting, and McNamara would hold court. If it was a political problem, or if the agenda called for a State Department report on Asia, I was the briefing officer. Rusk simply did not participate. Rusk had the theory that he was a personal adviser to the president. He told the president alone what he thought, not what the State Department thought, whereas most secretaries felt that their job was to represent their department's thinking. We never knew what Rusk told the president behind closed doors.

Prior to Kennedy's assassination, was McNamara hawkish even though Kennedy intended to get out of Vietnam?

McNamara didn't argue for escalation of American involvement, but he did claim that we were winning with military aid and advisers. Of course, I argued that Vietnam was going to hell in a hat. My information was based upon intelligence that Vietnamese political leaders in all the major cities were providing. McNamara based his assessment upon what the South Vietnamese generals told him.

But didn't McNamara profess early on that he thought Vietnam was a winnable war and that it was just a matter of time before the communists were defeated?

He said that often. McNamara wrote in his book that the time to get out of Vietnam was just after Diem was overthrown. Here's what really happened. The meeting that McNamara was referring to was an NSC meeting held at the State Department because Kennedy wasn't present. Dean Rusk chaired the session. McNamara and I had a big fight over a fact-finding trip where [Marine Corps Maj.] Gen. Victor Krulak [Joint Staff] after talking only with South Vietnamese and American Army officers, concluded that we were winning the war. Paul Kattenburg, who was a staff officer at State and an expert on the region, interrupted and backed me up, stating that we should immediately find an honorable way to get out of Vietnam. McNamara exploded and started screaming at Kattenburg. It was on that occasion that McNamara refers to in his book that he thought we should have gotten out of Vietnam. That gives you his capacity for self-delusion.

McNamara regularly shuttled back and forth between Washington and Saigon?

McNamara would tell me without any warning that he was going to Vietnam. I would insist that a State Department representative accompany him. McNamara would inform me that he had to be at the airport in thirty minutes to catch his plane and that there was no time to take on an additional passenger.

McNamara only talked with the top generals during his visits?

Right. What could he possibly find out that we already didn't know? He talked to the same generals who sent us cables. The generals wouldn't let him go down and talk with the colonels and troops. It's remarkable how ill-informed and half-assed many of the major decisions were made in Washington. And many of these decisions were personalized, removing any objectivity from the decision process.

McNamara wrote, in *In Retrospect,* that he misread China's objectives and that the fundamental reason for America's failure in Vietnam was because there were no experts on Asia to consult.

That was baloney. Hell, there were dozens of experts; they just weren't high ranking. For example, there was Allen Whiting, author of *China Crosses the Yalu,* one of the top China minds in the country. There was Edward Rice, a career foreign service officer who spent years in China. Then there was Marshall Green who served as deputy assistant secretary of state for Far Eastern affairs and as consul general in Hong Kong. All three spoke fluent Chinese. The Vietnamese and Chinese experts were saying that we couldn't win the war for a variety of reasons. I was convinced that we couldn't win a land war in Vietnam, so why start one? I did what I could to keep us from getting in deeper. As Kennedy had instructed me, my job was to prevent the United States from slipping or creeping into a war. And we didn't while I was at the State Department.

McNamara accused you of circumventing the chain of command and causing the assassination of Diem.

I didn't circumvent the chain of command. There was an NSC meeting in August 1963 that he failed to mention in his book. Ambassador Frederick Nolting was being replaced by Henry Cabot Lodge. As assistant secretary, I accompanied Lodge to Hawaii where we had a conference with CINCPAC, Adm. Harry Felt. We had heard rumors that Diem's brother, Ngo Dinh Nhu, was going to crack down on Buddhist pagodas, so we sent a message to Diem that if the rumor were true, the U.S. government would condemn him and his government. Diem said he wouldn't do it. Three days later, while we were in Hawaii, Nhu attacked the Buddhist temples and killed unarmed monks. Lodge immediately flew to Saigon. I returned to Washington on Saturday, August 24, and received the so-called August cable that said the generals had met with Lodge and had shown him evidence that Diem was going to arrest and kill them. The generals had no other choice but to take matters into their own hands in self-defense. He asked what was the U.S. position. In those days, we received cables like that once a week. So I wrote back a potboiler that said the U.S. government would not take part or take sides in such disputes; that we would examine any new government on its own merits. This was on a weekend. Kennedy was in Hyannisport [Massachusetts]; Rusk was at the United Nations in New York; John McCone [CIA director] was off on a second honeymoon; and McNamara was out of town. So we drafted this potboiler—this standard reply—and sent it around to various places. Rusk inserted a paragraph that said, if control of Saigon were lost, the United States would endeavor to support the war through the port in Hue, which could have been interpreted as a go-ahead with the coup. Rusk's statement changed the entire nature of the cable. So now the potboiler was an encouragement for a coup; it was a green light. Rusk's paragraph was boiled down to a single sentence that said the same thing in much more veiled language. On Sunday, Ambassador Lodge replied with a cable that he would inform Diem that the generals were plotting against him and to get Nhu out of the country. Lodge said that he had done nothing and would do nothing until he heard back from me, because if he went to Diem and told him about a coup, Diem would kill all the generals. That Monday, August 26, there was an NSC meeting that McNamara never mentioned in his book. Kennedy did something that I never saw him do before or since. He came into the meeting obviously mad but not at any particular person or the draft of the cable. Kennedy said that we could go with the original cable (i.e., encourage the generals but meet with Diem), or we could support Lodge's recommendation, which was to encourage the generals, but don't tell Diem; or we could cancel the whole goddamn cable because nothing had been done. The only people to know about the cable were Lodge and those of us in the room. Kennedy then went around the table and asked each of his cabinet what their recommendations were. Everyone voted for number two, to include McNamara, which called for a coup, but not to tell Diem. This would give the coup a better chance of succeeding.

That was a pivotal point in the war.

Of course it was. But the whole case that McNamara makes about me engineering the coup was crazy. In the first place, if I had ever written a cable that Kennedy didn't approve, I would have found myself out on the street the very next morning. Do you think that Jack Kennedy would let anybody survive who did something like that? Not on your life.

In the short span of time between the assassination of Kennedy and when you resigned in February 1965, did you think that President Johnson was gearing up to escalate America's involvement in Vietnam?

No, I wouldn't put it that way. Johnson was clearing the deck to make any decision possible. I don't think he intended to escalate the war at that time. But I think he thought that he may have to, in which case he would have to get rid of Bobby Kennedy, Averell Harriman [under secretary of state], Mike Forestal, and myself. And he did.

During this window of time, was McNamara ratcheting up America's military for war?

Yes. McNamara, Dean Rusk, and Walt Rostow wanted to send American troops to Vietnam because they felt that the South Vietnamese couldn't stop the Viet Cong; however, they had no intentions of invading North Vietnam. Later, Rusk wanted to cross into North Vietnam but not all the way to Hanoi. He thought that by invading only part way, the Chinese wouldn't intervene, yet it would scare Hanoi enough to pull out of South Vietnam.

The assassinations of Kennedy and Diem were critical events in Washington's decision to send American fighting men to Vietnam?

Diem's death didn't matter because Kennedy would not have allowed the U.S. to get pulled into a war. But, within days after the assassination of Kennedy, Johnson issued an NSC action memo stating that he didn't want anybody to go to bed at night without thinking about what we all could do to further the war in Vietnam. Every time we turned around, there was another memo from the president about Vietnam. Then he made Averell Harriman roving ambassador instead of undersecretary and removed other key people for the region at the State Department. This made it very clear to me that he was clearing the decks so that he could be free to do anything he wanted to do in Southeast Asia. About that time, I was scheduled to attend an international conference in Sydney, Australia. While in flight, I told my wife, Eleanor, that I had to resign. Lyndon Johnson was moving toward a war; I had to get out of Washington before that happened. I was absolutely against a war in Vietnam. When I returned to Washington, I submitted my resignation to Harriman.

Did Johnson know about Kennedy's intention to withdraw?

I don't know if Lyndon Johnson knew about Kennedy's intention to withdraw. I think a guy with his political skills knew that Kennedy was never going to get us into a shooting war, but it became perfectly clear to me that Johnson wanted a war. You can speculate why; whether he did it to take away attention from his other problems, or whether in his simple-minded way—although his mind was convoluted in other ways—he connived the Vietnam War. Certainly, as I told you, there wasn't a single expert on Southeast Asia that I knew who thought we should go to war there.

What was Johnson's motivation to expand the war?

I think his motivation was some kind of simple-minded anticommunism. It was either black or white; whereas Kennedy recognized that the communists had different colors and shades. It wasn't just black and white.

Was McNamara Johnson's lackey?

I think so. Johnson used to take McNamara's ego in front of all the cabinet members and squeeze it like a lemon, and McNamara would come up smiling. I wouldn't stand for anyone treating me the way Lyndon Johnson treated McNamara. Once, McNamara didn't play the active supporter, and the minute McNamara expressed doubts about U.S. policy, Johnson sent McNamara to the World Bank. There were only two relationships you could have with Lyndon Johnson. One was to have so much independent political power that he had to pay attention to you, like Senator Richard Russell, or a sycophant like his aide, Jack Valenti. Johnson made Averell Harriman, whom he couldn't seduce but also was too powerful to fire, roving ambassador for everything but Asia. There was nothing in between. I was the first to go because I didn't have any independent power. All I had was expertise. Whereas, Kennedy treated me exactly as he treated Russell, or McNamara, or Rusk, and he meant it. That's why people were so loyal to him. Loyalty goes down as well as up.

Who did Johnson listen to about prosecuting the Vietnam War?

I don't think he listened to anybody. He had his own world view and his own opinions about how to wage the war. Lyndon Johnson was a superb politician. He made estimates based on his political knowledge on what he could get away with or what would be supported. He would never do anything that he thought would be repudiated. He did what his gut told him and whether he could get support or not.

Would you have stayed in government if McNamara were not Secretary of Defense?

No. The minute Lyndon Johnson became president, he systematically, over the next three or four months, removed from influence on Vietnam all the people who opposed the war. What he did to me was very clever. He had somebody dig into my background and discovered that my father had been in charge of the Philippine military academy. He offered me the ambassadorship to the Philippines to push me out of Washington. It took me thirty seconds to see through his ploy. I told him "no, thanks" and went to Columbia University where I taught and wrote books and articles about international affairs. I probably had more influence in my twenty-five years of writing than I did at the State Department.

JOHN KERRY

How do you ask a man to be the last man to die in Vietnam?
How do you ask a man to be the last man to die for a mistake?
—SPEECH BEFORE THE SENATE FOREIGN RELATIONS COMMITTEE, 1971

A Senate aide had forewarned me that John Forbes Kerry rarely talks about his combat experience in Vietnam. So when I enter his third-floor chamber in the Russell Senate Building, I'm not surprised that the tall, lanky junior senator from Massachusetts tells me that he almost didn't grant me the interview.

Over the years, I have found that incumbent politicians, American and foreign, with few exceptions, tend to be calculating, unrevealing, and well rehearsed. At first I sense that Kerry is no different. He eyes me with skepticism and informs me that our time is limited because of another meeting he must attend.

Still, I am intrigued by this Yale University graduate with a privileged upbringing who was driven to serve his country twice in Vietnam, only to return to the United States to lead an antiwar movement against the government for which he shed blood thrice.

Seated behind me is his speechwriter, pen and paper in hand. It's the only instance of all my interviews in which I wasn't alone with the subject. I suspect that the young man is there to make sure I don't misquote the senator or perhaps to learn something about his boss that he otherwise would not have heard.

Born into a wealthy Boston family, Kerry could have been granted a deferment upon graduating from Yale in 1966 and gone to graduate school, as did most of his contemporaries. Although critical of Washington's Vietnam policy, he joined the Navy and volunteered for Vietnam because he believed in service to his country. In 1968, he volunteered for a second tour to command a patrol boat in the Mekong Delta where he became, as he describes it, cannon fodder. "It was a wonderful time in all its craziness. There was a great bond, a great connection that forged. It was a time of enormous contradiction between living and dying."

When Kerry returned to the United States, he was disillusioned by the senseless killing of American soldiers. Unable to accept Washington's refusal to pull out, he resigned from the Navy and, after much soul searching, joined the militant Vietnam Veterans against the War. Being both a patriot and a war objector, he was a paradox for the Nixon administration to handle.

I read about the leading roles that Kerry and Senator John McCain played in bringing to a conclusion the POW/MIA dilemma and normalizing relations in 1995 between Washington and Hanoi. I also read about an antiwar demonstration at the Capitol steps where, twenty-nine years ago, a thousand Vietnam veterans led by a young Kerry threw their medals and ribbons over a barricade to denounce the war. It was a symbolic statement staged for the media that overnight was seen around the world. On April 22, 1971, dressed in military fatigues, his combat decorations pinned to his chest, Kerry stood in a Senate hearing room before Senator Fulbright and the Senate Foreign Relations Committee. His scorching indictment against America's involvement in Vietnam reverberated throughout the halls of Congress: "There is nothing in South Vietnam, nothing which could happen that realistically threatens the United States of America. And to attempt to justify the loss of one American life in Vietnam, Cambodia, or Laos by linking such loss to the preservation of freedom, which those misfits supposedly abuse, is to us the height of criminal hypocrisy, and it is that kind of hypocrisy which we feel has torn this country apart."

I ask myself, as I look across the desk at the fifty-six-year-old senator: What drove him to shuck his uniform and to fight a different kind of war against Congress and the president of the United States? He must have known that his actions would kill any political aspirations that he might have had at the time.

You volunteered to go to Vietnam?

I did. In 1965, while I, like many of my classmates at Yale, was trying to decide what to do after graduation, Lyndon Johnson issued his now famous call for five hundred thousand more troops. The draft ratcheted up significantly. Like many of us in our generation, I had a choice to seek a deferment by going to postgraduate school or enlist. At that point, I wasn't morally opposed to the war. I was a bit ambivalent about it, but my sense of responsibility to service to country far outweighed any other thoughts I had about America's involvement. So, I applied for Officers' Candidate School [OCS] and was accepted. I entered OCS in August 1966 after graduating from Yale and volunteered for duty in Vietnam.

What was the mood in the country then?
It was changing rapidly. I signed my induction papers at the end of 1965 and graduated from Yale in the spring of 1966. I delivered the graduation speech about Vietnam in larger, foreign policy terms and about America's role in the world and what we were attempting to do there. This was before the uproar on college campuses. I think the first draft card was burned in 1967. I was in uniform and far removed from America when the Pentagon march took place. And then came 1968, which obviously was the year of all years in terms of change, turmoil, upheaval, and confrontation in America. I was on a guided-missile frigate in the Gulf of Tonkin [off North Vietnam] when Martin Luther King Jr., was killed. I returned to Long Beach [California] the day Bobby Kennedy was killed. During my leave in the summer of 1968, I attended a Eugene McCarthy speech in Massachusetts and was swept up by the questions that were asked him. It wasn't until I set foot in Vietnam in October 1968 that I learned for myself what was really happening on the ground. Then, I understood.

What did you understand?
I understood the contradictions, the strategic complexity, and the historical imperatives about the place. I understood the social, political, and structural problems that were part of the war and the lack thereof. I could see firsthand that America's strategy wasn't going to work. It was just plain as day to me once I was on the ground. I could make judgments about the capabilities of the Vietnamese forces that we were working with. I could see the level of corruption and the failures of our own strategies in terms of winning hearts and minds. I could really see it and believe it and live it. Each day added to my sense of wrongness, to my sense of how ill advised our country was.

Did you have a sense of hypocrisy of being there in uniform?
No, not at all. I believed I was doing my duty. My responsibility was to serve my country. It was my choice, and I was proud of it. I was proud of my men and what we accomplished. The fact that I thought the war was wrong didn't mean I liked the Viet Cong or the communists. I abhorred their behavior and the way they treated the

Vietnamese people. That wasn't the issue. The issue was could we, the United States of America, strategically achieve our goals? Was Vietnam worth American lives? And under what circumstances should the politicians in Washington ask their people to make that sort of sacrifice? It was very clear to me that you don't do it unless you intend to win; unless you have a strategy that can win; unless you provide the full support necessary to win; and unless you sell the commitment to the American people before you start. All these lessons that came out of Vietnam were very clear to me then. I felt a deep sense of responsibility to speak out about what I had seen in Vietnam when I returned home. We had some very intense discussions about this among the men in my squadron. But, no, I didn't feel hypocritical for being there. I felt proud to be a United States serviceman, and I felt proud in the way I executed my responsibilities.

What was your feeling while you were in Vietnam about the bureaucrats in Washington?

I thought that they were increasingly out of touch and incapable of seeing what Neil Sheehan so brilliantly articulated: "Some of them could see it, but by in large their leaders were hung up in a series of stereotypical historical belief systems that didn't confront reality."

Did you have any political aspirations then?

I was interested in politics, and I had public service aspirations. I was certainly directed into the public issues arena, but how it would play out, I had no idea. To answer your question, I wasn't committed to running for office. In fact, once I came back and opposed the war, I threw any future political aspiration to the wind.

When you were in Vietnam, did you buy into the domino theory as justification for your being there?

Occasionally, we would have some heated discussions about the domino stuff, and whether China or Russia would intervene if we took the war north. But, no. My total focus was on fighting the NVA and VC.

Did you enjoy combat?

Yeah, at times I did. There was an excitement, an exhilaration in combat. You come out of a battle as aware of the fact that you are alive as any time in your life. There was a high to that. I think a lot of people have described it as an adrenaline rush. There's an intensity

Capt. Gil Dorland (right) in the Mekong Delta in 1964.

Associated Press war correspondent Peter Arnett covered the war in Vietnam from 1962 to after the fall of Saigon in 1975.

Peter Arnett

Lt. Gen. Mike Davison led the joint U.S.-South Vietnamese incursion into Cambodia in 1970 to destroy North Vietnamese supply depots.

Gen. Mike Davison, USA (Ret.)

Pentagon *"whiz kid" Daniel Ellsberg in Vietnam circa 1967. A former Marine, he was sent to Vietnam by the Pentagon to help implement pacification programs. Later, he leaked the Pentagon Papers to the* New York Times *and incurred the wrath of the Nixon administration.*

Daniel Ellsberg

Gen. Alexander Haig, USA (Ret.)

Lt. Col. Alexander Haig (right) confers with Maj. Gen. John H. Hay (center) in 1967. In 1969, Haig joined President Nixon's National Security Council. He also served as Secretary of State during President Reagan's first term in office.

New York Times *reporter David Halberstam (right front) in the Mekong Delta with U.S. Army Capt. Ken Good (center) and South Vietnamese troops in October 1962. He was the first U.S. newspaper correspondent to stake out Vietnam full time. His book* The Best and the Brightest *was a scathing assessment of the arrogance and lies that produced the U.S. quagmire in Vietnam.*

Tom Hayden

Antiwar activist Tom Hayden (left) on a visit to North Vietnam in 1967. He made two controversial trips there to establish a dialogue between the peace movement in the U.S. and the North Vietnamese government.

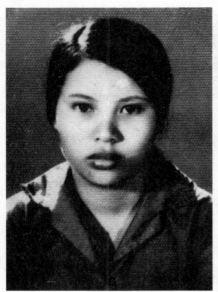

Writer Le Ly Hayslip, author of When Heaven and Earth Changed Places, *witnessed the ravages of war as a young woman in South Vietnam. Oliver Stone based his film* Heaven and Earth *on her life.*

Le Ly Hayslip

Roger Hilsman served as Assistant Secretary of State for Far Eastern Affairs at the time the Kennedy administration made pivotal policy decisions regarding U.S. support for South Vietnam. He firmly opposed the introduction of U.S. ground troops.

Roger Hilsman

Senator John Kerry

John Kerry (back row, second from the left), now a U.S. Senator from Massachusetts, joined the Navy and commanded a patrol boat in the Mekong Delta during the war. He became disillusioned with the war by the end of his second tour of duty and headed the militant Vietnam Veterans Against the War.

Kissinger presided over U.S. foreign policy during the Nixon and Ford administrations and was the chief U.S. negotiator at the Paris peace talks.

Anthony Lake

Anthony Lake (present day) served at the U.S. Embassy in Saigon from 1963–1965 and in the State Department's Bureau of Far Eastern Affairs for three more years. Later, he became Kissinger's special assistant on President Nixon's National Security Council.

Cau Le

Col. Cau Le was one of the most highly decorated men in the South Vietnamese army. He was decorated for bravery in combat twenty-eight times and received South Vietnam's Medal of Honor as well as the American Bronze Star and Silver Star.

Lt. Barry McCaffrey in Vietnam in 1965. He was wounded three times during the war. In the Gulf War, he commanded the Army's 24th Mechanized Division, and later served as President Clinton's drug czar.

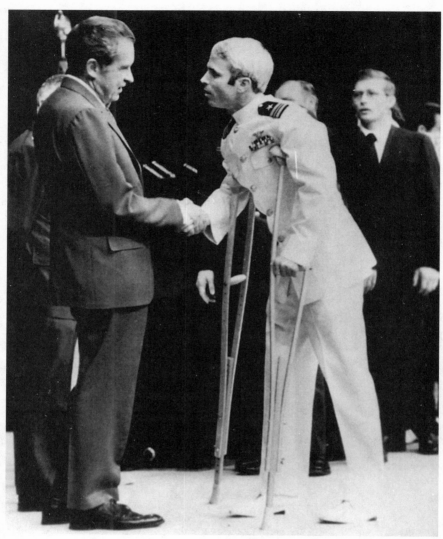

Senator John McCain

John McCain, now a U.S. Senator from Arizona, shakes hands with President Nixon soon after being released from the infamous "Hanoi Hilton" prison in North Vietnam. After his Navy A-4 Skyhawk was shot down over Hanoi, he became a prisoner of war for over five years.

Noted historian Lt. Col. H. R. McMaster (present day), author of Dereliction of Duty. He graduated from West Point in the early eighties in the shadow of the Vietnam War.

Katie Trotter McMaster

CIA station chief Thomas Polgar (left) in South Vietnam. His warnings about the impending fall of Saigon in 1975 were ignored.

Thomas Polgar

Maj. Norman Schwarzkopf standing in front of a Huey helicopter in Vietnam in 1966. He was twice wounded during the war. Later, he gained fame as the commanding general of the Allied offensive during the Gulf War.

James Webb as a Marine lieutenant in Vietnam. Since then, he has been an acclaimed writer. He also served as Secretary of the Navy from 1987–1988.

Gen. William Westmoreland, USA (Ret.)

Gen. William Westmoreland was chosen by President Johnson in 1964 to command U.S. forces in Vietnam.

to it that's very challenging. Anybody who didn't feel it was scared stiff. Not to say that I wasn't scared. I was terrified at times. And there was a lot of instinct involved. As you know, you react instinctively. Let me just say that there are ups and downs to that curve of exhilaration. It was not something we eagerly sought out like an adrenaline fix or anything like that. We were happy to have it behind us, but, when it presented itself, you did what you had to do.

Did you feel any moral ambiguity in killing people?

I don't know quite what you mean by moral ambiguity. When we were in battle, we were doing our job to the very best of our ability. I wanted to win. I had no ambiguity about that whatsoever. I didn't like the communists, and I didn't like what they were doing to innocent people. I deplored communism. It's a failed, miserable way of life. But my questions then became, "Were we winning the hearts and minds of the people? Did we gain a foothold that had a chance of sustaining itself without having American soldiers endlessly dying to defend it?" There were too many times that I went out on missions with Vietnamese soldiers only to discover that they disappeared when the going got rough. After a few times of that, you question what's going on. I think that's what evolved. That's why I've been so adamant about preparedness before committing ground troops in a Kosovo or wherever. I won't put American soldiers in harm's way unless the United States is prepared to win.

When you returned from Vietnam, when did you change your mind about America's involvement?

I had already changed my mind while I was in Vietnam. As I said, I was going through this struggle over there. As I began to see things clearer, I knew our policy and reason for being there was screwed up. I did my duty to the best of my ability, but I had no illusions about what we were doing wrong. Many of the boat skippers and men thought the same as I did. It was a very shared feeling.

Did you resign from the Navy when you returned in 1969?

No, I was originally posted in New York as an aide-de-camp to an admiral. I was sort of decompressing during that period. I was a bit out of touch with everything. And then it hit me around the end of 1969 that I had to speak against America's involvement in Vietnam. I couldn't contain it inside me, particularly after a very close friend of mine was killed. That's when I realized that I couldn't just sit back and do nothing while my friends were still over there. I had work to do.

Did you speak out individually, or did you join a group of protestors?

Initially, I was alone. I didn't want to be part of any group. I spoke out at Rotary Clubs and wherever people would listen to me, and one thing led to another. Ultimately, I did bump into some Vietnam vets who were also speaking out. Figuring that was the most effective way to communicate my message, I joined them to speak as one voice. It was about then that I came into contact with Vietnam Veterans against the War.

You talked to Congress?

I resigned from the service and became a spokesman for the Vietnam Veterans against the War. I testified before the Senate Foreign Relations Committee in 1971 and vented the frustrations of a lot of veterans. Up until then, I had done a lot of work in VA hospitals and witnessed the treatment of veterans. It was not pretty. The hospitals were not equipped for dealing with the conditions of the people coming home. We began a major campaign to improve the services in the hospitals and started the first Post-Vietnam Stress Syndrome Disorder outreach. A lot of good came out of it. We got vets' benefits and allowances raised and the GI bill extended. A lot of hidden, unseen work came out of that advocacy, but the principal point was opposition to the war.

In your activism, did the government attempt to shut you up?

They were engaged in intimidation. I remember a meeting in St. Louis, Missouri, where the FBI was all over the place. They had guns laid out on the front seats of their cars. It was pretty direct. And another incident that took place in a park in D.C. after I had spoken before the Senate committee. My wife and I wanted to decompress. All of a sudden, I saw this guy up on a hill and other guys peering at us. I felt I was the target of our own police. America has been through strange periods, and that was one of them.

Did you feel you were at war again?

Not at war, but I felt very uncomfortable as a hard-fighting American patriot and idealist that my government targeted and treated me that way. It was very disturbing and a real eye opener.

When did you first start to realize that your antiwar efforts were having an effect?

I began to realize this after I testified before Congress in April 1971. The public's response was enormous. It elicited a very strong response from people in the country who saw real veterans with prosthetics, stumps and missing limbs and scars, and Purple Hearts and Silver Stars, and all kinds of things that were real.

Did you have any sense of betrayal to soldiers still fighting in Vietnam?

No, I felt true to what I was doing. I was very strong in my conviction that our actions could save American lives. To this day, I believe that we minimized the number of kids that would have been shipped over there. We actually helped bring about the return of prisoners of war, even though many of them did not like us then. In the end, we had a profound impact on this country's commitment and understanding of the war. Richard Nixon and Henry Kissinger and other political leaders would not have felt the imperativeness to Vietnamize the war had it not been for our efforts. I think that we gave energy to the antiwar movement in 1971 that was waning and losing focus. I did feel very self-conscious about friends and veterans that didn't understand what I was doing. I am very sympathetic to their point of view and have no rancor or bitterness whatsoever for anyone who saw the situation differently. I understand and respect their perspective. But I cannot tell you that I wasn't hurt by the vilification from those veterans who saw my actions in a bad light. That was hard on me. Obviously, I didn't want that. What I did was controversial. It would have been a lot easier for me just to be one of the anonymous returnees and do nothing.

Members of the Joint Chiefs of Staff were also in disagreement on how the war was being conducted. Should the military chiefs have resigned when their advice continued to be disregarded by the administration?

That's a judgment that I could never make, and one that's entirely personal and very difficult. I don't want to lay that one on them. I think the culpability here is not in people that didn't act, but with those who were charged with a greater level of responsibility and didn't act appropriately. In the end, I think that is one of the great tragedies of Robert McNamara. He tried to explain to America, in his book, his evolution of the war as almost an apology. I thought he made matters far worse by claiming an intellectual superiority of knowing that the war was wrong at the outset. I don't understand why he did that, except maybe to reconcile himself with some of his friends in Cambridge who were disappointed in him. But, in the process, he assumed the burden of a moral bankruptcy much greater than anything one may have thought. If he did indeed know that Vietnam was so wrong in the beginning, it begs the larger question of how he then could have been either so complicitious or ultimately so silent. The responsibility lies principally among the politicians. Vietnam was a political war, politically driven, politically sustained, and ultimately politically terminated. I don't blame the military. They did the best they could under the circumstances. Many of them did shout and scream, and some careers were indeed affected by virtue of their attitudes toward the politicians.

Was Vietnam McNamara's War?

Robert McNamara obviously played a pivotal and central role in designing and prosecuting the war, but he was not alone. There were plenty of architects working with him to share complicity in strategic errors and judgments. We shouldn't forget that more Americans and Vietnamese were killed in Richard Nixon's so-called "honorable exit" than were lost in the entire earlier stages of the war. The Nixon era was the time of the greatest embitterment in this country because it was the time of the greatest confusion about what America was attempting to achieve.

Would you describe in one word the underlying attitude that allowed the United States to escalate the war in Vietnam? Was it arrogance? Was it triumphalism, as Kissinger called it?

I've grown up enough now that I would never succumb to one word. It wasn't just one word. There's hubris; there's myopia; there's ignorance; there's historical ignorance; there's Cold War mentality. There were a lot of different ingredients. When you think about it, it was almost a natural progression of the outgrowth of America's failure to win in Korea, of the Eisenhower years, of Kennedy's exuberance and energy, and of confluence about China's and Russia's willingness to intervene. One of the most remarkable things to me is to go back and read Neil Sheehan's *A Bright Shining Lie*. I must say that I was not aware until I read Neil's book about how much lying and coverup was going on in 1963 and '64 and '65. I was stunned by those early battles where the generals had lied. Had I known a lot of that stuff earlier, I would have been ten times angrier. It's just incredible how early that went on.

Should the president and key cabinet members, such as the secretary of defense, have military experience?

The answer is yes, it is better to have had military experience. Is it a prerequisite? No. Look at Franklin Roosevelt, who was a great war leader, and Ronald Reagan did his share of exploitation and immersions. So it's not clearly a prerequisite, but the president must have leadership skills and clarity of principles and goals before he puts the country in harm's way. For the secretary of defense and the various secretaries of the armed forces, as well as senators who serve on the foreign relations committees, prior military experience is invaluable. To know what it means to stand in line for long hours, not to have a warm shower, and to be in dangerous situations all bring important ingredients to the decision-making process.

Congress cut off the funds that virtually ended U.S. participation in Vietnam. What were your feelings then as to the cutting off of funds? And now that you are a legislator, what is Congress's responsibility to American soldiers when sending them into harm's way?

Good questions. First, cutting off funds by Congress represented the absolute failure of policy but the absolute victory of American people asserting their choice. It's a very traumatic, draconian step. It is not the best way to get out of something or to carry out policy. But, in Vietnam, it became the only way, which was a great tribute to the structure of government that our forefathers put together. Ultimately, the opinion of the American people surfaced to where Congress reflected it and took action—much too late and after tragic loss of lives. Cutting funds is not the best option in the execution of foreign policy. It is far better to have the executive branch work with Congress to achieve objectives rather than have such a draconian ax come down on a policy. But it ultimately was a triumph of the system in Vietnam.

HENRY KISSINGER

For the sake of our long-term peace of mind, we must some day
undertake an assessment of why good men on all sides found no way to
avoid this disaster and why our domestic drama first paralyzed
and then overwhelmed us.

—HENRY KISSINGER, *Years of Renewal*

He sits on a divan in a large, unpretentious office overlooking Park Avenue, a telephone conveniently within arm's reach. I have the sense that he's always near a phone just in case the president of the United States or another world leader calls.

"What can I do for you?" he asks, knowing full well why I'm there. General Haig had told me a week earlier that he had run into Henry Kissinger at a cocktail party and that Kissinger had queried him about the upcoming interview and me.

Haig, in his book *Inner Circles,* describes his first meeting with Kissinger in late 1968, when he was being interviewed to be Kissinger's military assistant. "Only the owlish, rumpled Harvard professor was present. This elemental Kissinger was noticeably plump, impressively learned, transparently ill at ease with a stranger—and very funny."

Kissinger was born in Furth, Germany, emigrated to the United States when his Jewish parents fled the Nazis in 1938, and was naturalized an American citizen when he was drafted into the U.S. Army in 1943. During World War II, he saw action in the Battle of the Bulge with the 84th Infantry Division and was discharged in 1946 as a staff sergeant. He graduated summa cum laude from Harvard University in 1950 and received a Ph.D. four years later. Entrenched in academia, he suddenly came into the spotlight in 1957 with his acclaimed book, *Nuclear Weapons and Foreign Policy.* With the support of Governor Nelson A. Rockefeller, he became Nixon's national security adviser in 1969 and, in 1973, was sworn in as the fifty-sixth secretary of state.

I had been told that Kissinger, with his place in history guaranteed, is very reluctant to talk one-on-one with scribes carrying tape recorders. In 1972, he allowed Oriana Fallaci, the famous Italian journalist, to interview him, which resulted in the publication of demeaning quotes that Kissinger could not recall saying.

Although he is no longer the power player who could get away with making outrageous remarks, such as: "There cannot be a crisis next week. My schedule is already full," I sense that the seventy-six-year-old statesman hasn't changed that much since his days in government. I also sense that he's still the same man whom David Halberstam compared with Robert McNamara: "Kissinger was a great infighter, but he was subtle and deft. You'd walk down the hall with Kissinger and you didn't realize that you'd been separated from your testicles. Whereas McNamara comes at you with brute force and tries to discredit you with numbers and whatever."

What questions could I possibly ask this icon that haven't already been asked a thousand times, or that he hasn't written about in his volumes of books?

On my flight from Miami to La Guardia, I had read a declassified "Secret/Sensitive/Eyes Only" White House memo written by Secretary of State Kissinger to President Gerald Ford after the fall of Saigon. It dealt with lessons of Vietnam: "It is remarkable, considering how long the war lasted and how intensely it was reported and commented, that there are really not very many lessons from our experience in Vietnam that can be usefully applied elsewhere despite the obvious temptation to try. Vietnam represented a unique situation, geographically, ethnically, politically, militarily and diplomatically. We should probably be grateful for that and should recognize it for what it is, instead of trying to apply the 'lessons of Vietnam' as universally as we once tried to apply the 'lessons of Munich.' The real frustration of Vietnam, in terms of commentary and evaluation, may be that the war had almost universal effects but did not provide a universal catechism."

I wonder if Kissinger has since changed his mind? Were there no lessons to be learned? Were fifty-eight thousand American lives sacrificed for no redeeming purpose whatsoever? I remind myself to ask Kissinger what he now thinks about this before the interview is completed.

I dig into my briefcase, pull out two minicassette recorders, and place them on a coffee table separating us. I want to get started because his executive assistant had warned me earlier that Dr. Kissinger would be pressed for time because of a last-minute trip to Europe.

"Why two recorders?" Kissinger asks. There's a genuine curiosity in the low-monotone, accented voice that is as famous as the man. I explain that I have two recorders in case one malfunctions.

"Yes, of course," he replies.

Rather than begin my interview at his earliest involvement in Vietnam, or when he helped to plot Nixon's secret plan to end the war quickly, or when he negotiated the Paris Peace Accords with Le Duc Tho, North Vietnam's chief negotiator and Kissinger's corecipient of the 1973 Nobel Peace Prize, I decide to start on America's final hour in Saigon.

"Mr. Secretary, what were you thinking when the last helicopter lifted off the embassy rooftop at the fall of Saigon?"

He looks at me with those drooping, bloodhound, blue-gray eyes that someday will be on Mount Rushmore. "Were you on the last helicopter?" he asks me.

Never, ever, would I have anticipated such a response, which perhaps is part of his genius. "No, sir, I wasn't," I respond.

He hesitates, perhaps wondering where I was going with this opening question. "It was a very sad moment," he says. "An appallingly conducted war, an American disaster, self-inflicted, and unnecessary."

Did you envisage such an ending in the early 1960s?

No. I didn't know very much about Vietnam in the early 1960s. But I don't think I would have favored such a large-scale military commitment. I probably would have favored military action in Laos, which could have been the turning point in the war. If we had resisted in Laos, the North Vietnamese wouldn't have had the Ho Chi Minh Trail to infiltrate South Vietnam. But once the war evolved, I thought we had to win.

Was it arrogance on the part of our politicians that pulled us into Vietnam?

I think a kind of triumphalism here in America contributed a lot to our involvement in Vietnam. And we see again some of it reemerging in the likes of Kosovo, Somalia, and Haiti.

Vietnam has been referred to as "McNamara's War." Can we point the finger at Secretary McNamara for our tragic loss?

I like McNamara very much as a person. However, he was not a war leader. He should have been head of HEW [Department of

Health, Education, and Welfare]. He looked at Vietnam from a very mechanical point of view as a statistical problem. And he gave up very early in the conflict. All along I didn't believe that a war of attrition could be won in a guerrilla war. I was always in favor of going into the sanctuaries and cutting off the Ho Chi Minh Trail.

So, you thought McNamara was not the right man for the job?

Again, I want to stress that I like him and respect him, but he was not a war leader.

Did Kennedy have intentions of pulling out of Vietnam as many have speculated?

That's what they all say now, but I see no evidence of that. Nobody has any proof.

What did you think?

Well, Kennedy was assassinated about three weeks after we triggered the overthrow of President Diem. I think the overthrow of Diem committed the administration to the people we put in to replace him. Diem was overthrown because he was suspected of not being very enthusiastic about pursuing the war. He was accused of neutralist tendencies that people forget today. Yet, his journalistic critics attacked him for doing the exact same things that the U.S. government did eight years later.

When did you become involved in Vietnam?

I first became involved in Vietnam when [Ambassador] Henry Cabot Lodge invited me to go out there to consult with him in 1965. I returned in 1966 and once more in '67. I went three times before I conducted on behalf of President Johnson a sort of a peace negotiation. My view was that we had involved ourselves in a war that we knew neither how to win nor how to conclude. Our military approach was wrong; we couldn't win using the strategies that we were pursuing.

Could you be more specific?

First of all, I did not agree with the Westmoreland strategy of search-and-destroy because that enabled the enemy to set the level of our casualties. I believed in putting the population in secured enclaves. I thought that it was better to have 70 percent of the country under 100 percent control, than to have 100 percent of the country under 70 percent control. Gen. Creighton Abrams more or less followed that strategy after we came into office because we insisted on it. Secondly, I thought we had to go into the sanctuaries.

What was your position on bombing the North?

I would have preferred to have attacked supply depots, if necessary, with ground forces. I wasn't such an advocate of the air campaign because I don't think that it did a hell of a lot of good. We paid a heavier price for it than it was worth. Later on, I strongly supported Nixon's B-52 campaign. But, in the Johnson period, I thought our strategy was too inconclusive.

Are you saying we should have invaded North Vietnam with American troops?

Not so much an invasion, but we should have cut the Ho Chi Minh Trail and occupied the Cambodian sanctuaries. I think we had them defeated at the end of 1972. A lot of books are coming out now that support that thought.

Early in the war, did you subscribe to the assumption that China would intervene if we invaded North Vietnam?

I don't know what I thought at the time. Later on, once I was in office, I thought China was too worried about Russia to intervene. While they did enough to keep their revolutionary credentials, I don't think China was the major factor that some people in the Kennedy and Johnson administrations thought it was.

When I talked with General Westmoreland, he said that his major fear was the intervention by China. The Chinese could afford to lose massive numbers of troops, whereas we couldn't. Military strategies were conditioned on this one assumption.

That was true during the Kennedy and Johnson administrations. We were afraid of Chinese intervention because of our experience in Korea. They didn't follow the fact that China and Russia were really confronting each other, but that wasn't so easy to see. It took us in the Nixon administration a few months to understand. We came in January 1969; by June, we understood it.

Did you buy into the domino mind-set?

It wasn't a mind-set. It was correct.

Why didn't the Paris peace treaty work?

First of all, the peace treaty was marginal to begin with, because it was at the end of a drawn-out period of harassment and systematic congressional pressures. It didn't work because Congress wouldn't vote the money for economic aid and because they wouldn't vote the money for military aid. And because it prohibited military intervention to preserve the treaty. No peace agreement could work under those conditions. Korea would have collapsed under those conditions.

Did you realize then that the peace agreement was on faulty ground?

Yes, but we had no other alternative to pursue under the restraints imposed by Congress upon the administration.

Did you think that the North Vietnamese had any intention of honoring the peace agreement?

Not unless they were compelled to do so. Hanoi only understood the threat of American reintervention and the maintaining of South Vietnam as a viable and strong society.

What was your feeling about Congress at the time?

I thought then, and I think now, that they were responsible for the collapse of Vietnam.

Why did Congress behave the way they did?

First of all, there was a Democratic Congress in a Republican administration. Secondly, the liberal [George] McGovern element was the dominant force. They thought there was something fundamentally wrong with America, and, unless America lost in Vietnam, it would never come to its senses. So we had this strange situation where many people were actively working to defeat this country in order to save their country.

That's indeed ironic. Did you trust Congress?

It's not a question of trust. There were many people in Congress that I trusted, respected, and liked. People like Senator [Hubert H.] Humphrey, whom I personally adored. But I thought their overall impact on Vietnam was disastrous.

Did the peace movements force Congress to reverse its support of South Vietnam?

You can't take any one thing by itself, but the peace movement created a general atmosphere of lawlessness, of assault on the government, of trying to bring the government down by paralyzing it. All these things contributed to a hysterical atmosphere. All the generations sort of threw in the towel.

Why did you accept the North Vietnamese presence in the South when many experts believed that had President Nixon continued the Christmas 1972 bombing, Hanoi would probably have agreed to withdraw?

[Slow grin] I don't know where all these experts who believed this were at the time. The problem was, the North Vietnamese had agreed to pull out of Laos, but they never did. We had offered a cease-fire from 1970 on. A new Congress was coming in early January. Negotiations with Hanoi were reaching a head at that point. If Congress had ordered us out of Vietnam, it would not have agreed to pass the supplemental to an appropriations bill. Congress had already passed resolutions within the Democratic caucus to do this. So, our judgment was that we had provisions against NVA reinforcements and against either their adding troops or adding new equipment. We thought these were adequate safeguards that would bring about the gradual withdrawal of the North Vietnamese forces.

In your book, you wrote that you had advised President Nixon to go before Congress to outline his strategy for Vietnam and to demand a clear-cut endorsement of his policy.

I thought that was what he should have done early in his term. He was more experienced in politics than I was, and he felt that he would never get a clear-cut answer—that the debate in itself would weaken him. And, also, he thought it was an abrogation of executive responsibilities and the weakening of the presidency, turning us into a parliamentary system.

In hindsight, do you think we could have won the war?

I think in hindsight that we should have probably done in 1969 and '70 what we did in 1972. We should have tried to go for a knockout when we still had a lot of troops in there. If it hadn't been for Watergate, there is absolutely no doubt that we would have bombed the hell out of them in April and May 1973. If it hadn't been for Watergate, the president would have been able to get, if not all, most of his economic aid requests. The North could not have reinforced as they did. I'm certain that Vietnam never would have collapsed in 1975. But I can't predict what would have happened over a ten-year period.

Could we have had a political victory without a military victory?

No. The North Vietnamese fought for thirty years, and they weren't going to quit without being militarily defeated.

Did the United States underestimate the North Vietnamese determination?

It wasn't a question of determination; it was a question of the people who got us into the war. Kennedy and Johnson assumed Hanoi thought like Americans—making cost-benefit calculations. But, the North Vietnamese were willing to pay a much higher price than we were.

What lesson have we learned from Vietnam?

If we go into a war, we have to be prepared to win or we shouldn't go at all. We have to have a winning strategy. Our basic strategy for Vietnam was a novel strategy that had nothing to do with the military. We just wanted to hang in there long enough until we could democratize South Vietnam and make it stand out compared to its neighbors. There was never time for this. It would take much too long. It was not a military war. It was a Great Society war—a war geared to our perception of domestic politics.

The phone rings. I glance at my watch. It's noon sharp, time for the former secretary of state to leave. He sets the phone down, looks over the top of his spectacles at me, and asks a question. Of all my interviews, Kissinger was the only subject of the nineteen on my list to ask me my opinion. I sense that he's genuinely interested in hearing my thoughts. It would have been so easy for him to dismiss me.

Kissinger: You were in Vietnam. What do you think of the war?

Dorland: Washington politicians—bureaucrats—did their young people and the country wrong.

Kissinger: Do you believe we could have won the war?

Dorland: I do, had military victory been the objective.

As I shake his hand to leave, I tell him that I believe his literary work will live long after he goes, much as Winston Churchill's did. He smiles. I think he agrees.

ANTHONY LAKE

*I come away from Vietnam with an intense feeling that our principal
mistake was to lose touch with reality. . . . The gulf between
Washington, where personally decent men made policy about people as
if they were merely playing chess, and Vietnam, where so many
Americans and Vietnamese died their individual deaths, still upsets me.*
—ANTHONY LAKE, *The New York Times Magazine* (JULY 20, 1975)

He was a last-minute addition to the collection of people whom
I wanted to interview for the book. Only after the others had
been interviewed did I realize that Anthony Lake's perspective as a
young foreign service officer assigned to the embassy in Saigon, and
later as special assistant to Henry Kissinger at the National Security
Council, could make a valuable contribution to the book. Most
important, I wanted to ask him about allegations in various publica-
tions that Kissinger and President Nixon threatened Hanoi with the
use of nuclear weapons to force the North Vietnamese to pull out
of the south. As Kissinger's right-hand man, he certainly would know
the answer.

A 1961 magna cum laude graduate in history from Harvard University, Lake joined the American diplomatic corps and volunteered for
assignment in South Vietnam. He arrived in Saigon in April 1963.
Like other young Army advisers and reporters, he saw that the war
out in the bush was not the war being portrayed by the military brass
in Saigon and by the Johnson administration. In 1965, he returned
to Washington. For the next three years, he saw the war as a staff
assistant in the Far Eastern Bureau of the State Department.

In a 1975 article for the *New York Times Magazine,* he wrote that,
while he was at the State Department, "I was increasingly bothered
by the gap between the Vietnam I remembered and the Vietnam that
was treated as an abstract object of American interest and debate.
In Washington, we lost sight of Vietnam as a real place, with real
people."

By 1969, Lake opposed the war. He was a Democrat; and he was
not a Nixon enthusiast. Nonetheless, Henry Kissinger tapped him

to be his special assistant, and Lake accompanied the president's national security adviser to Paris for secret negotiations with the North Vietnamese. By then, as Lake later wrote in his *Times Magazine* piece, "I was sick of a war that defied termination."

Lake's relationship with Kissinger is perhaps best depicted in Walter Isaacson's book, *Kissinger, a Biography.* "Lake had emerged as more than just Kissinger's special assistant; he was his fair-haired young intellectual, an idealistic foreign service officer with the brains and breeding that Kissinger admired." Isaacson also notes, "Kissinger was particularly devastated by Lake's resignation [April 30, 1970], and he asked Haig to try and change his mind."

For the next two years, Lake worked for Senator Edmund Muskie of Maine during his bid for the Democratic presidential nomination. Lake followed this assignment with two years of directing the International Voluntary Services, a private version of the Peace Corps, and four years at the State Department during the Carter administration. In 1980, he left government for academe as a college professor of international relations.

In 1992, Lake joined Bill Clinton's presidential campaign as the then Arkansas governor's senior foreign adviser. In 1993, he returned to the White House as President Clinton's first national security adviser.

I phone Professor Lake's office at Georgetown University. His secretary informs me that the professor rarely grants interviews, but, in this case, he would make an exception. We agree to talk on the telephone because time is of the essence; my manuscript is already being edited at the publisher.

Lake's voice is soft and laced with hints of a scholarly professor, which, of course, he is. He stops in midsentence to say "quote" and "end quote" where they are appropriate, as though he were dictating into a recorder. Considered a "pragmatic neo-Wilsonian" in his approach to foreign policy, he often laughs at himself, which suggests a man who does not take himself all that seriously. His time being pressed, we dive immediately into the first question.

You arrived in Vietnam in April 1963.

I had been trained for six months in Vietnamese. As a first-tour junior officer, I would be in various assignments at the embassy over the course of two years. But, the assumption was also that a major part of my time would be spent in the field doing provincial reporting. This entailed going into the villages and reporting what I observed to the embassy. I began in the consular section, which brought me into contact with a number of Vietnamese and also with American citizens, especially merchant seamen, who had gotten themselves in trouble. Strictly on a professional basis, I got to know just about every bar and low-life dive in Saigon. This was also a good way to practice my Vietnamese and to learn some words they never taught us at the Foreign Service Institute.

How old were you when you first went to Vietnam?

I was twenty-four. But, I got a lot older in the two years that I was there.

When were you assigned to be Ambassador Lodge's assistant?

About the end of November 1963; after the coup [that overthrew President Diem].

Did you have any knowledge that the coup was going to happen?

None at all, not until a machine gun in our garden started firing at the Presidential Guard barracks across the street. I think that was the first fighting in the coup.

You had no knowledge then of Ambassador Lodge's role in the coup prior to it occurring?

As I said, I had no idea a coup was about to take place. I was in the consular section at the time.

Were you a subscriber to the domino theory?

I think my own motives in asking to go to Vietnam—and I did volunteer—had less to do with the domino theory than with the excitement of President Kennedy's call for the advancement of democracy around the world. I had also become very interested in Asian affairs. Vietnam simply seemed like an interesting place to be involved in Asia. But, no, I don't recall any of us really discussing the domino theory while we were at the Foreign Service Institute.

Did you believe nationalism was the driving motive behind Hanoi's war efforts?

Yes. I had read Vietnamese history, and I was aware of two thousand years of Vietnamese struggle to remain independent of China and the first Indochina war against the French. But that was almost an academic understanding. I only began to understand the importance of nationalism when I was there. For example, I can remember that the signs we saw in the villages while traveling around the countryside referred far more frequently to the fight against "foreign invaders" and Saigon's dependence on the United States than to any social or economic agenda. It became increasingly clear just how powerful was the nationalism that lay at the heart of this.

Robert McNamara wrote in his book that there were no experts on the region during 1963 and 1964 when you were at the embassy and that was a cause for flawed assumptions in Washington's strategic planning. Do you agree with McNamara?

No. I don't want to readdress this whole argument, which is more complicated than that. But, in fact, before I went to Vietnam, I visited the Bureau of Intelligence and Research (INR) at the State Department to read and to talk to their analysts. One of those analysts, whose name deserves to be remembered, was Louis Sarris. Steeped in Vietnamese history, Sarris was profoundly skeptical of our involvement in Vietnam. I think his career suffered as a result. He was certainly an expert, as were others as well, and he clearly made his arguments in his work.

When you were an assistant to Ambassador Lodge, did you question U.S. policy and the buildup of American forces in Vietnam?

Not really, although I began to question some of the reporting from the field. I would read the official reports, which were almost invariably optimistic. Then, I would talk to young reporters like my friends Neil Sheehan and David Halberstam, who had witnessed the same events and had a totally different take on them. When I was in the field in Central Vietnam in late 1964 and early 1965, I witnessed firsthand what was a near-total collapse of the South Vietnamese government's position in the region, which reinforced my skepticism.

Could we have won the war at that time?

No.

Did you believe that then?

No, I did not. In the 1960s, most of us, and I'm referring to the younger officers and reporters who were increasingly questioning the war, had not yet arrived at the conclusion that we could not win.

We believed that we could identify younger Saigon political officials and military officers who were not corrupt and who were prepared to prosecute the war in a more sophisticated, political context. None of us was prepared to conclude that it was hopeless because, in part, we hadn't tested alternative propositions. And, in part, whenever you're engaged in such a struggle, whether it's playing football—as I had done very badly before—or whether it's a war, it's very hard to say that it's hopeless because then everything that is being done is useless or worse. It took me some years to arrive at the very bitter conclusion that we could not win the war, and therefore we had to stop it as quickly as possible.

Were the embassy's communications to Washington optimistic, or were they pessimistic as you saw the situation?
Generally optimistic.

Why wasn't the pessimistic point of view communicated to Washington?
It was communicated, but it was not a majority opinion. I also believed at the time—in Vietnamese political terms—that perhaps a solution could be reached if we worked more closely with groups such as the Buddhists. I developed a bit of a reputation of being a "Buddhist sympathizer," mostly because I was working Central Vietnam where the Buddhists were particularly strong and was developing a hostility to the Saigon government. I remember reading, en route to Vietnam, Graham Greene's *The Quiet American*. As you may recall, he was a young diplomat who actually worked for the Agency and who believed in finding a "third way." I remember thinking then that Greene was naïve; what did Graham Greene know about Vietnam? I reread the book in the 1980s with great sadness because I realized then that probably there had been a "third way" for a settlement.

What was that third way?
Finding groups like the Buddhists who were not absolutely committed to the war on either side, who were noncommunists, and who might be the focal point for a political solution.

If we may fast-forward to 1969, what did your job entail as special assistant to the president's national security adviser, Henry Kissinger?
I did most of his staff work and accompanied him to the secret negotiations with the North Vietnamese in Paris during 1969.

Were you involved in the design of Nixon's secret plan to end the war quickly?

Yes, I was, although I had strong doubts about it. The idea of the plan was to threaten the North Vietnamese with very strong measures if they did not agree to a diplomatic solution by a certain date in late 1969. This reflected the experience that then Vice President Nixon had had with Eisenhower's reputedly having ended the Korean War in 1953 through the threat of force—implicitly nuclear force. But I was not aware at the time, and I don't recall now, any nuclear aspect of the threat in 1969.

There was no mention, or discussion, as to the use of nuclear threats against North Vietnam in Nixon's secret plan?

I can't say that nobody in the bureaucracy ever talked about it as far as I can recall. To my knowledge, and I witnessed a great deal of what was going on, I never saw any reference to or heard any discussion of a nuclear threat.

But there are recently published books that allege President Nixon and Dr. Kissinger threatened Hanoi with the use of nuclear weapons.

Whatever you read in books, it's always Rashomon—different people have different memories. Again, I'm being careful here. I cannot say nobody ever heard Nixon or Kissinger ever say nuclear. But, to my knowledge—and I think I was a pretty good witness at the time—nuclear weapons were never seriously discussed or mentioned to the North Vietnamese. I never saw that.

Were you against the war in 1969?

Yes, although I often disagreed with the reasons of some of those who opposed the war. I certainly was opposed analytically to the arguments that were made by some as to why the war had ever occurred. I did not believe that it was the result of the American economic system or result of the Pentagon's desire to test new weapons. I do think it was a combination of different motives, primarily the doctrinal straitjacket that we were caught up in at the time. We knew the answers as to when to intervene around the world before we even asked questions about the specific countries. It was also the result of a growing domestic political problem in the U.S., in that the more each president became committed to winning the war in Vietnam, the harder it was for that president to survive losing it. So we staggered on.

Did you believe in 1969 and '70 that we could have won the war?
No. That was the basis of my opposition. The reason why I thought we couldn't win then, and couldn't have from the early 1960s on, was not because I thought our troops fought badly. In fact, they fought very well; and, for the most part, they were not behaving as they were caricatured here. We could have kept the government in Saigon going for an indefinite period so long as we had our troops there; but that's not winning. The definition of success had to be our ability to leave the country and to leave behind a government that could, on its own, command the loyalty of its people—that could survive without an American military presence. To come to your point about nationalism, the more we did for the South Vietnamese government, the more we damaged its nationalistic credentials and the farther away we were from the success that would allow us to leave—a terrible paradox. As I said, unhappily, we could not win the war. I say unhappily because of the lives that had been lost. I concluded that we had to end the war as soon as we could. That is why I argued while I was working for Kissinger, and, to his credit, he listened to my arguments.

How did you find working for Dr. Kissinger?
[Long pause.] I found it exhilarating in the opportunity to argue my case and to be involved in events that mattered. It was difficult working in the White House, which I was not happy doing and, even more, just feeling discouraged about where the policy was going. That was why I left on the day of the Cambodian incursion.

Was President Nixon the driving force behind U.S. foreign policy in Vietnam, or was it Dr. Kissinger?
Both, but in the end when there were disagreements—and there were—it was the president.

What was your impression of working indirectly for President Nixon?
I didn't see that much of President Nixon. I was a career foreign service officer assigned to the White House. I wasn't involved in a partisan way. There was a stunned hush in the White House mess

when I said that I was a registered Democrat. I had never been a Nixon enthusiast.

Then why did you accept the job with the Nixon administration?

Because of my fascination in working at such a job and because I thought I could have more influence in stopping the war from within.

In 1969, did you envision such a tragic ending to the war five years later?

I didn't know how it was going to end. But I did believe at the time and certainly in retrospect, that the main barrier to achieving an agreement was the American position that went back to the Johnson administration, that stipulated there had to be a mutual withdrawal. That meant the U.S. wouldn't leave South Vietnam if the North Vietnamese didn't. The difficulty here was that in order to keep domestic American public opinion on board as much as possible, Nixon had begun "Vietnamization"—which meant we would withdraw American forces. The North Vietnamese were not idiots and recognized then that there was no reason to give in on mutual withdrawal because the U.S. was unilaterally withdrawing. The demand for mutual withdrawal then was abandoned in late 1971 and opened the way for the Peace Accords in 1972.

Did the North Vietnamese negotiate in earnest?

It's hard to say. In 1984, I met with a senior Vietnamese official who had been involved in the talks. I asked him if the proposals that were made in 1972, including the abandonment of mutual withdrawal, would have been an agreement in 1969. I was surprised when he said, "No, because it was necessary that they first militarily defeat you." I still sometimes wonder why he said that. Was it because they had no intention of agreeing in 1969, even if the Americans' side had been more flexible? Or was it because my hypothetical question was simply unimaginable, and he couldn't for some psychological reason imagine the alternative?

Did Dr. Kissinger and the president think that we could have won?

I don't know. They were so focused on trying to get a diplomatic agreement that I wasn't able to tell.

Which involved "sticks and carrots" tactics?

Yes. The stick was the secret bombing and then invasion of Cambodia and, later, the invasion of Laos and then the bombings in 1972, especially after the North Vietnamese offensive, which, incidentally, was launched without the knowledge of the Russians. Hanoi was trying to drive a wedge between Moscow and Washington at the time we were developing détente, which was threatening to Hanoi. The carrot was better relations.

Were you part of the planning effort for the Cambodian incursion?

In early 1970, I was no longer Kissinger's special assistant, although I was continuing to work on various Vietnam projects for him in the Old Executive Building. I was not involved in the military planning and didn't know its exact character. The weekend before the incursion, Kissinger called into his office a few of us whom he thought would be opposed to it. He didn't tell us that there would be a full American participation. He said that there was a plan for a South Vietnamese move across the border with American forward air controllers. That was what we then debated. We offered various reasons why we thought it was a bad idea. At the end of the meeting—and I had done much of the arguing—Kissinger said that he knew what I was going to say before I said it. I remember thinking that then I could resign because it was clear that I had no influence at all. So long as I thought I had any influence, it was my obligation to stay on. That night, Roger Morris [NSC staffer] and I wrote a resignation letter and gave it to then Col. Alexander Haig, Kissinger's military assistant, and asked Haig to deliver it to Kissinger on the day of the incursion into Cambodia.

Was there any discussion as to the impact a Cambodian incursion would have on the antiwar movement, which at that time was relatively quiet?

In that meeting with Kissinger, it was one of the arguments that we made, but it wasn't the major argument. I just could not write speeches any longer that disagreed with the people who were opposing the war, which included both Morris and myself, especially since I didn't have any real influence.

Did the threat of China intervening influence White House decisions as it had in previous administrations?

It was a consideration with regard to military actions on the ground against the North. But, no, China wasn't a major factor in the war plans being prosecuted at the time. We were more interested in finding ways to open relations with China, partly in order to reduce Chinese support for North Vietnam.

Why did Nixon have your phone wiretapped after you left the administration?

I wasn't consulted, so I wasn't aware of all the reasoning that went into it [laughter].

How did you know your phone was tapped?

Many people suspected their phones were tapped, especially in those days, but I didn't know it until a couple of years later when Seymour Hersh wrote his story in the *New York Times.* Mine was but one of a number of taps; I believe there were seventeen of them. The tap on my phone began only after I had resigned and left government. It then continued during the period when I was beginning to work on my doctoral thesis at Princeton and then continued while I was working for Senator Muskie and his presidential campaign. The White House had advance word of some of Senator Muskie's speeches so that they could be prepared to answer them. That is not my view of democracy in action.

CAU LE

He [Le Cau] arguably has more combat time, as well as more POW time, than any known American.

—James Webb, *VFW*, September 1991

From the outset of this project, I wanted to find a voice that could represent the unsung heroes of South Vietnam's army. I didn't want a general who had fled to the United States prior to the fall of Saigon. I wanted a soldier who had shed blood on the battlefield in defense of his country, a warrior who had remained in South Vietnam after the communist takeover.

I had shared this quest with James Webb, who said he knew just the person, a Colonel Cau Le, or Le Cau in Vietnamese. "Cau's as good as they come," Webb said. "I'd have him on my flank anywhere, anytime."

I meet with Cau at the Hyatt Regency Hotel near Reagan National Airport in Alexandria, Virginia. He drove down from his home in Philadelphia with his wife, Kieu Van. His voice is soft and punctuated with a very distinct Vietnamese accent. At 5 feet 4 inches and 120 pounds, he is deceptively fragile looking for a man who was wounded three times, decorated for bravery in combat twenty-eight times, and received Vietnam's Medal of Honor and America's Silver Star and Bronze Star medals—the highest awards for valor in combat that the United States can bestow on a foreign soldier.

A 1963 graduate of the Vietnamese Military Academy, Cau spent the next twelve years fighting for his country. He was promoted to regimental commander at age twenty-eight, when his regimental commander and his American adviser were both killed in a 1969 battle. A month before the fall of Saigon in 1975, NVA soldiers captured him in a swamp when he was cut off from his troops. His ankle had been shattered from stepping on a land mine. Like many of his comrades in arms, he was sent to a communist reeducation camp known for its brutality. For the next thirteen years he was a POW.

His wife, who supported their five children by working as a nurse, was permitted to visit him once a year for fifteen minutes. The journey took her more than three days to reach the prison camp deep inside the jungles. He did not see his children until he was released in 1988. Cau resettled in Philadelphia with his family in 1990, and has since worked for the city's district attorney's office as an advocate for Asian victims of crime.

Looking younger than his fifty-six years, there are no visible signs of five years spent in a "hell cell," as he calls the solitary-confinement box that had no direct lighting, running water, or ventilation. To keep his sanity and to survive, he sang to himself. It doesn't take long to sense the love and passion that Cau still holds for his country and his differences with the media about the fighting capability of the ARVN. He's quick to point out that the press didn't tell the whole story.

He likens his survival to the willowy reeds in the swamps that bend with the wind. But when I mention communism, his whole persona tightens and his voice hardens. I can feel the intense hatred that burns inside him for the communists who destroyed his homeland. Indeed, Cau was the voice that I sought to speak out for the more than quarter million South Vietnamese soldiers who died at a casualty rate forty times that of Americans.

When you were commissioned a new lieutenant in 1963, was the South Vietnamese army capable of defeating the Viet Cong?

When I graduated from the Vietnamese Military Academy as a lieutenant in 1963, the fighting was between the local Viet Cong and the ARVN. I thought defeating the VC would not be a difficult matter. As a platoon leader with the 23rd Infantry Division in Ban me thuot, Central Highland, I fought against the local VC. My soldiers were brave, diligent, persistent, and patriotic; however, they greatly needed better training and equipment.

Why didn't you have better weapons?

All of our equipment came from the United States. The American government was not interested in providing the ARVN with modern weapons. It wasn't until 1968 that we received M16 rifles and better weapons. It was regrettably late.

Did the Vietnamese people perceive the Viet Cong as communists?

The Vietnamese people were confused about the Viet Cong, who cleverly hid their communist characteristics. The Vietnamese Communist Party camouflaged its identity under the title Vietnamese Labor Party. The communists proclaimed that they fought to protect national independence from foreign invaders and employed terrorist tactics and assassinations to exploit public support.

Did you see NVA soldiers at that time?

No, I had no contact with the NVA in 1963, but the Vietnamese Marines did in Phuoc Tuy Province. I personally didn't see the NVA until winter 1965 when my company was attacked in the Tuy Hoa Valley, Phu Yen Province. The NVA was equipped with automatic weapons (AK47), while my unit had only old World War II, semiautomatic Garand M1 rifles. We took heavy casualties. That evening when my unit withdrew, I saw NVA soldiers, wearing khaki uniforms, cross an open rice field in a long line. I called for artillery, but the battery couldn't fire because there was no ammunition left for that day. I received only two smoke rounds to scare the enemy.

Ngo Dinh was president in 1963. Did his being Catholic in a predominantly Buddhist country cause problems for the military?

No, I don't think so. President Ngo Dinh Diem was a very strong leader. I liked him and believed that the ARVN would need him to defend South Vietnam from communist invasion. His Catholic character would effectively support our military goals because Catholicism does not tolerate communism. Later, his two powerful brothers, Bishop Ngo Dinh Thuc and Ngo Dinh Nhu, his political adviser, unduly influenced President Ngo Dinh Diem. Unfortunately, his oppression of the Buddhists led to the 1963 coup d'etat.

Did you think in 1963 that the United States was behind Diem's assassination?

Everyone knew that Washington had given the Vietnamese generals the green light to carry out the coup against President Ngo Dinh Diem. The American government didn't want to assassinate Diem, it just wanted Diem to leave Vietnam. The decision to execute Diem was made by the coup's leaders.

Why didn't Diem remove his younger brother, Ngo Dinh Nhu, when Washington asked him to?

Ngo Dinh Nhu had served as the most powerful member of President Ngo Dinh Diem's ruling circle. He controlled the secret police, the Can Lao Nhan Vi Party (the ruling party of the government), and the national strategic hamlets programs. Nhu didn't want to voluntarily step down from power, and Diem hesitated to get rid of him. Diem had a strong character, but he needed his brother Nhu to do the dirty work. Nhu was very clever, but he made big problems when he burned Buddhist temples and beat up monks. Diem should have sent Nhu out of Vietnam when President Kennedy advised that he be removed, but Diem had a strong nationalistic character and didn't like being pressured by Washington.

Did the United States betray your country by giving the green light for the coup?

When President Ngo Dinh Diem was assassinated, there was no qualified successor to govern the country. I think Washington miscalculated the coup.

After the assassination of Diem, the parade of generals who led coup after coup in South Vietnam had to affect the morale of your troops?

Absolutely. The generals were not politicians; they were military men. They should have taken care of their men and not gotten involved in politics. They didn't have the political capacity to run the country. It was a total tragedy for the country. Many times, generals were promoted not because they were competent but because of their loyalty to whomever was president at the time so that they didn't make a coup. The coups created a political instability in South Vietnam. The Viet Cong exploited this by increased military activities that led to the deterioration of the country's security. ARVN troops had to fight harder to stop the VC but lacked support from above. The ARVN troops felt frustrated and angry.

Then why did you stay in the army?

I attended the Vietnamese Junior Military Academy in 1949 when I was six years old. Later, I went to the Vietnamese Military Academy, which was modeled after the U.S. Military Academy at West Point. After graduating, I was a professional soldier who enjoyed the challenges of a military lifestyle. Despite all the political changes, I dreamed of helping build a strong South Vietnamese army to stop the communists.

When U.S. troops entered Vietnam in 1965, ARVN troops were given secondary roles?

The ARVN consisted of three categories, regular, regional (RF), and popular forces (PF). When the American troops entered South Vietnam in 1965, our regular units were given the mission of pacification and essentially became regional forces. On the other hand, U.S. soldiers took over the responsibility of ARVN regular forces. In 1968, my battalion, which had been reduced to a regional force, was spread out over a large area to protect many villages. The only fighting that we experienced was against local VC. Our mobility and effectiveness were greatly diminished. Because the ARVN was used basically for security purposes, the Americans had a higher casualty rate. The media wrongly blamed Vietnamese soldiers for refusing to fight. Had ARVN been allowed to fight side by side with American troops, when American forces withdrew, ARVN would have been well prepared to take over the fighting mission. Such a policy also would have led to lower American casualties and more victories. On one occasion in April 1968, two of my companies fought side by side with an American tank company in Ninh Tinh. We eliminated almost one battalion of the 95th NVA regiment. We were very proud of the victory, and our confidence was increased.

You said that the media wrongly blamed the ARVN of refusing to fight.

That's correct. Many authors and journalists have not written the whole truth. They said that the ARVN were not good soldiers. That is wrong. As a man who spent twelve years in combat, I can honestly say that we had many brave, diligent, and patriotic soldiers in our armed forces. They fought valiantly and selflessly against the communists year after year. Many sacrificed in silence and gave their lives to the country. Over one-quarter million Vietnamese soldiers died defending the cause of freedom. There was a language and cultural barrier between foreign journalists and the South Vietnamese military. This created a lack of communication and misunderstanding between the two. Sometimes, the foreign media underreported the heroic actions of ARVN. For example, in 1972, the 23rd Infantry Division, with American fire support, had defeated three NVA divisions in Kontum Province, but the major news agencies weren't interested in the story. There were also numerous ARVN generals who fought bravely at the end of the war who would rather die than surrender. Gen. Nguyen Khoa Nam, IV Corps commander, and division commander Gen. Le Nguyen Vi and others will go into Vietnamese history as great heroes despite being forgotten by the media.

You are saying that the media was unfair in its reporting?

I'm saying that the media didn't have the full story. Hanoi and NVA contemptuously dismissed foreign journalists' requests to visit because they considered foreign reporters as a dangerous enemy who might damage their well-controlled public image. On the other hand, these same reporters were welcome in South Vietnam. This created a situation in which foreign journalists gained critical access to South Vietnamese military. Some of them exploited this favor to create sensational headlines at the expense of ARVN. I once met the photographer of the popular picture that showed Gen. Nguyen Ngoc Loan shooting an unarmed Viet Cong prisoner. The photographer expressed regret for taking the picture because General Nguyen was his friend. During the 1968 Tet Offensive, the NVA captured over five thousand civilians in Hue citadel. Later, they withdrew and massacred these civilians in the jungles. Some of them were buried alive. The media didn't report this story as often and prominently as the picture showing Gen. Nguyen Ngoc Loan killing one Viet Cong. The media accused ARVN of killing women and children. This was wrong because they didn't know the whole truth. The communists considered the war between the North and the South as a Peoples' War. Everybody was either soldier or war supporter. They taught young boys and girls to spy on ARVN activities and to throw hand grenades at the ARVN soldiers. Women transported weapons, food, and ammunition for the NVA and VC. They shot ARVN soldiers and, when captured, dropped their weapons and pretended to be civilians. This created a difficult situation for ARVN. They had to defend themselves against an enemy that sometimes included women and children. The media didn't depict the whole story. The fact is they should have written about the NVA and VC pushing young children and women into the war.

Could the ARVN have defeated the North Vietnamese in 1968 had it been properly trained, equipped, and provided American firepower and air support?

Certainly. We had defeated many NVA and Viet Cong units during the Tet Offensive in 1968. With the American firepower and air support, we could have defeated the NVA.

Were ARVN officers capable leaders?

Yes. The younger generation of officers was college educated and trained in officer training schools with the support of American advisers. Some officers graduated from the Vietnamese Military Academy and had years of combat experience. They were good leaders. Older officers were trained by the French in a totally different style of warfare. Many of them were former NCOs without any education. ARVN soldiers were very tough and dedicated fighters when they had good leaders, but some of the senior generals were political appointees. This had a very bad effect on the morale of the troops. My division commander, Lt. Gen. Nguyen Van Toan, was absolutely corrupt. He was relieved, but, a few months later, he was promoted to corps commander because he was loyal to President Nguyen Van Thieu. It was disgraceful.

What did you think about President Nguyen Van Thieu?

He wasn't as independent and strong as President Ngo Dinh Diem. He depended on American support to lead the country. When America cut off military aid, he lost his confidence and panicked. He made costly, wrong decisions when he withdrew the II Corps from the Central Highlands and when he abandoned the cities of Hue and Da Nang in the First Corps. These strategic mistakes led to the collapse of South Vietnam.

When you were battalion commander in 1970, did you have the right equipment to defeat the NVA?

We had good equipment and support at the time to defeat the NVA. We had M16 rifles, M72 rocket launchers, adequate ammunition and fuel, and U.S. air support. In 1970, ARVN controlled the battlefields of South Vietnam. My battalion even had the capacity to raid huge NVA supply depots in Cambodia along the Ho Chi Minh trail. We caught the NVA by surprise and captured thousands of weapons, tons of rice, and medicine. Other ARVN units achieved similar successes.

Why didn't we go into Cambodia earlier?

I don't know. The decision to fight in Cambodia belonged to Washington and President Nguyen Van Thieu.

Did you think South Vietnam could win the war in 1973 and 1974?

Yes, I believed we could win the war with continued American support.

When the war was drawing to an end in 1975, did you have weapons and ammunition to fight with?

We didn't have enough ammunition and supplies to fight big battles. We could only fire five artillery rounds a day for each gun. There was a limited gas supply for my trucks. We had a shortage of batteries for radio communications and parts for tanks. When we made heavy contact with the enemy, we severely lacked fire and other support, which reduced our ability to fight considerably.

The NVA was in South Vietnam?

The NVA was in South Vietnam since 1965. There were over two hundred thousand troops, about twenty divisions. We had captured many NVA soldiers. Despite this, Hanoi strongly denied NVA presence. That was a big lie.

Did you know then that you were going to lose?

No, I never thought that we would lose the war. Despite the cut in military aid from the U.S., we still fought, as President Thieu said, a "poor man's war." I believed that when the NVA violated the Peace Accords of 1973, the American government would retaliate as President Nixon had promised.

What were your feelings about Washington politicians for cutting off military aid?

I felt frustrated because the NVA still had the full support of Russia and China, whereas the ARVN had to rely on no one but itself. I also felt betrayed when Washington's politicians refused to support South Vietnam in the final months of the war in 1975.

Besides hoping that the Paris peace agreement would work, did you think that the North would win?

No, I never thought that the North would win. In previous major battles such as the 1968 Tet Offensive and the 1972 Easter Offensive, the North proved that they could not defeat the South.

Many journalists and pundits have praised the NVA.

I think the journalists and pundits saw the NVA only from a distance. The media lacked a lot of critical information because the communists blocked the foreign press from visiting NVA troops. In reality, there were many NVA deserters and negatives that the media never reported. NVA soldiers were strongly controlled by communist members within each unit about what they could say or do. Their leaders deceived NVA soldiers. They were told that South Vietnamese people were under the oppression of foreign invaders. When the NVA soldiers entered Saigon in 1975, they were shocked because the people of the South had more freedom and wealth than the people of the North. The NVA had used this lie to encourage its soldiers. From 1965 to 1975, the NVA suffered a higher casualty rate of almost four to one compared to that of the ARVN. The overall casualties of the NVA during the Vietnam War was about one million, whereas that of the ARVN was roughly one-quarter of a million. This shows that from a purely military point of view, the NVA had tactically lost against the ARVN. The NVA also behaved atrociously during the war. As I told you earlier, the NVA captured five thousand civilians in Hue citadel in the 1968 Tet Offensive and mercilessly murdered them in the jungles. The NVA were war criminals.

You're talking about their leaders. Weren't the North and South Vietnamese soldiers basically the same?

Yes, I knew the NVA soldiers for years when I was a prisoner of war. We were similar in many ways. The NVA leadership controlled its soldiers very tightly, but the individuals were basically no different than us.

You were captured in 1975?

I received an order to move my regiment from Tam Quan District, Binh Dinh Province, to Qui Nhon City. Tens of thousands of South Vietnamese refugees out of fear of the eminent arrival of the Communists followed my soldiers for protection. I couldn't maneuver my battalions because of the civilians mixing with my soldiers. When I tried to lead one of my units through a rice field to bypass the crowd, I stepped on an antipersonnel mine. The explosion broke my right ankle. My men carried me in a hammock for a few days. I told them to leave me because I didn't want them to slow down and be caught by the enemy. They refused to leave me. Unfortunately, the VC captured us near a swamp on the morning of March 31, 1975. My captors left me under the care of a peasant family and paid me no attention because they thought that I was a sergeant. The military code specified that we do not give our rank when captured by the enemy. A week later, the VC found out through other prisoners that I was a colonel. They demanded that I send a message to my soldiers calling for their surrender. I refused. Then they took me to a secret prison that was code-named T20. This camp was located on the border between Kontum and Quang Nam Provinces. They held me there for a few months after the fall of Saigon.

What happened then?

I was transferred from T20 prison to Ky Son reeducation camp in Quang Nam Province. I stayed there for three years under the control of NVA soldiers. In 1978, they moved me to Tien Lanh reeducation camp, also located in Quang Nam Province but in a different district controlled by VC police. A few months later, I was moved to Dong Mo, a secret camp where I stayed for a few months. At the end of 1978, I returned to Tien Lanh. At this point, the VC had completed building new cells. I stayed in solitary confinement for five years from 1978 to 1983. I was then relocated to a maximum security section at Tien Lanh until my release in February of 1988, after which I served one year of probation.

Did you see any American prisoners?

No. There were only Vietnamese prisoners.

Were the Viet Cong harder on you than the NVA?

Yes. The VC hated us more than the NVA. The local VC had suffered heavy casualties from my regiment during the war. The NVA, on the other hand, fought at many different locations throughout the country and didn't carry personal revenge.

You were in solitary confinement for five years?

From 1978 to 1983, they kept me in a small box without direct light, running water, and reading materials. There was only a tiny window for air. I was poorly fed. One time, I was so hungry that I ate a rat. It was terrible.

How did you keep from going crazy?

I sang all day long. Singing lifted my morale and vented my anger. One of my favorite songs went like this: "Cac anh di ngay ay da lau roi, cac anh di den bao gio tro lai; xom lang toi trai gai van cho mong." It meant "You have gone away long ago. When are you coming back? In our village, boys and girls are still waiting for you." I truly enjoyed this song because it eloquently expressed my feelings and my love for my people and my country. The love for my family had guided me through this hardship. My wife sent me letters and award certificates of my children's academic achievements. I would read them over and over again. I felt there was a connection between me and my family despite the long distance and years of separation between us. I was also an optimist. My favorite saying was, "When destiny gives you a lemon, make lemonade." There were countless incidences in prison when I turned frustration and anger into a driving force to survive. I always hoped that one day I would be reunited with my family.

Were you tortured?

The guards didn't physically torture me, but they mentally abused me. They threatened to kill me many times. They crushed my mentality and resistance through starvation and refusal to provide medicine when I was seriously sick. I remember one time they chained my ankles for two weeks straight.

Did they try to brainwash you in reeducation camp?

Every POW had to work under harsh conditions for eight hours a day, six to seven days a week. We lacked food and clothes and were basically starved and cold in the winter. Besides punishing our bodies, they fed us communist propaganda. We had to learn political lessons that accused the Americans as war criminals and neocolonists and proclaimed the ARVN puppets of America. The Vietnamese Communist Party, on the other hand, was praised excessively. They told us that communism would defeat capitalism globally. Every night, each POW was told to criticize other POWs and himself. Every POW lived in a state of fear and distrust with others.

Did you see your wife while you were in prison?

My wife worked as a midwife. She held two jobs to raise five young children. She could only afford to visit me once a year for fifteen minutes under camp regulations. In 1978, after a long and difficult journey, she was not allowed to see me. She typically had to travel 1,000 kilometers each way from where she lived in Bien Hoa City to my prison located in a mountainous area. She took the train, bus, and motorcycles to get there. Sometimes, she had to walk miles in the jungles because there was no other means of transportation.

Why did the Communists finally release you?

Pressure from international and many Vietnamese organizations abroad influenced the communists' policy. I was also one of the last remaining POWs at the camp.

Had Vietnam and Saigon changed under Communist rule when you went home?

When I was released from Tien Lanh camp, I took the bus home. My fellow passengers were very sympathetic when they learned that I was a former South Vietnamese soldier. They collected some money and food for me. I greatly appreciated this gesture. I felt that they still loved the ARVN soldier. When I held the money in my hand, I couldn't recognize it because the communists had changed the currency. It was then that I realized everything had changed. When I arrived in my village, I had to ask for directions several times before I could locate my house. The communists always declared that everyone was guaranteed food and clothes. Everybody would have a chance to go to school. In reality, the people struggled to survive and often were without food and clothes. Many children were forced to leave school in order to work to survive. Ironically, a new social class of government officials and police became rich from bribery and corruption. On the other hand, the people were getting poorer and poorer.

What work did you do before emigrating to the United States?

I applied to teach in a high school but was refused because of my ARVN background. I then opened a basic English class at home and taught Amerasian children and their families who were about to emigrate to America.

Why did you survive the war when so many other ARVN soldiers didn't? Do you believe that a higher power chose you to live and eventually come to the United States?

I can't answer that, but I do feel blessed. I fought continuously for twelve years. I was wounded three times and spent thirteen years in prison as a POW. For years I didn't think I could survive. Somehow I prevailed and was fortunate enough to have an opportunity to move to America. I have a burning desire to go back to a Vietnam free of a communist regime. I want to go there to honor the South Vietnamese and American soldiers who died for the ideals of freedom and democracy.

BARRY McCAFFREY

Combat was the most totally absorbing, selfless,
and worthwhile thing I had ever done in my life.
—BARRY McCAFFREY TO JOSEPH L. GALLOWAY,

U.S. News & World Report (MARCH 4, 1991)

In 1990, at the outset of Desert Storm, Maj. Gen. Barry McCaffrey was the youngest and most decorated division commander in the U.S. Army. A veteran of two tours in Vietnam and one in Dominican Republic, he did not go to battle to look for a fair fight against the Iraqi forces in the Gulf War. His mission was to hit the enemy with everything he had and minimize American casualties. "War," he told a reporter, "is killing people and destroying their weapons and equipment." At first, he was against sending American soldiers into Kuwait and Iraq for fear of taking excessive casualties. But once the decision was made, the 24th Mechanized Infantry Division's "left hook" maneuver caught Saddam Hussein's Republican Guard completely by surprise; only one American was injured.

On another battlefield two decades earlier, the U.S. Army's stratagems failed to adhere to the principles of overwhelming power and surprise before committing American forces. McCaffrey and Gen. Norman Schwarzkopf took with them to the Arabian Desert the bitter lessons of Vietnam's piecemeal commitment and graduated response. It was McCaffrey's note to me about Vietnam—"Our young soldiers deserved better"—that inspired me to write this book.

The taxi moves by the White House, turns onto 17th Street, and pulls up in front of a tall brick building. McCaffrey meets me at the door to the office of the director of the Office of National Drug Control Policy, the country's "drug czar." His hair is white; his chiseled face resembles the battle scowl that cartoonists sketch. He looks like a general. To outsiders, McCaffrey is a tough, no-nonsense, top executive. But, deep down, he's still a fun-loving infantryman who mixes his precise dialogue with GI jargon.

McCaffrey was born into a military family; his father was a West Pointer, class of 1939. He grew up on military bases where he met friends of his father who would later lead America's war effort in Vietnam. In 1970, as a three-star general, William J. McCaffrey was in charge of all Army forces in Vietnam. Barry McCaffrey points out that his father is his mentor, his confidant, and his sounding board for major personal decisions.

A 1964 graduate of the U.S. Military Academy and barely a year out of school, McCaffrey was fighting on the streets of the Dominican Republic with the 82d Airborne Division, the same unit in which his son Sean would serve twenty-five years later as a young lieutenant in the Kuwaiti desert. After his return from the Dominican Republic in 1966, McCaffrey promptly signed up for Vietnam as an adviser to the South Vietnamese Airborne Brigade and returned to Vietnam in 1968 as a company commander with the 1st Cavalry Division.

Thrice wounded, his fear of coming back in a box was almost realized in a fierce battle during his second tour. Now a retired full general, whose last active-duty assignment was to head the U.S. Armed Forces Southern Command in Panama, McCaffrey is a member of President Clinton's cabinet and the National Security Council. As a political appointee close to the presidential throne, I wonder how much he'll temper his responses. Within minutes, I know the answer: He's holding back nothing.

You first volunteered for Vietnam upon graduating from West Point in 1964?

I did. I was convinced that Vietnam was where the next big war was going to be. I wanted to be part of it. I volunteered for the 82d Airborne, thinking that it would be one of the first American units to go, but the 82d was deployed to Dom Rep [the Dominican Republic] instead. The intervention in the Dom Rep was so different from what followed in Vietnam. In Santo Domingo, we were hailed as liberators. The fighting, although heavy during the initial intervention, was followed by peacekeeping operations under OAS [Organization of American States] political control. It was actually quite fun. We were heavily involved in civic action, and the people were grateful for the peace we consolidated.

Why did you want to go into combat?

Romanticism. I was taken by the notion of fighting with an American combat unit. I had been immersed in military history since I was ten. All my relatives had fought in wars. My dad saw extensive combat in World War II and Korea. The Dominican Republic was so exciting that, when we returned to the States, four of us drove up to Washington to volunteer for Vietnam. The 173d Airborne Brigade had just been deployed, and we were convinced that the war was going to be over soon. I remember the assignment officer at the Pentagon asking me whether I wanted to be a platoon leader or a battalion commander. I told him that I wanted to be a battalion commander. He said, "Congratulations, we're sending you to be an adviser with the Vietnamese Airborne Brigade. You'll be the same as a battalion commander." I said, "Hot damn, sign me up." Shows you how naïve a young airborne lieutenant can be. That was the end of romanticism for me—that first tour in Vietnam.

So you became an adviser.

The first tour in Vietnam, I was an adviser to an ARVN parachute infantry battalion. Ton San Nhut Air Base in Saigon was the home base for the national strategic reaction force. The American advisers were handpicked from elite American units. All of us were extremely impressed with the enormous courage of the Vietnamese units. They had great soldiers. Their offensive spirit was unbelievable. We spent a lot of time standing by in Saigon or in a provincial capital to be committed in counterattack to support developing battles. I saw all of Vietnam and fell in love with the country, the people, and the culture. The fighting was intermittently severe with heavy friendly casualties; two of my U.S. captain senior advisers were killed only weeks apart. Our U.S. team of NCOs was incredibly courageous and also suffered corresponding heavy losses. I was wounded twice and learned to dig like an animal to stay alive under mortar and artillery fire. The life of an infantry battalion in the Vietnam jungles fighting North Vietnamese regulars was a brutish, dangerous existence. To this day, I'm in contact with retired M. Sgt. Rudy Ortiz, whose example of valor and tutoring in combat skills turned me into an effective field officer.

Did you discuss with your dad America's involvement in Vietnam before you volunteered?

My dad was horrified by the whole idea of getting involved in a land war in Indochina. He talked to me about it at great length and about the fundamental mistakes of the Korean War. He was very much opposed to our intervention from the start. Once we were committed, however, he and his generation of military leaders—who had seen such heavy combat in World War II and Korea—tried with all their might to lead us to victory. Dad served more than three years in Vietnam as General Abrams's deputy.

Did you buy into Washington's explanation for sending American troops to Vietnam?

I understood the reasoning in an intellectual sense. It was clear to me that this was communist aggression and that they were going to swallow up other countries. I went to Vietnam with more tools and understanding than probably 99 percent of the American soldiers. I had Vietnamese language and cultural training. I had written academic papers on Vietnam as a West Point cadet and read Bernard Fall's books. But, once there, I disconnected from the geostrategic aspects of the war. I was just energized by the honor of wearing the red beret and camouflage fatigues of the Vietnamese Airborne. That was my whole world. I had this incredibly romantic, dangerous, and important life.

There has been a lot of bad press about the will to fight of the South Vietnamese Army. Were they good fighters? Were their leaders capable?

The South Vietnamese military was, of course, a mixed bag. The senior leaders were, in many cases, corrupt and disorganized. They certainly lacked the political will, focus, determination, discipline, and patriotism of the North Vietnamese. Many of the South Vietnamese units were ferocious fighters whom I respected and learned from. Vietnamese Airborne units were as good as any shock unit in the world. The Vietnamese Marine Brigade, the ARVN Ranger Battalions, the ARVN First Division in I Corps, and many other units also fought bravely and effectively. At the end of the day, however, the communists had the legitimacy of Ho Chi Minh's revolution against the French. The South Vietnamese didn't understand that land reform and corruption were key political issues. Finally, the Russians and Chinese had more staying power. The U.S. became disillusioned with a war that was inadequately understood. Our strategy was flawed. We tired of the huge losses and the slaughter of our boys.

You also volunteered for a second tour. You already had two Purple Hearts and the Distinguished Service Cross. You were pushing your luck. Why?

Guilt. I had an idyllic tour as an aide to Maj. Gen. Chet Johnson in Panama. He was a grand old soldier, a survivor of the Bataan death march, and a wonderful man to work for. He was lining me up to go to graduate school at Harvard and then to teach social sciences at West Point. Then, in 1968, the Tet Offensive hit. Horrible pictures were shown on AFN television every night. It looked like Stalingrad. I couldn't take it. So I called the Pentagon and asked to be sent back to Vietnam. Then, I told the general who had grander ambitions for me than fighting in that crazy war.

What was the general's reaction?

General Johnson was scared when I told him that I was on orders. He treated me as a son and had seen a lot of death in his time. My wife Jill was scared, too, but she understood. Jill always understood. There was never any discussion or argument about my going. She bundled up the two children and went home to her family in Southern California. Her dad was an admirable man and a WWII vet with three combat parachute jumps in the Pacific Theater with the famous 11th Airborne Division. He safeguarded my young family during three combat tours early in our lives. Jill's brother was also on the line in Vietnam at the same time during my first tour. He volunteered to serve with the 101st Airborne Division and was promoted to sergeant in combat as a team leader of a long-range recon unit.

Did you have any premonitions that this time you might have a rendezvous with death?

I really did. I said good-bye to Jill and my two children. Her dad was going to drive me to the airport. I was so sure that I would never see her again that I threw up on the sidewalk. By then, American casualties were up to something like 460 dead per week. I had no illusions about what was going on. But, when I got there, the Tet Offensive was over. I volunteered for and was assigned to the famous 1st Cavalry Division. We suddenly found ourselves temporarily as an army of occupation doing all kinds of peacetime stuff. Then, in November 1968, the war exploded, and my 1st Cav brigade was ordered to make an emergency deployment from the North in I Corps to the Cambodian border in III Corps area where we promptly got the shit kicked out of us. It was unbelievable. I took command of B Company, 2-7th Cavalry, at three in the morning when the company commander, who was a friend of mine, was killed. By the end of two weeks, I was the second-longest serving company commander in the battalion. All the others had been killed, wounded, or relieved. My company was in contact with the enemy almost continuously for three weeks. Many of us eventually were killed or injured; we had close to 100 percent casualties over time. Our young soldiers were nearly all draftees. They were a joy to work with. They had enormous courage and were ferociously devoted to each other.

Why are some of us spared, and others aren't?

I don't know why. Some people would say that there was no bullet made with their name on it. This sure wasn't my view. I knew I was going to get clocked eventually, so I was observant about digging in—and about survival instincts and techniques. I never took a chance unless I was forced to, and then I was hyperaggressive. I wasn't depressed about being killed, but I was very conscious of it. Since then, I've always wondered why I survived. So many fine young soldiers—so many friends—were killed or maimed.

What were your thoughts about Washington's handling of the war during your second tour with an American unit?

I operated off a 1:50,000 map like the rest of the infantry captains. If you weren't on my map, I didn't care who you were. All I wanted to know was where the support artillery, commo relay stations, and lift helicopters were; that was it. We stayed in the field nearly continuously and in frequent combat. Our horizons were narrow and focused on survival.

Were our soldiers good fighters?

Americans are natural fighters. The soldiers in my company, including NCOs and second lieutenants, were essentially all draftees with modest military training. They arrived with rudimentary knowledge of weapons and tactics. Naturally courteous and fun loving, they had innate team skills. As soon as they figured out that the company would take care of them—and that the sergeants and officers knew what we were doing—they turned into aggressive fighters. They were in good health, physically strong and resilient. Many had completed a year or more of college. Beer drinking, bad grades, and no family connections got them drafted. They came into the Army knowing that they'd been screwed but feeling they had to do their duty. Many of the young soldiers had dads and uncles who were veterans. My first sergeant, Emerson Trainer, and I were basically the only RA [Regular Army] old guys in the company. Both of us were on our third combat tours and had been wounded twice before. The first sergeant had been a private in the Korean War with the same company, B Company, 2d Battalion, 7th Cav. He was badly wounded and married a beautiful Japanese girl while hospitalized in Japan. To this day, he and I have remained friends. I admired him greatly. He was a model NCO with outstanding leadership skills, courage, integrity, and concern for his soldiers.

You're quite high on your men.

You bet. Our company has been having periodic reunions with growing attendance since the end of the war. These men are admirable to this day. An overwhelming number have done very well in life in terms of jobs, education, and family, but they can never forget the bond of love, misery, and excitement born of combat in Vietnam. Basically, we were a tough, determined, dangerous group of soldiers. We had incredibly fast and responsive artillery, as well as armed helicopter and fighter-bomber support. Our air medevac and backup hospital care were excellent. Our field nutrition was adequate. We received mail regularly. If you weren't killed or maimed too early, you would get a great five-day R&R outside of Vietnam.

But combat was no cakewalk.

In retrospect, life in the field was unbelievably hard. You carried more than a hundred pounds of gear, primarily ammunition and water. We were heavily armed; the company had nine M60 machine guns and normally one 81-mm mortar. All of us carried M16 rifles with four hundred rounds of ammo, an entrenching tool, two hand grenades, some smoke grenades, C4 demolitions, and a mortar round. We also hauled a bunch of claymore mines, trip flares, and booby trap devices. Everyone had a gas mask and a couple of CS grenades. We all wore helmets with chin straps fastened. While moving in the jungle, we had leafy camouflage on our web gear and packs. Each squad carried a pick and D-handled shovel plus empty sandbags. All soldiers had gloves to protect their hands while digging or using machetes to chop trail. Our soldiers always had multiple medical problems—ripped skin, infections, eye injuries, foot problems, lower GI difficulty, and crotch rot. We were wet, baked, and exhausted from lack of sleep and constant movement. Our uniforms were frequently in shreds; we were filthy and smelled like wild animals. Visitors who came by helicopter would be nauseated by our stench and appearance. Nevertheless, we were clean-shaven and kept our hair cut even in the field. Long stretches of boredom and misery could turn into bloody mayhem at any minute. Helicopter assaults were the only brief periods of coolness and contact with technology. The end of a helicopter assault would bring either a silent reembrace by the dense jungle or the terror of an opposed landing.

And when you made contact with the enemy?
Battles were frequent and unpredictable. We normally initiated contact first by suddenly walking into NVA encampments deep in the jungle or encountering enemy units moving on trails. We would try to attack rapidly and aggressively with two platoons while the reserve platoon and mortar platoon blew down trees to open a helicopter pad. Artillery would mass rapidly on the enemy and start hammering. At some point, I would gauge that our volume of fire had pinned down the enemy force and then we would attack violently. A volley of a hundred or more hand grenades, sometimes mixed with CS gas, would normally initiate the attack. Then we'd attack firing full automatic with our bugler blowing the charge to terrorize the enemy unit. I still have the company bugle. They sent it to me in Walter Reed hospital after I was wounded. It was a tough last day, three killed and thirty-five wounded in desperate fighting. My left arm was almost completely blown off by an enemy light machine gun firing at close range.

Most of our fighting men were sons of blue-collar workers. Would Washington have looked differently upon the war had sons of influential Americans been on the front lines?
Of course. When President Nixon changed the draft to a random lottery with few exemptions, it sucked the energy out of the war. Now dads with kids and electrical engineering degrees would be forced to serve. This policy put a new face on the war. At the same time, we should remember that 70 percent of those killed whose names are listed on the Vietnam Memorial were volunteers.

The stories about what was happening back in the States must have had a demoralizing effect on you and your men.
Yes. I was getting stories from Jill in Southern California about her friends asking how her husband could be so stupid to be in Vietnam. Why didn't he take measures like the others to get out? It got to the point where I told my troops that the reason we were fighting was because the 120 of us soldiers in the company depended on each other. We were fighting for the Army—not America. I told them to divorce themselves from the stuff going on back home.

You must have taken special umbrage at some of the antiwar activists, like Jane Fonda.
I despised Jane Fonda. To this day she bothers me although I've ameliorated my viewpoint somewhat. But Jill never has. Talk about fierce. She won't go to a movie with Jane Fonda in it. Jill will turn off the TV if Fonda is on the set.

Did you have a drug problem with your men?
Very, very little. The drug problem wasn't in the field with rifle companies; it was back in the rear on brigade firebases. Our combat capability was severely degraded by drug and alcohol abuse as the war went downhill. By 1971, drug abuse and racial conflict were enormous problems in the rear areas. Combat units, for the most part, were far less affected by it.

Could we have won the war?
In retrospect, of course. First of all, it was a matter of political will. Graduated force was the worst thing we did in Vietnam. Force is a vector. Force has direction but also intensity and magnitude. What we did in Vietnam was to shape our strategy carefully, gradually escalating violence against the North Vietnamese. They were about as tough and capable an enemy as we've ever faced historically, and we let them adjust to our action. We allowed them to develop a global political and resource support system. We let them intervene and win in our domestic political environment. Unquestionably, we could have demonstrated our ability to use levels of violence to swamp their decision-making capacity. The approach we chose represented a grand strategic failure. South Vietnam's fate was sealed when the U.S. Congress voted to cut off their ammunition and fuel. South Vietnam fell not to an internal insurgency, but to a massive, classic, armor-led invasion. By the way, it wasn't all the politicians' fault. The military leadership also used inappropriate tactics and strategy. Our military helped screw this one up.

Didn't Washington screw up early in the war by not attacking sanctuaries in Cambodia and Laos?
Washington refused to recognize publicly that the North Vietnamese Army was in Cambodia in full strength. I was a rifle company commander in '68–'69. We went into LZ Billy, three kilometers from the Cambodian border, and were run out by the NVA. They were coming out of Cambodia with clean uniforms, fresh haircuts, and

brand-new weapons. They were beautifully organized and logistically better off than we were—but we were forbidden to fire across the border. The whole thing was crazy. The notion of sanctuaries was outrageous to me and to all of us who operated on the Cambodian border. When we were up at the DMZ in the north on my first tour, thousands of North Vietnamese crossed the river in broad daylight and attacked us. We were almost wiped out. They were considered untouchable in their sanctuaries during some periods of the conflict.

Should we have used nuclear weapons and avoided the loss of fifty-five thousand American lives?

I can't rationally imagine us ever using a nuclear weapon again. Nuclear weapons are for deterrence and to prevent further nuclear proliferation. They're not war-fighting tools. I hope we never have to use them.

Did the threat of China intervening enter your mind?

We knew all about the Chinese, but I'm not sure that country had much influence on my thinking. We weren't there to conquer China; that wasn't our political objective. Our aim was to force the North Vietnamese to give up their goal of subjugating South Vietnam. The U.S. built up its forces to a half million troops. We applied enormous resources over an extended period of time without a strategic focus. We didn't heed Clausewitz. We didn't think through the logic of our situation. In my judgment, the lion's share of the blame goes to the political leadership, but I also want those of us in uniform to assume responsibility. We didn't employ military power to achieve a defined purpose; we just hung on in a meat-grinder engagement and fought our opponents in the arena of their greatest strength—on the ground, in the jungle, and at close range with automatic weapons and hand grenades.

U.S. policy and strategies were conditioned by fear of China. Should we have ignored the possibility that China would intervene if we pushed the war north?

The key to winning the war in Vietnam was not to fight China but to apply an overmatching level of violence in an explosive manner to overload the North Vietnamese decision-making capacity. We also needed to understand the nature of the war in the South, which I don't think Washington ever did. We should have armed our South Vietnamese allies with appropriate technology, equipment, and training as step one of the conflict instead of waiting until the end of the war before properly equipping them. When I was with the Vietnamese Airborne, they had World War II M2 carbines, .30-caliber machine guns, BARs [Browning automatic rifles], obsolete helicopter support, and faulty communications. I often wondered why we didn't give our Allies modern weapons. And we had the wrong guy there. Poor General Westmoreland. If he had been a brigadier general in 1941, he would have been wearing five stars by the end of the war. They would have built a statue of him at West Point. We never had a more dedicated, honorable, handsome general officer in our country's history. But he was totally ill-suited to think through what we were doing in Vietnam. He never did get it. This is all, of course, hindsight on my part. During the war, I was a line officer focused on tactical combat operations. My perspective limit was the range of an M16 rifle.

Why was Westmoreland the wrong guy?

He didn't understand that the Vietnamization program should have been going on in 1965, not delayed until 1971. Land reform was the key to stopping the insurrection at its core, particularly in the Mekong Delta. We also had three CINCs running the war in Vietnam. We had SAC [Strategic Air Command] strategic air power, Pacific air and sea power, and MACV. We needed one unified air/land/sea command. The division of power and accountability was completely nuts. A major contributing factor in our failure may have been the mindset of my dad's military generation. I have tremendous respect for them. They were honorable men with incredible courage, dedication, and years of combat experience in World War II and Korea. Their discipline was absolute. They were apolitical and didn't even vote. However, they were faced with political inanities from McNamara and his operations research "whiz kids." My father knew that U.S. involvement in Vietnam was wrong, but his generation—and I knew most of the two and three-star generals in Vietnam because they were my dad's war buddies—strongly accepted unquestioned civilian control of the armed forces. So when they saw things that were stupid, and McNamara had been stupid, this group didn't adequately challenge their orders. They thought the proper course of action was to state an opinion and then numbly obey.

Should the Joint Chiefs of Staff have resigned en masse?

Absolutely. I thought about that dilemma for years. Dad worshipped Gen. Harold K. Johnson, the Army's chief of staff. He was one of the finest people we ever had in uniform, but he was wrapped up in personal honor rather than institutional honor. When he realized we were going in the wrong direction and couldn't correct it, he should have gone to the mat with his political bosses and then quit. He had no excuse for remaining obedient and mute. There were too many of us getting ground up, and many people in uniform were questioning what the hell was happening.

The force of McNamara's personality was so overwhelming that he browbeat the joint chiefs and generals in the field into submission.

I agree. But again, their corporate ethic was one of respectful, dutiful obedience to authority. They were smart, well-traveled people. They knew about politics, but they weren't equipped intellectually to handle arrogant, blowtorch personalities like McNamara and his "whiz kids."

You're not a big McNamara fan?

I remember, when I was a cadet at West Point, being unsettled by one of McNamara's "whiz kids" giving a lecture. The guy derided the lessons of history and the generals who still thought in terms of World War II. That sort of thinking and the micromanagement of the war by bureaucrats in Washington were destroying the armed forces. To many of us, McNamara exemplified a brilliant mind that knew the price of everything and the value of nothing. The guy was a tragic figure. His book is simply disgusting. The gall of seeking empathy by claiming he knew Vietnam was a lost cause but still continuing to send thousands of Americans over there to lose their twenty-one-year-old lives. However, the country learned a lot because of Mr. McNamara. We have a far more balanced understanding of the relationship between military force and U.S. society than we did before Vietnam. We all should read H. R. McMasters's *Dereliction of Duty*. It's a powerful book that chronicles the consequences of the failure of wisdom in managing military power.

There's been finger-pointing in the press about "political generals" in the Pentagon succumbing to the Oval Office's micromanaging of military operations in Kosovo. Have we not learned from Vietnam?

You're referring to people who say on television that if Washington listened to "real" combat soldiers, we never would be in this mess.

I don't see how we can call the joint chiefs "political" officers. Adm. Jay Johnson is a Navy fighter pilot, and Gen. Hugh Shelton has been carrying a gun from the time he was old enough to do so. He earned a CIB [Combat Infantryman Badge] and a Purple Heart. I was one of the "Pentagon Generals" and hope I'm not viewed as a person who doesn't know what life is like in a front-line combat unit. So, I'm not quite sure what some of these critics are saying.

Earlier you lauded the North Vietnamese as tough fighters. Could the South Vietnamese have held them back had the U.S. Congress not cut off its funding?

In my judgment, we lost the war when Congress voted to cut off their ammunition and fuel. From that moment on, the South Vietnamese army knew that it was just a matter of time before they collapsed. Everything started to unravel after that vote. I had watched the North Vietnamese Army at close range and greatly respected the communist soldiers; however, communism was alien to the Vietnamese tradition, the Confucian ethic, and rural village life. The North adopted an ideology that did provide iron discipline, integrity, and direction. The North Vietnamese generals and political leaders were absolutely superb. I have enormous regard for the NVA regimental commanders who would spend days personally reconnoitering their target—and then would go back to bring up their units and lead the attack. These men were real professionals. Nevertheless, I think the South Vietnamese could have defended their country successfully. Our strategy set them up to lose. We expected them to fight the same kind of war we had waged with firepower and helicopters. Then we turned off their ammunition and fuel as we left. Predictably, they succumbed not to insurrection but to a major invasion of tanks, artillery, and rockets. This final onslaught overwhelmed them. Had Washington demonstrated an unwavering resolve to support South Vietnam, democracy could have prevailed.

We were defeated on the streets of America?

The war had gone on too long. There wasn't a purpose; the strategy was flawed; and the tactics didn't make any sense. Our efforts were going nowhere. The war was a national tragedy. We got into it without thinking—and out of it without thinking. We completely abandoned the South Vietnamese. They went under like an ox hit behind the ear with a bullet. I was teaching social science at West Point when Vietnam started to fall. Two of us volunteered to return and help get our people out of there. It was disgraceful what we allowed to happen to the South Vietnamese who had supported us and trusted us. Our conduct was shameful.

You were the commander of the 24th Mechanized Infantry Division in Desert Storm. Did Washington politicians micromanage military operations there as they did in Vietnam?

Although Desert Storm wasn't without flaws strategically and tactically, it was a good example, in my judgment, of the proper relationship between political power and military strategy. Our national leaders used military force respectfully and decisively. They didn't get involved in micromanaging details. They gave the CINC, Gen. Norman Schwarzkopf, tremendous latitude. Personally, I didn't want to invade Iraq and Kuwait for fear we'd take several thousand casualties. We hoped that our political leadership could have tricked the Iraqis out of Kuwait, but the armed forces were given the authority, equipment, and training for a quick victory. It was the opposite of Vietnam. During Desert Storm, I was sure the CINC and JCS chairman knew what they were doing. I had absolute trust in the president and secretary of defense. This is the way to win a war.

You are now part of an administration in which the president, the secretary of defense, secretary of state, and national security advisor have had no military experience. Do you think they should?

It's interesting that you say that. We greatly admired defense secretary Dick [Richard B.] Cheney during Desert Storm, and he had been draft-deferred as a graduate-school father of small children. He, along with most young Republicans with whom I worked in the Bush administration, had never heard a shot fired in anger. So I'm not sure that combat is a prerequisite even for the secretary of defense. But I do think our political leaders must trust the military professionals enough to consider their advice. Then, the political leadership can decide whether or not to accept it. The way we get into trouble in America is when civilian leaders disregard the military calculus about how to employ power to achieve political objectives. Our presidents and key advisers must understand both history and military power—and have confidence in their advisers. Dr. William Perry, who was secretary of defense during my tenure as CINC US SOUTHCOM, is a superb public servant. He's on a par with Gen. George C. Marshall. A draftee sergeant with a Ph.D. in mathematics, he loved soldiers and their families enough to safeguard their interests and the welfare of our country. He's a model for what America needs as civilian leadership for national security.

Any final thoughts on your Vietnam experience?
The war ended twenty-five years ago in 1975. Most of us are now twenty-five to thirty-five years removed from Vietnam combat. I still have pain in my heart about Vietnam. I don't think the country deserved the chaos and oppression that the communist victory brought. Hundreds of thousands fled through the jungle to Thailand or to the sea to escape the cruelty and retribution that followed. The historians are still trying to sort all of this out, sifting through mountains of documents. It has been my impression, and I'll say it again, the country learned a number of vital lessons. First of all, we must not commit our youth to war without the support of the American people. In a democracy, lack of such support produces catastrophic divisiveness and a weakening of the national will that is essential to winning. Second, we must not send our sons and daughters to war without a clear understanding of national aims and the cost of achieving them. Third, we need to understand that war is not theoretical business. When we make a decision to fight, the victory will be paid for in blood. Combat has costs; it is never free. Finally, we learned as individuals that to survive and succeed, when conditions are appalling and your life is on the line, requires moral and physical courage, competence, self-discipline and, most importantly, trust in your buddies.

JOHN McCAIN

Vietnam changed me, in significant ways, for the better.
It is a surprising irony that war, for all its horror,
provides the combatant with every conceivable human experience.
Experiences that usually take a lifetime to know are all felt,
and felt intensely, in one brief passage of life.

—JOHN McCAIN, *Faith of My Fathers*

Regardless of how many times I read or hear stories about John McCain's five and a half years in the Hanoi Hilton (Hoa Lo prison), I am always amazed at the distance he has traveled since his release from captivity. I wonder as I enter the senator's second-floor office in the Russell Senate Office Building, if he would be a U.S. senator and Republican presidential candidate had his A-4 Skyhawk not been shot down over Hanoi?

Ten days earlier, I had requested an interview with the senator and half expected to be turned down or, at best, put on hold because of his feverish schedule. But McCain's office called a few days later to say that he would be delighted to talk with me. Granted, McCain was a darling of the media during his campaign for his easy accessibility in the back of his campaign bus, Straight Talk Express, but to carve out over an hour of his hectic schedule for a book that wouldn't hit the stores for months was indeed revealing of the man's character.

Dubbed the "crown prince" by his North Vietnamese captors because of his military lineage that dates back to the Revolutionary War, John Sidney McCain III was expected from birth to carry on the family tradition. His paternal grandfather, Adm. John S. McCain, was commander of all U.S. aircraft carriers during World War II, and his father, Adm. John S. McCain, Jr., was commander of U.S. armed forces in the Pacific during the Vietnam War. Both retired as four-star admirals. The young McCain's reputation as a hell raiser at the U.S. Naval Academy (class of 1958) and as a naval fighter pilot, however, gave no indication that he was a "chip off the old block," that is, until his aircraft was hit by a communist surface-to-air missile. It was his twenty-third air mission over North Vietnam and his last. Forced to eject, he plunged into a lake in the middle of Hanoi and shattered both arms and a leg. For two and a half years, he was in solitary confinement in a 6- by 9-foot hole in the ground.

McCain sweeps into his office a few minutes late for our meeting. Photographs of Native Americans taken by Barry Goldwater, the deceased Arizona senator and 1964 Republican presidential contender, cover the walls. McCain's desk is stacked high with papers. He apologizes, but I can tell by the tightness in his face that he's already at his next appointment. We sit at a coffee table across from each other. His eyes are steady; deep lines in his face reflect a mounting weariness from his run for the Republican presidential nomination. I wonder what he would look like in uniform. Would he be more natural than in the rumpled suit that he's wearing? How would he appear as the next president of the United States?

As I fumble in my bag for a publisher's proof copy of his soon-to-be-released memoir, *Faith of My Fathers*, I can feel his eyes boring into the back of my head. Clearly, he wants to get the show on the road.

I place my minicassette recorder on the table and, out of deference to the torture that he suffered in prison, tell him to let me know if any question makes him uncomfortable. "I'll answer all your questions," he shoots back.

After the first few questions, he catches his breath and starts to unwind. There's still a lot of "swabbie" left in him that Congress hasn't drained out—the twinkle in his eyes and some choice four-letter words from a Navy flight deck. If there is any anger in him from his POW days, I do not discern it.

Sadly, I sense that America isn't ready for his type of integrity and candidness in the Oval Office. He does not have the faintest interest in sticking his finger in the air to take a consensus on which way the political winds are blowing. There's only one direction for this former Navy captain: Full steam ahead. A commander never takes a vote among his troops before determining whether to go to battle stations, which is unsettling to the party leadership that controls the big political machinery.

As we wrap the interview, I ask him if he thinks of himself as a philosopher. Much of what he says is laced with philosophical anecdotes. "I'm an idealist. A flawed idealist," he retorts. There's nothing phony about his response.

When a misfired Zuni rocket on the flight deck of the USS _Forrestal_ punched through the fuel tank of your A-4 jet—and you survived the holocaust—did you ask yourself, "Why me?" and not the 134 men that were killed?

I've had a very charmed life, having had several other narrow escapes. But, at the time, I wasn't so struck by the "why me" aspect as I was struck by the really terrible things I saw happen to eighteen- and nineteen-year-old kids. The 134 that were killed were mainly young members of the flight deck crew, some of whom I knew. So, at least at that time, I wasn't so much impressed with my own survival as I was agonized over the terrible loss of these young lives. Later on, because of accumulation of experiences that I've had, it has made me curious and given me a certain sense—and I'm not a fatalist because I believe man controls his own destiny—but I do believe that there must be at least some reason behind all of these extraordinary events which I survived.

After the _Forrestal_ went to Subic for repairs, you volunteered for combat on the USS _Oriskany_. Why? You had just barely escaped death on the _Forrestal_.

An officer from the _Oriskany_ came to my squadron looking for volunteers. The _Oriskany_ had lost a number of pilots and was under-manned. I volunteered because I wanted to remain in combat, to do what I perceived was my duty. I had been trained for this literally all my military career, and it had something to do with heritage and inspiration of my family. I also felt, in those days, that the cause was just.

I know that when many of us volunteered the first time for Vietnam, it wasn't just about stopping the communists. It had something to do with manhood, about testing character under fire.

I think so. When I mentioned that I wanted to fly in combat because that is what I had been trained to do, it was also—as you said—a test of manhood as well as skills.

Did you enjoy combat?

Oh, yeah. I found it invigorating, adrenaline inducing, and very exciting in many respects.

What did you and your fellow pilots think about Washington's handling of the war?

We were very disillusioned and angry that they restricted the bombing targets in the fashion that they did. I remember the first target that I had on the *Forrestal* was a military barracks. This was in 1967. I went up to the intelligence center and saw that it had been bombed twenty-seven times before; it was just a pile of rubble. We were prohibited from striking SAMs as they were off-loaded from Soviet ships in Haiphong harbor, transported north, and then fired at us. We were prohibited from hitting airfields with MiGs on them that they launched to attack us. Later, when I was on the *Oriskany*, we lost a pilot in Haiphong, and one of our guys rolled in and bombed the antiaircraft position that had shot down the pilot. They were going to ground him because he had struck a target inside the city of Haiphong. It was that kind of damn foolishness that frustrated many of us.

Did you think, at that time, that we could win the war?

I believed that we could win by bringing enough air power to bear not only in the North but also in the South. I also believed the propaganda that McNamara and the administration put out about our winning the war. But, I didn't have any real way of knowing about how the war was going in the South because of our cloistered existence and flying off an aircraft carrier. In those days, we didn't watch the evening news on television. Frankly, we had less information than the average American did.

Soon after you were on board the *Oriskany*, your plane was shot down over Hanoi. What rushed through you the moment that you realized you were hit?

I had no particular emotion because my training took over. My plane was hit; the wing was gone; and I knew I had to get out of the airplane as quickly as possible. So my reaction was almost automatic. It wasn't as if I felt a rush of emotions. My adrenaline was obviously already high because we were flying into a heavily defended area, but there was no panic. I was hit; the plane wouldn't fly; eject.

When did emotions kick in?

A certain amount of fear struck me when I was pulled up on a lakeshore, and they began beating and bayoneting me. I thought that maybe I wasn't going to survive, but I was so badly injured that the prospect of dying didn't have too powerful an impact. It puts you in a daze where you can take a lot more pain than you would otherwise.

What kept you going?

Faith in God; faith in my country; faith in my fellow prisoners. Even after the bombing stopped in October 1968, we all believed that the United States would bring us home.

Anger must have had an effect on your ability to resist.

It made me less fearful, as did my intense contempt for the guards, the turnkeys, and the interrogators. And you had to keep your sense of humor. If you can laugh at your captors, you can chop them down from their inordinate size.

Did you travel outside of your body to lessen the pain while being tortured?

I'm not sure that I was ever able to divorce my mind from my body completely, but I certainly was able, at least, to compartmentalize the pain so that it would not overwhelm me. You can build up a much higher threshold of pain over time so that you're able to reduce its impact.

Human contact—even a tap on the wall—and some sort of mental aerobics must have been critical to keeping your sanity.

Absolutely. Just a tap on the wall every few days, or some other kind of communication, was crucial to overcoming the debilitating effects of solitary confinement. Those prisoners who didn't communicate—either because they were prevented from doing so or because they were afraid to do so—mental problems got the best of them. One time, I was put into a cell called "Calcutta" for about four months and was completely isolated from the others. I couldn't communicate with anyone. I was able to get through that because I had already gone through a hardening experience. Had it happened to me at the beginning, it probably would have broken me.

And the brainwashing the North Vietnamese put you through about America losing the war?

I, like the others, believed that everything they told us, or played over the loud speakers, was propaganda.

Did they play Jane Fonda over the loudspeakers?

Yeah. She was an airheaded young actress and incredibly stupid, naïve, when she climbed into an antiaircraft gun emplacement and said she'd like to join with her Vietnamese brothers and sisters and shoot down an American pilot. That really offended me; that crossed the line. But as for the rest of the antiwar people, I didn't waste my time thinking about them.

As I told you at the beginning, I don't want to dig into what went on inside the prison. But there must have been an act of bravery you witnessed that stands out?

Yeah, there is. Mike Christian, a Navy pilot shot down like myself, had sewn an American flag with a needle he made from bamboo and scrap clothing. In the afternoons, Mike would take the flag out of hiding and hang it on the wall. All of us would recite the Pledge of Allegiance before we ate our soup. Well, the guards somehow found the flag, confiscated it, and beat Mike senseless. [McCain grits his teeth, pained by the memory.] They punctured his eardrums and broke several ribs. When the guards were done, we cleaned him up as best we could and put him back on his mat. As I was falling asleep, I glanced over to a corner where there were some dimly lit lightbulbs. Mike was bent over—needle and thread in hand, eyes nearly swollen shut—sewing together another flag so we could give our Pledge of Allegiance. In my book, that was real heroism.

During the five and a half years you were in prison, did you ever envision someday being in politics?

Never. My ambition was to get back in the Navy and resume my flying career.

Did you believe that we were involved in a senseless war?

No, I never thought that. My questioning of the war—its purpose, its utility—was not scrutinized until after I got out of prison and went to the Naval War College. I spent a good deal of time there studying the war, its origin, the Pentagon Papers, Bernard Fall's books, Halberstam's *The Best and the Brightest,* and all the stuff from the French occupation. It was only then that I began to evaluate the war.

Any conclusions?

You bet. We tried to win the conflict on the cheap, with no clear strategy for success. That, when we got into the conflict, there was a fundamental misconception of the nature of the enemy; there was an overreliance on our ability to go anywhere "bearing the burden," in Jack Kennedy's words. The combination of all those factors made good Americans turn against our efforts in Vietnam for legitimate reasons. The American people couldn't see a strategy for victory, and indeed there wasn't one. So, over time, they turned against the conflict. The defining moment was when Walter Cronkite—the most respected man in America at that time—announced on nationwide television after the Tet Offensive that he didn't believe we had any further reason to be in Vietnam. That was the seminal event in the whole antiwar sentiment in this country.

Had we had a definite policy with victory being the goal, do you think now the ending would have been different?

Sure, but you have to take into consideration the restraining factors on Lyndon Johnson and Kennedy before him—and even Nixon to a certain degree—although not so much him because of the change in relations between the U.S. and China and the U.S. and the Soviet Union. There was justified concern that China would enter the war as they did in Korea. That cautioned and constrained area activity that was engaged by the military. The answer should have been either go in and disregard the possibility of China intervening by ending the conflict as quickly as possible, or we shouldn't have gone at all if we believed that it would trigger a wider conflict. But, we should never have gone halfway.

Do you think now that China would have intervened?

It's still not clear to me what China's ambitions were at that time and how far they would have carried those ambitions, and whether the Russians would have been a restraining factor or not. You can draw a lot of scenarios, but I think that the domino theory was probably overhyped by our experience in Korea. However, I believe had we not fought in Korea, it would have had a profound effect on Asia, on Japan, and on every other country. So it's a tough call. But, to enter the Vietnam conflict in the belief that a few thousand men and some airpower were going to stop Ho Chi Minh was stupid. Lyndon Johnson gave a speech at Johns Hopkins University in Baltimore in 1965 that basically offered a bribe to the North Vietnamese. For a long period of time, he could not understand why Ho Chi Minh didn't accept it. It was a fundamental misunderstanding of what Ho Chi Minh's ambitions were.

It's always easier to look backward.

Yeah, except that there are certain fundamentals that you can't ignore. Obviously, those are that you don't go into a conflict in a half-hearted fashion without a clear strategy for victory.

What other lessons did we learn from Vietnam?

I think that McNamara's reducing our efforts to body counts, to pacification programs, and to other alternatives to waging a conflict in a vigorous fashion led the United States down a primrose path to disaster. Trading American bodies for Vietnamese bodies was no strategy, regardless of the ratios and glowing reports and optimistic scenarios fed to the American people. And then the Tet Offensive, even though it was a tactical disaster for the North Vietnamese, caused the public's confidence to crumble. I think the McNamara line and all the myriad of other things that he and his "whiz kids" came up with were no substitute for a winning strategy. We needed a strategy that encompassed fundamentals, such as you can't give your enemy sanctuary; you can't allow them to resupply their troops freely in the field without impediment; and hitting them hard at the source rather than at the end of the command and supply chain.

You weren't a McNamara fan?

I believed that he was arrogant, and I believed that he didn't pay attention to the military. He had fired Adm. [George W.] Anderson, who was the chief of naval operations and whom a lot of us respected and admired. We didn't like McNamara and his "whiz kids." Their reputations were already well known for their disregard for the advice and experience of the uniformed military.

Now that you're part of the Washington bureaucracy, what should the military do when it strongly disagrees with the politicians on how to run a war?

The military have two choices—obey orders or resign. They have no other independent course. If the Joint Chiefs in 1965, who all later said that they knew full well that McNamara's strategy was doomed to failure, had stood up and resigned en masse, I think that would have changed the American policy in Vietnam. Instead, most of them went along with McNamara in believing they could change policy from within. My judgment is that they should have quit. There have been other times in history when other military men had done it.

It's a hard call.

Yeah, I know it's a hard call, but they don't give away four stars because the job is easy. If the Joint Chiefs believed that our Vietnam strategy was doomed to fail, needlessly cost American lives, and divide our country in a way we have not been since the civil war, I would argue there was a higher obligation.

Apparently the military didn't apply lessons learned from Vietnam when the Oval Office persisted in micromanaging the crisis in Kosovo.

I believed that preparations for ground operations were absolutely necessary. When I asked Gen. Hugh Shelton, the chairman of the Joint Chiefs of Staff, at a Senate hearing why the ground-troop card wasn't played, he said that they couldn't get our allies to support this. That is not General Shelton's call. His job description is to provide the best military advice and counsel to the president. But General Shelton went over to the political arena and thereby acquiesced to what I believed was a terribly flawed military strategy— ruling out the option of ground troops. I severely criticized General Shelton for not providing the best military advice to the president.

According to Kissinger, Congress lost the Vietnam War by cutting off the funds. What is your view about Congress's responsibility when it comes to cutting off the money?

In my view, Congress has only two choices. Like the military, it cannot conduct foreign policy. Congress can either support the commander-in-chief, or it can stop the money. Congress always has been very reluctant to "cut off the money" when our men and women are committed. It's a responsibility, a burden, they wouldn't want to shoulder. It's obviously a very difficult choice, and, in Vietnam, it came very late and really not until our troops were out of the country. However, I think that Congress cut off the funding mainly for political rather than patriotic reasons.

Do you believe that the president, the secretary of defense, and key presidential advisers should have military experience?

It's interesting that this is the first administration in history where none of the top people have had any military experience to include the president, secretary of defense, secretary of state, national security adviser. But I don't think the president has to. Abraham Lincoln served two months in a militia. Franklin Delano Roosevelt didn't.

Ronald Reagan's military service was on a movie set. But I think you should surround yourself with people that had military experience. As for the secretary of defense, no, I don't even think it's an absolute requirement. The thing that bothers me is that there are fewer and fewer members of Congress that have had any military experience. They don't understand sufficiently the rigors of military life, especially those of the enlisted person.

Back to the first question of "Why me?" and why you survived the *Forrestal*, prison, and the other close calls. Is there some universal order that spared you for a reason?

I don't know. I was reminded some time ago by the death of John Kennedy that you must seize the moment and be prepared for the reality that today might be your last day. So that when that time comes—and it always does—you can look back and say that you did the very best that you could at maximizing your opportunities. The reason for my impatience is often caused by frustration in dealing with the legislative process, opponents, and other obstacles that keep me from achieving my goals.

How long did it take you to dump the baggage from prison when you got out?

It took me about a half hour. I never had a flashback, never had a nightmare. The shadow of Vietnam does fall over some of my thinking at times, but it's not an overriding factor. My decisions are based on my experiences, readings, and advice from people whom I respect. I try to look at challenges in their entirety, rather than bouncing them off my Vietnam experience. The gravest mistake we often make is fighting the last war. Contrary to popular belief, my experience in Vietnam was, on many occasions, an uplifting and wonderful experience because of the company I kept and the example set by others of honorable behavior and courage and compassion and love. This has caused me to seek the approval of those I served with along with my father and grandfather as my lasting ambition.

McCain stands and walks to the door to rush off to his next meeting. He exits, then pops his head back into the office. "Thanks," he says and disappears into the cold, vacant corridor.

H. R. McMASTER

I wondered how and why Vietnam had become an American war—
a war in which men fought and died without a clear idea of how their
actions and sacrifices were contributing to an end of the conflict.

—H. R. McMASTER, *Dereliction of Duty*

My initial list didn't include any participants who were not directly involved in the Vietnam War. I made one exception in Lt. Col. H. R. McMaster, however, after some of the subjects in my book referred to *Dereliction of Duty* as a "must-read" to understand the lying and chicanery in Washington that made Vietnam an American war.

Joseph L. Galloway, senior writer at *U.S. News & World Report* and coauthor of *We Were Soldiers Once . . . and Young*, best sums up the significance of McMaster's work: "Here's everything you didn't read in Robert S. McNamara's book. Vietnam did not simply happen; it was not an accidental Cold War collision that killed 58,000 Americans and a million Vietnamese. Men of power and responsibility caused the disastrous war and left their fingerprints all over it—and here are their names and what they did and said and decided in secret. McMaster has mined newly declassified records and, in these pages, sheds fresh light and understanding on how the best and the brightest, shielded by a bodyguard of lies and the words 'Top Secret,' maneuvered and manipulated our country down the road to war and bitter defeat."

I found Lt. Colonel McMaster commanding the 1st Squadron, 4th Cavalry in Schweinfurt, Germany. He said that he would be honored to be included in such a notable group of subjects, but, because of his current assignment, we agreed to conduct the interview via e-mail. One of McMaster's air troops was being deployed to Kosovo, so he would be spending considerable time in the Balkans. Previously, he had commanded Eagle Troop of the 2d Armored Cavalry Regiment in combat against Iraq's Republican Guard in the Gulf War.

A career Army officer and a 1984 graduate of the U.S. Military Academy at West Point, McMaster started writing *Dereliction of Duty* as part of his master's thesis in history at the University of North Carolina at Chapel Hill. He completed the prerequisites for his Ph.D. concurrently with his M.A. and finished penning his dissertation and his book while teaching history of the Korean and Vietnam wars as an assistant professor in history at West Point.

The primary source of information for his research was recently declassified secret documents that showed the widespread responsibility among the Joint Chiefs of Staff for the eventual disaster in Vietnam. This led to his burrowing into memoirs, taped meetings and telephone conversations, and oral histories and memoirs of military and civilian officials, including the president and his chief advisers, who were involved in the decision-making process of the war.

McMaster writes in his book's preface: "It would be impossible for an Army lieutenant, obtaining his commission in 1984, not to be concerned with the experience of the Vietnam War. I thought to better prepare myself to lead soldiers in combat it was important to learn from the experiences of others, and the most recent U.S. war seemed as good a starting place as any. I read personal accounts written by junior officers, but found to my surprise that the Army I entered barely spoke of Vietnam. The emotions connected with sacrifices made in a lost war ran too deep to permit the veterans of that conflict to dwell on their experiences. . . . I wondered how and why Vietnam had become an American war—a war in which men fought and died without a clear idea of how their actions and sacrifices were contributing to an end of the conflict."

McMaster tells me that he did not take a sabbatical from his teaching assignment at West Point to complete the massive research that went into his book; he wrote at night and on the weekends. "My wife Katie thought I had lost my mind, but I couldn't have done it without her support." He knew that he was onto a very important story and felt compelled to tell it. "It was either write the book or be a bore at cocktail parties for the rest of my life."

Did you start out with the premise that there was dereliction of duty on the part of certain people in the military and politics and that the book's contents would validate your premise? Or did dereliction become obvious the deeper you plowed?

I began my research to clarify the role of the Joint Chiefs of Staff in the decisions that led to an American war in Vietnam. I believed that fully half of the story of how and why Vietnam became an American war was missing. It soon became clear to me, however, that I would have to place the role of senior military advisers in context of all the President's advisers and influences on the decision-making process. I gained access to previously classified materials, including handwritten notes of the most confidential meetings and tapes of telephone conversations between Lyndon B. Johnson (LBJ) and his inner circle. What I found was astonishing and led to the conclusion that much of the conventional wisdom on Vietnam was inaccurate. My subject area broadened, and it became clear to me that the period November 1963 to July 1965 was the most critical in understanding the gradual escalation in Vietnam from an advisory and support effort to a massive air campaign, to the commitment of large numbers of soldiers and Marines. I found that the American war in Vietnam was not the result of a tidal wave of Cold War ideology. Far from inevitable, the war was only made possible by lies aimed at the American people, the Congress, and even members of Lyndon Johnson's administration. Lyndon Johnson based his decisions primarily on his domestic political agenda—getting elected in 1964 and passing the Great Society legislative package in 1965—rather than on the political and military situation in Vietnam or America's global and regional interests. Over time, the administration was unable to distinguish between the truth and its own deceptions. Rather than impersonal forces, the disaster in Vietnam was a human failure. The causes of that failure were many and reinforcing: arrogance, weakness, lying in the pursuit of self-interest, and an abdication of responsibility to the American people. I did not come to that conclusion based on any preconceived ideas. I reached that conclusion based on an examination of the full body of evidence.

How did you verify your conclusions? Did you have a systematic procedure? Were many/some of your conclusions subjective on your part?

I believe that the conclusions in *Dereliction of Duty* are grounded firmly in the evidence. I used a multiarchival research technique and conducted interviews to place the documentary record in context of personalities and advisory relationships. I examined, made copies, and took notes on documents in the Lyndon B. Johnson Library, the Naval Historical Center, the Marine Corps Historical Center, the National Archives, the U.S. Army Military History Institute, the National Defense University, the Library of Congress, the Center of Military History, and the Joint Staff Historical Office. I arranged the evidence in a general chronology and then grouped the documents by subject within that chronology. I laid out the documents on a large conference table and pieced the story together, outlining the chapters and writing the chapter right from the documentary evidence. In short, I did not know what I was going to write until I examined the entire record. This approach permitted me to connect Joint Chiefs of Staff meetings, National Security Council meetings, telephone conversations, cables and public pronouncements on the same specific topic.

What were LBJ's objectives in Vietnam?

One of the most striking aspects of how and why America went to war in Vietnam is the absence of clearly defined political goals or objectives. One of the chapters in *Dereliction of Duty* is entitled "War Without Direction." The initial objective was to guarantee the freedom and independence of South Vietnam. Over time and under the leadership of Lyndon Johnson, the objective became one of stalemate based on the administration's unwillingness to commit the level of force necessary to impose a solution consistent with U.S. interests. Johnson sought instead to commit only the level of force that would be politically acceptable and was determined to avoid a debate in Congress that might jeopardize his domestic goals—getting elected in 1964 and passing Great Society legislation in 1965. Members of Johnson's administration argued that ambiguity in connection with the objective in Vietnam was an advantage because that ambiguity gave them "flexibility" in the domestic political arena. Not only was Johnson's approach undemocratic, it removed an important corrective to what was an unwise policy.

You noted that Robert McNamara lied. What specifically did he lie about?

LBJ's and McNamara's approach to the war was fundamentally dishonest. They created the illusion of success to keep Vietnam from becoming a prominent issue in Congress. In March 1964, McNamara, with the assistance of Gen. Maxwell Taylor [chairman of JCS], lied about the opinion of the Joint Chiefs of Staff in connection with the viability of gradually escalating the American military effort in Vietnam. Throughout 1964 and 1965, McNamara assisted the president in obscuring the potential long-term costs and consequences of the war. He lied to the Joint Chiefs of Staff about the nature of the president's decisions to keep them on the team and to prevent them from raising objections to LBJ's policy, particularly to

Congress. In August 1964, McNamara lied about American actions that led to the first Gulf of Tonkin incident and evaded questions concerning the reliability of reports concerning the second attack. In February and March of 1965, McNamara lied about the mission given to the first American ground combat units arriving in South Vietnam. In June and July of 1965, McNamara lied to the Congress about the scope of General Westmoreland's troop request and the cost of providing even the initial number of troops that General Westmoreland had requested. What was more important than the fact that he lied, however, is the effect that his lies had on the course of events. His dishonesty was a severe impediment to the administration's ability to deal effectively with the complex problem of Vietnam. Over time, it became difficult for the administration to distinguish between reality and its dishonest portrayal of the situation in Vietnam. McNamara's lies also permitted the administration to circumvent the Constitution and deny the Congress the ability to influence decisions that involved war. Not only was his approach undemocratic, it removed an important corrective to what was an unwise policy.

Did you uncover a pattern for lying that dates back to his tenure at Ford Motor Company?

There is an excellent, elegantly written book that sheds light on McNamara's character and his propensity for lying. I recommend *The Living and the Dead* by Paul Hendrickson.

Did McNamara lie to appease the president?

McNamara appears to have acted as a very talented and persuasive sycophant who gave the president the advice that he wanted and that supported Lyndon Johnson's desire to forestall a debate on Vietnam. Ironically, LBJ did not want to go to war in Vietnam, but every decision that he made during his attempt to build a consensus behind a fundamentally flawed policy moved the nation in that direction. McNamara was dishonest about matters other than Vietnam to support what the president wanted to achieve. For example, soon after LBJ assumed the presidency, McNamara lied to congressmen about savings in the Department of Defense budget to assist the president in gaining approval for expensive domestic legislation.

How much control did McNamara have over the JCS?

McNamara took a divide-and-conquer approach to the Joint Chiefs of Staff. McNamara actually described those tactics to LBJ in a phone conversation. The JCS tendency to offer single-service solutions to the complex problem of Vietnam and the chiefs' desire to protect the interests of their services made them vulnerable to such an approach. Rather than advice, what LBJ and McNamara wanted from the JCS was silent support for decisions already made and the legitimacy lent to the administration's policies by the chiefs' uniforms.

How did LBJ and McNamara control the JCS?

McNamara and Johnson kept the JCS "on the team" by obscuring the nature of decisions already made and by promising more resolute military action and a larger commitment of military force in the long term in exchange for the chiefs' support in the short term. Revealing in this connection are recently declassified notes of meetings among the JCS, LBJ, and McNamara that took place between April and June of 1965. In these meetings, LBJ referred to himself as "the coach" and to the JCS as "his team."

Why didn't members of the JCS resign en masse? Was there any evidence that they considered resigning?

Army Chief of Staff Harold K. Johnson considered resignation after LBJ decided against mobilization for Vietnam, but he decided instead to stay on and "try and fight and get the best posture we can." Other stories about General Johnson driving to the White House with his stars in hand and turning around at the last minute and the JCS contemplating resignation en masse are apocryphal. Resignation, however, is not the primary issue, and the focus on it has prevented debate over the JCS role in this critical period from revealing the most important conclusions. The most important point is that the JCS failed to give the president and his civilian advisers their best advice. The nature of civil-military relations depended in large measure on individual character. Despite the fact that all members of the JCS believed that the president's policy and McNamara's strategy of "graduated pressure" were fundamentally flawed, they failed to challenge the assumptions on which the policy and strategy were based. They also failed to develop a comprehensive estimate of the situation or a strategic alternative to the administration's approach. They chose instead to work within what they knew to be a fundamentally flawed policy and strategy in an effort to intensify the war by degrees. The JCS failed, as well, to give candid assessments to Congress. That lack of candor assisted the president in forestalling debate. In short, the JCS compromised principle for expediency and gave tacit approval to a strategy that led to a large but inadequate commitment of troops, for an extended period of time, with little hope for success. McNamara and LBJ were far from disappointed with the Joint Chiefs' failings. LBJ had little use for military advice that recommended actions inconsistent with his domestic priorities. McNamara's arrogance and disregard for military experience and for history led him to draw principally on his civilian staff in the Department of Defense. Perhaps one of the most significant observations from this period is that, ultimately, an administration can get the military advice it wants by virtue of whom it appoints and how it crafts advisory relationships.

Twenty-five years after leaving government, McNamara wrote in his book that he was against expanding the war in 1963 and wanted the removal of U.S. forces from Vietnam? Did you uncover any evidence to support this?

The evidence does not support McNamara's claim. The often-cited withdrawal of one thousand U.S. advisers from Vietnam just prior to the U.S.-supported coup in Saigon in November 1963 was designed to place pressure on the Diem regime in connection with the repression of Buddhist opposition. McNamara advocated all of the incremental actions that led to an American war in Vietnam—covert raids against the North and into Laos beginning in early 1964, the Gulf of Tonkin strikes in August 1964, initiation of the Rolling Thunder air campaign in February 1965, the introduction of the first ground combat units in March 1965, and the introduction of large numbers of U.S. troops in July 1965.

Did the United States consider using tactical nuclear weapons in North Vietnam?

Consideration of the use of nuclear weapons appears to have been a holdover from the Eisenhower administration's strategy of "massive retaliation." Use of nuclear weapons in Vietnam was discussed in 1954 during the First Indochina War in connection with the siege of Dien Bien Phu. The JCS also discussed nuclear options with the Kennedy administration during the Laotian Crisis of 1961. The evidence is clear, however, that Eisenhower and, later, Kennedy, never gave those options serious consideration. As LBJ considered military options, he was very much concerned with fears of an escalation of the war to include China and the Soviet Union. Nuclear weapons were not only irrelevant to the problem of Vietnam, the

Johnson administration and McNamara, in particular, viewed their use as unconscionable and dangerous. By the early 1960s, the JCS seemed also to have arrived at that inescapable conclusion.

McNamara admits in his book, *In Retrospect*, "the foundations of our decision making were gravely flawed," meaning he badly misread China and its intent to intervene if the United States took the war north. Did LBJ and McNamara intentionally exaggerate the danger for political reasons?

The Johnson administration often discussed Vietnam in the context of the Korean War, and that analogy highlighted the danger of escalation. Although the fear of escalation was genuine and present, LBJ did exaggerate that danger for political reasons. He used it to parry JCS calls for more resolute action in Vietnam. LBJ, for example, stated that he had decided against mobilization to keep the "political noise level" low so as not to antagonize China. Commandant of the Marine Corps Gen. Wallace M. Greene, Jr., however, recognized at the time that the decision was designed to "keep the political noise level down in the United States" and to prevent congressional and public debate over Vietnam policy.

McNamara noted in his book that there were no American experts on Southeast Asia. Was this another lie?

McNamara's statement is disingenuous. LBJ was anxious to contrive a consensus on Vietnam, a consensus based in large measure on lies to the American public, Congress, and members of LBJ's own administration. Anyone who challenged the administration's approach was excluded from meaningful discussions. This was the case with John McCone, CIA director, and Vice President Hubert Humphrey. Dissenter George Ball had been assigned the role of "devil's advocate" during Vietnam deliberations, and his arguments were not seriously considered.

Was there evidence of an industrial-military complex perpetuating the war?

There is no evidence to indicate that the "military-industrial complex" played any role in LBJ's decisions.

Did JFK indeed intend to pull back U.S. effort completely after the 1964 election? He had already withdrawn one thousand men. Was there any reliable evidence as to what JFK would have done had he lived?

Although there is anecdotal evidence that JFK was willing to withdraw from Vietnam after the November 1964 election, the actions of the administration belie that conclusion. As mentioned previously, the decision to withdraw one thousand advisers was meant to pressure the Diem regime in Saigon to end the brutal repression of Buddhist protests. The withdrawal was accomplished on paper without an actual reduction. The Kennedy administration's role in fomenting the overthrow of the South Vietnamese government saddled the U.S. government with responsibility for its successor. The coup and Diem's and his brother's subsequent assassinations had the effect of deepening America's involvement in what thereafter became a new war. Comparisons between administrations are of limited utility as the situation in Vietnam changed over time and each president confronted fundamentally different conditions.

Did you find evidence that LBJ wanted to expand the war in early 1965 or earlier?

Although LBJ had made a high-profile visit to Vietnam as vice president, he was on the fringes of Vietnam decision-making. He did, however, oppose the overthrow of the Diem regime and believed that the Kennedy administration had "killed" America's longtime ally. Those who advocated Diem's overthrow, such as Roger Hilsman [assistant secretary of state for Far Eastern affairs], Amb. Henry Cabot Lodge, and Secretary of State Dean Rusk, lost influence over Vietnam policy after Kennedy's death. LBJ's main concern upon assuming office, however, was to portray continuity. He recognized that he had achieved his lifelong dream not through the genuine support of the American people but through his predecessor's death. LBJ did not want to go to war in Vietnam, and he did not plan to do so. LBJ thought that he would be able to control U.S. involvement in Vietnam. That belief, based on the strategy of graduated pressure and Robert McNamara's confident assurances, proved in dramatic fashion to be false.

You state in your book that there was evidence that the war was lost before U.S. troops deployed to Vietnam in 1965.

The way in which the United States went to war in the period between November 1963 and July 1965 had a profound influence on the conduct of the war and its outcome. There was no effort to reconcile the administration's determination to limit the American military effort in Vietnam with the military assessment that the United States could not possibly win under those limitations. There was no effort to define U.S. goals or what "winning" meant. The JCS and the administration became fixated on the means, rather than on the ends, and on the manner in which the war was conducted instead of on a military strategy that could connect military actions to achievable policy goals. Military and civilian officials automatically equated military activity—bombing North Vietnam and killing the enemy in South Vietnam—with progress. They did not give sufficient thought to the nature of the war and the political and military sources of the enemy's strength. The fundamental dishonesty of LBJ's approach to Vietnam also had long-term consequences. As American casualties in Vietnam mounted and the futility of the strategy became apparent, the American public lost faith in the effort. As the American public discovered that it had been consistently misled about the nature and scope of American involvement in the war; circumstances surrounding critical events, such as the Gulf of Tonkin incident in 1964; and the potential long-term costs and consequences of the war, opposition to the war effort became more widespread. By 1968, the American government was besieged by opposition to the war.

Did you uncover any directives or evidence noting a tolerable number of American deaths that Washington would accept?

Over time, the aim of U.S. military forces in Vietnam shifted from ensuring the freedom and independence of South Vietnam to preserving U.S. international credibility. John McNaughton, a principal civilian planner in the Department of Defense, for example stated that the U.S. objective ought to be primarily to "avoid a humiliating defeat." According to McNaughton, the U.S. had to "get bloodied" to demonstrate that it would use military force to support its foreign policy. To McNaughton and others, such as William Bundy [assistant secretary of defense], committing the U.S. military to war in Vietnam and losing was preferable to withdrawing from what they believed was an impossible situation. At one point, McNaughton stated the number of casualties that he felt would be acceptable to the American public. Although this thinking underpinned the administration's approach to the war, no evidence reveals that LBJ or McNamara discussed the number of "acceptable" casualties explicitly. General Westmoreland and the JCS were not privy to many planning memos because the administration was anxious to prevent a debate over goals and objectives and recognized that the JCS would object to anything short of a commitment to victory over Vietnamese communist forces and the preservation of an independent South Vietnam.

You mention arrogance in describing McNamara and his "whiz kids." Was arrogance the cause of the U.S. failure, assuming that we can label it with one word? And how could we describe the driving force in LBJ?

The answer is, in some ways, related to your previous question. McNamara and many of his principal civilian advisers viewed Vietnam as another business management problem that, they assumed, would ultimately succumb to their reasoned judgment and rational calculations. They thought that they could predict with precision the amount of force applied in Vietnam that would achieve results. Their approach ignored the uncertainties of war and the unpredictable psychology of an activity that involves killing, death, and destruction. To the North Vietnamese, for example, the bombing of targets in the North was not simply a means of communicating resolve. Once the United States committed what the enemy regarded as acts of war, it unleashed strong emotions and created a dynamic that defied systems analysis quantification. The future course of events in Vietnam depended not only on what McNamara and his analysts in the Pentagon decided but on enemy responses and initiatives that proved difficult to predict. McNamara and his "whiz kids," however, believed that they could control the application of military force with great precision from halfway around the world. They forged ahead oblivious of the human and psychological complexities of war. Arrogance was certainly a factor. As Gen. Andrew Goodpaster [former deputy to Gen. Maxwell Taylor] observed in an interview, "they didn't know what they didn't know." The American war in Vietnam stemmed from a complex web of decisions and chain of events. The characters of the men involved and the relationships among them were the critical determinants of how and why those decisions were made. Johnson and his principal military and civilian advisers share the responsibility for those decisions. Lyndon Johnson, however, got the advice he wanted. He disregarded the advice he did not want to hear in favor of a policy based primarily on the pursuit of his own political fortunes and his beloved domestic programs. His behavior and the behavior of the men around him rendered the administration incapable of dealing effectively with the complexity of Vietnam and represented an abdication of responsibility to the American people.

THOMAS POLGAR

*The last day in Saigon and the days that followed were
the saddest, most traumatic days of my life.*

THOMAS POLGAR

The front page of *The Washington Post* dated Monday, May 5,
1975, reads: "The Republic of Vietnam, for which Americans
fought and which they supported so long, no longer exists. The last
few weeks of that republic are the stuff of high drama. . . . It involves
a tough Central Intelligence Agency station chief who foresaw the
impending disaster and argued fruitlessly for an early U.S. pullout,
while struggling behind the scenes for a political settlement that
would buy time. . . ."

Polgar was born in southern Hungary to Jewish peasants and fled
to the United States in the 1930s to escape the anti-Semitic Nazi
tyranny in Europe. With America's entrance into World War II, he
was drafted into the U.S. Army and, because of his fluency in several
languages, trained to be a counterintelligence agent in the Office
of Strategic Services [OSS], the predecessor to the CIA. Later, he
parachuted behind enemy lines with a false Nazi Party ID card, and
operated as a spy. After the war, he worked closely with Gen. Lucian
Truscott, chief of the CIA's station in West Germany. In the late
1960s, he was the CIA's station chief in Buenos Aires, Argentina.
There, he disarmed a group of dissident American hijackers by offer-
ing them Coke spiked with drugs. As a result of Polgar's ingenuity,
he was given the highly coveted station chief's job in Saigon, even
though he had never been to Asia before.

Polgar first arrived in southeast Asia in 1971 for an area orientation
in Laos and Vietnam before assuming his new job in January 1972,
and he was among the last Americans to be lifted by helicopter off
the embassy rooftop on the morning of April 30, 1975, as Saigon
fell to the NVA. Much to his consternation on his return to Washington, top officials at State and at CIA Headquarters in Langley, Virginia, threatened those who were in Saigon during the final days
from talking, as though the debacle never existed. Those who spoke

out about America's betrayal of its South Vietnamese allies left behind were condemned as anti-American.

A short, stocky man, nearly bald, and looking remarkably fit at seventy-eight years, Polgar speaks with a distinct accent derived from his Hungarian birthplace and his childhood tutoring in German. I'm reminded of David Butler's description of Polgar in his book, *The Fall of Saigon*: "The face Polgar presented the world—a cross between Edward G. Robinson and Henry Kissinger—masked a sharp analytical mind that carried a young man from Hungary through a steady rise in American military and civilian intelligence."

Polgar and I sit in the study of his Florida home filled with mementos from his world travels and intelligence career. A birdcage is covered so the parakeets don't compete with our conversation.

At the top of my list are questions about the inglorious final days twenty-five years ago and what Washington was doing at that time. Slowly and very precisely, he unfolds the story about the disconnection between his intelligence operation in Vietnam and the bureaucrats micromanaging the war from Washington. He says that the distrust in the Agency went back to the Kennedy and Johnson administrations. Polgar knew about NVA plans months in advance of the final offensive that toppled Saigon, but Washington refused to accept human resource reporting without corroborating evidence from radio or electronic intercepts. His jaws tighten; his words are hard. "Because of a stupid bureaucratic decision, Washington had willfully blinded itself to the truth. It was ridiculous."

When you first set foot in Vietnam in January 1972, what was your assessment of the situation?

I first arrived in Vietnam in October 1971 on an orientation trip. I returned as chief of station on January 7, 1972. I was of the opinion then that the survival of South Vietnam depended on American support and when that support disappeared, so would democracy. I based that not only on the military situation but also on the fact that the South never had a national consciousness as existed in the North. The only force that held the South together was the American support. President Nguyen Van Diem more or less helped until he was assassinated in 1963. The sole element of political continuity disappeared with his removal. Then, there was a series of generals in charge of the country, but none could claim popular support. All were totally dependent on American aid. After I took over as chief of station in January 1972, the North Vietnamese launched an Easter

Offensive. They were militarily defeated, but it was a close call. I think that if it hadn't been for the intervention by the U.S. Air Force and good tactical leadership by Gen. Creighton Abrams, we could have lost South Vietnam in April or May 1972.

What led to the Paris Peace Accords?

The fact that the South Vietnamese held together and Nixon's desire to have a cease-fire prior to the elections in November 1972. At the time the accords were signed in 1973, I reported a situation assessment that became very controversial, the distribution of which the CIA Headquarters in Washington tried to suppress. I basically said that the cease-fire would last only until Hanoi believed that they could do something without U.S. retaliation. Then, the Arab-Israeli war of 1973 broke out. The price of oil suddenly skyrocketed. This killed U.S. budgetary assumptions to support Vietnam. The Pentagon diverted to Israel much of its military resources to include rifles, machine guns, ammunition, bombs, and helicopters. U.S. support promised to South Vietnam simply did not arrive. Congress passed the bombing ban and reduced military and economic support, thus abandoning South Vietnam with no weapons and ammunition to fight with. It was [an] unconscionable double cross by Washington.

And then Watergate unfolded.

The North Vietnamese were deeply afraid of President Nixon. They considered him incalculable, half crazy—he would do anything. As long as Nixon was in office, the North Vietnamese were not going to provoke him. They remembered the Christmas B-52 bombing of Hanoi. When Nixon left office in August 1974, the North Vietnamese tested President Gerald Ford by attacking Phuoc Long in January 1975. It was the first province capital to fall after the cease-fire. Despite the United States commitment that Nixon and Kissinger promised to Thieu to support the South against Hanoi's aggression, there was absolutely no response to North Vietnam's taking of Phuoc Long. Following its victory at Phuoc Long, the North Vietnamese politburo concluded that it no longer had to worry about American retaliation. So it went for broke.

Did you communicate the criticality of Phuoc Long to Washington?

Absolutely, but at that time the Democratic-controlled Congress was so hostile to Nixon that they took it out on Vietnam. In Hungarian, we have a saying that "You want to beat the donkey but you are only beating the saddle." Congress couldn't stop Nixon, but they could reduce appropriations for Vietnam. The reductions in appropriations taken against the background of increased oil prices completely upset all budgetary calculations for aid to Vietnam. Without money, they couldn't do anything.

Did you have advance intelligence about the NVA attack on Phuoc Long?

We knew that the NVA was going to strike in the central highlands, but we didn't know where. We didn't pay much attention to Phuoc Long because it was a very insignificant place. It was in the border highlands of Vietnam inhabited mostly by Montagnards. It, by itself, was insignificant, but Washington's failure to react was pivotal. Immediately after Phuoc Long, we received solid intelligence that Hanoi viewed our silence as a green light. If I may deviate for a moment, Henry Kissinger, whom I had known since 1968 and with whom I worked closely in 1972, said jokingly that "Washington can handle only one crisis at a time." By January 1975, or earlier, we had the Mid-East crisis, the Nixon-impeachment crisis, and the congressional revolt against the administration's Vietnam policy. I was at the meeting in San Clemente [California], in March 1973, when Nixon and Kissinger promised Thieu that if the Paris agreement was violated by North Vietnam, there would be instant and brutal retaliation by the Seventh Air Force stationed in Thailand. There was a four-star general, John Vogt, sitting in Thailand whose sole purpose was to back up that promise. He was never used.

Was it inevitable, as some pundits suggest, that the war was hopeless in the minds of Washington by 1972 when you took command of the CIA station in Saigon?

No. When I first arrived, I felt certain that we could maintain ourselves in South Vietnam the way we had in South Korea and Germany. Prior to departing for Vietnam, I had a meeting with Mel Laird, who was then secretary of defense. He asked me how going to Vietnam would affect me personally. I told him that I was concerned because I had a son who was in his first year in college, a daughter who was a high school junior, and a younger daughter still in grade school. The assignment would be a tremendous dislocation for my family. He assured me, that in three or four years, there would be American schools in Vietnam. So he, too, was thinking in terms of how things went in Germany or South Korea. There was nothing in his conversation that suggested we were considering total withdrawal. There was no inkling that America's fourteen-year role in Vietnam was going to draw to an end.

When did you first believe Vietnam was a lost cause?

I thought that we could have survived Phuoc Long; it had only symbolic value. But the collapse of Ban Me Thuot in March 1975 was fatal because the South Vietnamese lost most of two infantry divisions out of a total of eleven countrywide. This was followed, four or five days later, by the evacuation of the Central Highlands, with a total lack of coordination between planning and operations. I thought at that time that everything was lost. This I reported to Washington, leaving no doubt as to the outcome certain to come.

Did we ever have a chance to win the war?

Absolutely, but only in the sense of maintaining an American-supported, non-communist South Vietnam. In 1972, despite the North Vietnamese offensive, I was very optimistic. All my family came to stay with me in Saigon, including my son who was a student at MIT. Like most college students, he was opposed to the war. During the 1972 fighting, the South Vietnamese forces, with strong American air support, were able to retake the northernmost province of South Vietnam. On the same day that happened, there was a party at the Japanese Embassy to celebrate the Emperor's birthday. I asked the Polish ambassador, who regularly traveled to Hanoi, what he thought of the South Vietnamese victory. He said it didn't make any difference; South Vietnam will lose the war in Washington. And that's exactly what happened. But, yes, sustained bombing by B-52s would have done the job. And I think a simple retaliation after Phuoc Long would have discouraged Hanoi.

Why didn't Washington retaliate after Phuoc Long?

I don't think that President Ford had either the political strength or the personal will to reinsert Americans into a combat role in Vietnam—even by air. Don't forget that there was a tremendous anti-Vietnam War sentiment in the country and in Congress.

Had we bombed the dikes in North Vietnam, would Hanoi have capitulated?

I think had we threatened to bomb the dikes, Hanoi would have capitulated, but we weren't allowed to bomb the dikes. It was against

U.S. policy. Washington was afraid of Soviet and Chinese intervention. Remember what the Chinese did to us at the Yalu River.

From your vantage point as CIA station chief, did you believe then that the Soviets or Chinese would intervene?
Absolutely not, and I'll tell you why. I was in Berlin during the Berlin blockade. When the U.S. started the Berlin airlift, there were fainthearted people in Washington who believed the Soviets would shoot down our aircraft. Then we'd have to answer them—and then we'd have WW III. I was chief of counterintelligence under a very smart chief in Berlin, Dana B. Durand, who was later chief of the CIA's Soviet division. He developed the theory that the Soviets cannot be provoked or appeased. They have a fixed policy, and they will follow that policy regardless of what we do. The Soviets weren't about to shoot down our planes over Berlin. Likewise, I didn't think the Soviets would send troops to North Vietnam, which, by the way, wasn't such an easy task to accomplish logistically. It wouldn't take many of our bombers to cut the trans-Siberian rail line. I didn't think the Chinese would intervene either. The Chinese were perfectly willing to arm the Vietnamese to cause the Americans more trouble, but the Chinese and Vietnamese were hereditary enemies. The North Vietnamese didn't want Chinese on their soil. Be that as it may, that type of thinking dominated Washington.

Leading up to the final days of Saigon, what was the context of the messages Washington was sending you?
There really were no substantive messages because the CIA wasn't in the business of policymaking. My superiors could only tell me about what was happening in Washington, which had no relevance to the situation on the ground.

Certainly, as chief intelligence officer in Saigon, you must have advised Washington of the deteriorating conditions?
I did on numerous occasions, but Washington refused to give South Vietnam what it needed most—a battlefield pause to regroup and rebuild its forces. I had absolutely no hope at that point for South Vietnam to survive. In late March, when Ambassador [Graham] Martin returned to Vietnam from dental surgery in the States, conditions were already desperate. Yet the embassy operated on a normal schedule of 8 to 12 and from 2 to 6. There was a two-hour pause for lunch while we were in the middle of a war and refugees

all around us. I suggested the abolition of the two-hour lunch break. The embassy wouldn't buy it. I wanted to keep the embassy open to 8 or 9 o'clock at night to help process the refugees. The embassy said they couldn't afford to pay the overtime. By then, the North Vietnamese had taken military regions 1 and 2 and were deeply into military region 3, while we were arguing at the embassy staff meetings about where the new Ramada Hotel should be built in Saigon. If it hadn't been so tragic, it would have been laughable.

[Polgar pulls out a cable, dated April 9, 1975, that he sent to CIA headquarters in Washington, and reads it to me:]
The Ambassador is spending the bulk of his time trying to generate support to increase military and economic assistance to South Vietnam, and to maintain orderly business attitudes in the face of what is clearly worsening situations. The government of South Vietnam has not been able to gird itself for effective action while the communists are increasing pressure. Both communication and human-source intelligence suggest that the North Vietnamese have made a determination to continue to expand military pressure for the isolation of Saigon, with the ultimate military objective being total victory. It is certain that we are heading here for a debacle of historic proportion unless the necessary changes are effected in time.

What was Washington's response to your warning?
Washington said that they were going to send a message to Ambassador Martin authorizing him to evacuate Americans and key Vietnamese as fast as possible. But we couldn't evacuate key Vietnamese because immigration laws prevented the sending of Vietnamese citizens unless they had valid exit visas and valid U.S. entry visas. It wasn't until the 27th or the 28th of April—almost three weeks later—that we received a message from the attorney general directing the embassy to send Vietnamese citizens to the United States on parole status. That meant that they had no legal rights and could be deported at any time.

There were allegations that you supported a coup to topple President Nguyen Van Thieu.
That's false. I never recommended a military coup. There was no basis for one. It would have just further confused things. I cabled Washington that opposing political forces were thinking about moving against Thieu and that his days as president were coming to an

end. It was strictly an objective observation. I didn't believe Thieu had the flexibility required to deal with a government that would include communists. He was enemy number one of the North Vietnamese. Therefore, if we were going into negotiations, somebody else ought to take his place—somebody personally more acceptable to the North Vietnamese and preferably not a military officer.

Would the North Vietnamese have agreed to a peaceful resolution and averted such an embarrassing end for the United States?

Not then; it was too late. They would have agreed prior to the fall of Phuoc Long if we had met most of their political demands. It would have been a disguised surrender and brought communist influence into the government of South Vietnam. But there are communist influences in governments about the world that don't cause harm—like in Italy. Inevitably, the communists brought into the South Vietnamese government would have continued with the capitalist-consumer society that existed in South Vietnam, but we were explicitly instructed not to let it happen. We didn't want any negotiations that would result in a coalition government.

Did your spies indicate that Hanoi was prepared to compromise?

Yes, very much so. Even in the summer of 1974, perhaps even a bit later, the secretary general of the North Vietnamese Communist Party said that people who believed that only a military solution was acceptable were mistaken. He hinted that they were ready to negotiate. But the basis on which they wanted to negotiate was never the basis on which Washington wanted to negotiate.

What did Washington want?

Washington wanted an unshakable, anticommunist South Vietnam as the bulwark against communist expansion in Southeast Asia. The domino theory was very much in play. Had the United States persuaded the South Vietnamese government to seek some kind of a political solution when its relative position was still strong, an accommodation with the North Vietnamese taking the Viet Cong people into the government could have been achieved. Granted, it would have been a de facto communist victory, but it certainly would have been much less radical than what followed. We could have evacuated people in an orderly manner. We wouldn't have had to have these rooftop lifts from Saigon. The point is that, until the very end, Washington directed the South Vietnamese government and Ambassador Martin to take an uncompromising, defiant stand. So there was a complete disconnect among what was happening in Congress, the change in President Ford's mind, and what we were told to do in Saigon.

When did you know Saigon would fall?

It was absolutely clear by April 25 that the NVA would overrun Saigon.

The embassy must have been in a state of panic?

To the contrary. I couldn't even persuade the embassy to stay open during the weekend of April 26 and 27. It was business as usual.

The embassy was closed during the weekend of the final days of Saigon. You're kidding?

I wish I was. Only the CIA station was operating.

As if nothing was going on?

As if nothing was going on.

You must have been climbing the walls?

I was. It was unbelievable. The embassy's swimming pool and cafeteria were open on Saturday, April 26. I think the commissary was still open on the 28th. You know the old saying, "Everybody wants to go to heaven, but nobody wants to die." The people just couldn't conceive that, after all these years, the United States was going to abandon Vietnam.

Why didn't we surrender?

I would have been happy to negotiate a surrender, but it was never an American policy. On April 28, our orders were to still hold out, which made absolutely no sense. There was a complete disconnect between policy and the situation as it evolved on the ground.

When did Washington finally tell you to get out of there?

On Sunday, April 27, NVA rockets hit the waterfront in Saigon. It shocked us because we hadn't experienced an attack in downtown Saigon since 1968. Washington finally told us to evacuate Saigon on Tuesday, April 29, after NVA artillery hit Tan Son Nhut airport.

I went to the embassy at 4:45 in the morning. I had a premonition that I wouldn't be returning to my home. I took a small carry-on bag to my office containing medications, camera, documents, and passport but no clothing. I was the first senior officer on the scene. From the rooftop of the embassy, using binoculars, I could see that Tan Son Nhut was in bad shape. I phoned the deputy ambassador and suggested that he and the ambassador come to the embassy immediately. The deputy ambassador said he was on his way, but the ambassador was very sick. Martin had pneumonia, throat cancer, and dental problems. I said sick or not, Martin had to come. At the embassy, Martin placed a call to Kissinger and Adm. Noel Gayler, commander in chief, Pacific. Martin could hear, but he couldn't talk because of his medical condition. He whispered to me, and I would relay it on the phone. The decision was to evacuate most personnel except for those needed for a bare-bones, lean embassy. We were not to close the embassy.

Could you see the enemy from the rooftop?

On the morning of April 29, we could see the fire and smoke at Tan Son Nhut resulting from the heavy artillery attacks. We heard the explosions. Even then, to those of us at the embassy, it was inconceivable that the U.S. would give up everything that we worked so hard to maintain for so many years. On the morning of the 29th, Ambassador Martin still claimed to believe that the North Vietnamese were moving up the artillery only to assert psychological pressure.

Intelligence indicated differently?

That's correct. The Americans at the airport, including Defense Attaché Army Maj. Gen. Homer Smith, his staff, and the Air America people [civilian airlines owned by the CIA], reported heavy damage to the runways, which meant an end to the fixed-wing evacuation that had been in progress through April. The ambassador decided to see for himself. We told him that this would be an unnecessary waste of time, but he insisted and was driven to the airport. He could reach no conclusion other than what previously had been communicated to him. The runways were unusable. Back at the embassy, the ambassador asked for the helicopters at 10:58 A.M. Saigon time, our last option. Adm. Gayler issued the "Execute" order three minutes later. This was not, however, the signal to close the embassy.

You don't have fond memories of Martin?

To the contrary, I had a marvelous relationship with Martin even during the final week in Saigon. Our relations deteriorated after we got back to Washington. The bearer of bad news is never popular, and Martin was dancing to a different tune. He had to implement policy as dictated by Washington, which, as late as April 24 or 25, was still for us to hang in there and make no concessions to the communists. Whereas, my job was to collect and report intelligence, the substance and trend of which ran contrary to his policy. I once asked Dr. Kissinger how he found CIA intelligence in general. He responded, "When it supports my policy, it is very useful."

What other options did you have besides evacuating the embassy?

We could have stayed in Saigon with a skeleton staff and hoped the North Vietnamese would give us diplomatic recognition. The situation wouldn't have been unprecedented. The same thing happened in Hanoi when the communists took over from the French, although it was only a consulate general. We still had maybe 200 to 250 Americans at the embassy, and plans were being formulated even then for the staffing of a stay-behind embassy. At around 12:30 P.M. on April 29, the ambassador received a call from Secretary of State Kissinger that President Ford decided to close the embassy as soon as the last American was evacuated, but he gave us no authority to evacuate Vietnamese as a group. The attorney general had authorized the evacuation of specifically named, so-called key indigenous personnel, but we never heard of plans to move fifty thousand or one hundred thousand or any other number. We then had a battle of wills. Secretary of Defense Jim Schlesinger wanted to move out all Americans as quickly as possible, taking Vietnamese only when it didn't interfere with the movement of the Americans. In the meantime, the ambassador slowed the departure of Americans because he recognized that as long as there were Americans, the airlift would continue and more Vietnamese could be saved.

There were problems with the evacuation helicopters?

Yes. The helicopter lift did not get off smoothly. There was a disconnect between Washington and the Navy in the South China Sea. L [launch] Hour was interpreted differently. The Marine infantry, scheduled to secure the landing sites in Saigon, were not on the same ships as the helicopters. As a result, we lost three precious hours, in addition to the time lost because of the ambassador's trip to the airport. These hours cost us dearly at the end. It wasn't until four hours after the evacuation order was given that the first helicopter arrived at the embassy. It was a very confused day. We didn't know how many Americans there were to evacuate. We didn't know how many Vietnamese and their relatives to move. The Vietnamese operated on an extended family rule. We figured an average of four people per American family, whereas the average Vietnamese family was seventeen or eighteen. It was a complete mess. As it turned out, only a fraction were evacuated. [There is a pause as Polgar contemplates the final hours of Saigon.] We broke our word to the Vietnamese. We pulled the rug out from under them. We couldn't even evacuate all the employees of the embassy. We ruined people's lives. Many families were separated.

Had Washington heeded your warnings earlier, could there have been an orderly exit?

No. First, our orders were to support the continuity of the noncommunist South Vietnamese government. If we had taken out the key embassy employees, military and political leaders, the police and guards, we would have had an immediate collapse—which Martin was told to prevent at all costs. Second, we didn't have transportation to evacuate that many people. Pan American and the other commercial airlines ceased flying about two weeks before. And would you believe it, Pan American was fined by the Federal Aviation Agency because it carried Vietnamese to the United States without proper visas. Air America planes had a range that didn't go beyond Hong Kong. We took a chance and sent one C-46 Air America plane to Hong Kong to refuel and to continue on to Taiwan. The Hong Kong authorities confiscated the plane because it carried Vietnamese without Hong Kong visas. Thailand and other Southeast Asian countries wouldn't accept any Vietnamese. So the big question was how to move the Vietnamese. There were ships in the port of Saigon, but the experiences with ships in the ports of Nha Trang and Da Nang when those cities fell were disasters. Once people started to board, panic set in and babies were trampled and people were crushed and fell into the sea. The ambassador didn't want to take a chance on mass riots at Saigon's docks. It was an absolutely hopeless situation.

Please describe the final moments in Saigon.

After the successful evacuation of the defense attaché's complex, which was then blown up at midnight, April 29, the only U.S. government personnel in Saigon were in the embassy. They consisted of the ambassador, his senior staff, the Marine security guard, and a few Army officers. There were, however, still many Vietnamese and other Asians on the embassy grounds. Helicopter flights continued to lift mixed loads of Americans and Asians. By the early morning hours of April 30, the flights thinned out. Ambassador Martin insisted that more flights were needed, while Washington set limits, which were, however, not enforced until around 4:30 A.M. when the Airborne Command Center transmitted in the clear [Polgar reads]: "The following message is from the President of the United States and should be passed on by the first helicopter in contact with Ambassador Martin. Only twenty-one lifts remain. Americans only will be transported. Ambassador Martin will board the first available helicopter and the helicopter will broadcast, 'Tiger, Tiger, Tiger,' once it is airborne and en route."

That was it?
That was it. The ambassador got up, without words, and walked to the elevator. The rest of the senior staff followed. As we trudged up from the sixth floor to the landing zone on the roof, no one spoke. We knew how we felt. We had no uniforms, but we were a defeated army. The remaining flights brought out the deputy chief of mission and the Marines. The president's order that the remaining flights would carry Americans only resulted in an uncertain number, but certainly in the hundreds, of Vietnamese, Koreans, and other Asians left behind on embassy grounds. It was our last betrayal in Vietnam.

How did you feel?
The last day in Saigon and the days that followed were the saddest, most traumatic days of my life. I felt a mixture of guilt, pain, and sorrow. I grieved more than when my parents or my brother died. They died of natural causes and I bore no responsibility in their passing. It was different in Vietnam. Thoughts came and come again. What else could I have done? What did I fail to do? What might have made even a small difference?

Can you single out one person in Washington responsible for the debacle?
I don't think it would be fair to single out any one person. We were at the end of a long process, and there were many people cooking the stew. The Ford administration was never enthusiastic

about Vietnam. When the latter's defeat became definitive, there was no motivation for a continuing hassle with Congress. The administration could not advocate pulling out from Vietnam. For obvious reasons, no American politician would propose surrender. Hanoi got them out of their dilemma. The administration used Graham Martin as the fall guy, directing him to pursue a policy that simply had no chance of succeeding and for which there was no domestic support. The Arab-Israeli war of 1973, the oil shortage, and the Nixon resignation were ingredients of the lethal dose that killed South Vietnam while the Soviet Union and China continued to support Hanoi. South Vietnam had no influential friends in Washington.

A final note?

It is worth noting that after the fall of Vietnam and the loss of many billions of dollars and of American prestige, there was no comprehensive congressional investigation. A subcommittee of the House Foreign Affairs Committee took a day of testimony from Ambassador Martin. I was never asked to testify. I was not debriefed on Vietnam by the CIA or by the State Department. It seemed that all wanted to forget.

NORMAN SCHWARZKOPF

I'd gone to Vietnam for God, country, and mom's apple pie.
But by September I was fighting for the freedom
of my South Vietnamese companions and friends.

—NORMAN SCHWARZKOPF, *It Doesn't Take A Hero*

Had Saddam Hussein not existed, there most likely never would have been a "Stormin' Norman," as the country came to know him. On February 23, 1991, as commander of nearly three-quarters of a million Allied forces amassed on the northern Saudi Arabian desert, Gen. Norman Schwarzkopf unleashed a massive ground attack that destroyed the Iraqi army in one hundred hours. A six-week air bombardment totaling 106,000 Allied air sorties had masterfully set up the battlefield for a feigned amphibious landing on the Kuwaiti coast followed by a mechanized "left hook" that caught the Iraqis completely by surprise.

In sharp contrast to the conclusion of the Vietnam War, when America turned its back on returning veterans, General Schwarzkopf addressed both houses of Congress and then led the largest victory parade in the nation's capital since World War II and a ticker tape parade in New York City. America's military and political leaders had indeed learned from their predecessors' mistakes twenty-five years earlier. As an adviser in 1965 to the South Vietnamese Airborne Brigade and, three years later, as an infantry battalion commander in a disintegrating U.S. Army, Schwarzkopf experienced firsthand what happens on the battlefield when politicians in Washington play field commander and the country is not firmly behind the military before committing troops. The lessons that he took to Desert Storm are foremost in my mind as I enter the general's thirtieth-floor office suite in downtown Tampa, Florida.

At first, I do not recognize the former bear of a man that TV journalist Barbara Walters had brought into America's living rooms. He's 40 pounds lighter than when we saw him in camouflaged fatigues. The walls that I half anticipated to be plastered with photos of the general in battle gear standing next to Arab sheiks are instead adorned with wildlife paintings and mementos from children. He points out that he and his wife Brenda devote time and personal resources to various charitable children's projects. "As I look back over my life, when I felt the best was when I was serving a cause for which I didn't receive anything tangible back," he says. When not attending to these projects, he lectures on leadership, a subject about which, he says, the public hungers to learn more.

Schwarzkopf is a second-generation West Pointer, class of 1956. His father was a brigadier general who later headed the Lindbergh kidnapping investigation as New Jersey's first police chief. Ever since his childhood, he envisioned someday commanding a decisively important battle, although his dream almost did not come true when, as a battalion commander in Vietnam in 1970, he tiptoed into an enemy minefield to rescue men from his unit. He says it was the most terrifying thing he has been through in his life.

He bristles when I mention that the press criticized the fighting capability of the South Vietnamese army. He says that he has the utmost admiration and affection for the soldiers and the officers of the Airborne Brigade with whom he lived and fought. The brigade commander was as brilliant a strategist as any with whom he served during his thirty-five years of service. On the other hand, the American military leaders at USARV headquarters were disgraceful, and cutting off military aid to the South Vietnamese was an absolute betrayal by the U.S. Congress. Twice wounded, he says that he understands the human price of war and the immense moral responsibility that political and military leaders have to avoid risking the lives of American soldiers by pursuing faulty strategies.

You volunteered for your first tour of duty in Vietnam when you had two years remaining as an instructor at West Point?

I was told that leaving West Point for Vietnam would be committing career suicide. But I volunteered because I was an infantryman, and Vietnam was an infantryman's war. I arrived at West Point in the summer of 1964. I had a three-year teaching obligation in the Department of Mechanics [mechanical engineering] after having just completed a two-year master's degree program at the University of Southern California in guided-missile engineering, neither of which had anything to do with being an infantryman. I was sitting back at West Point, fat, dumb, and happy, while other infantry officers were paying the price in Vietnam. The more I read about the war in 1964 and '65, the more I was actually convinced that that was where I should be. I was terribly uncomfortable with myself. But at the same time, everybody was telling me that nobody ever breaks out of West Point to go to war without first serving their three-year obligation. They warned me that I had better serve my three years or my career would be finished.

Did you have a sense that the war would be over soon and that you'd miss it?

That weighed heavily in my mind, but that wasn't the driving force. Deep down, I was an infantryman.

You must have had an urge to find out how you would perform under real fire?

Absolutely, that was always there. From the day I decided to go into the infantry, I wondered what I was going to do the first time somebody shot at me. What was I going to do in actual combat? Would I do my job, or would I be so terrified that I would run away like a coward? I can still remember exactly where I was lying the night before my first experience in combat and wondering how I would react the next day.

So you went to Vietnam without finishing your tour at West Point.

You bet. I became more and more comfortable about my decision after serving some time with the Vietnamese airborne. The airborne officers were truly patriots fighting for the freedom of their country. That sort of became my raison d'être of why I was there during that first tour. I was absolutely convinced that we were doing the right thing. I wore their uniform; I slept where they slept; ate what they ate. As you well know, there is nothing glorious about combat. It's sure as hell not like combat is shown in the movie theaters. We would go off for six weeks at a time in the jungles for a cause from which I wasn't going to receive anything tangible in return. I really had a tremendous sense of selfless service.

There has been a lot of bad press about the fighting capability of the South Vietnamese soldiers and their leaders.

I know. The press and some of the American advisers didn't have much respect for them. They said the Vietnamese were lousy fighters, no guts. They said their officers were dumb or just politicians. I used to get really angry when I heard that. It was such gross generalization.

It wasn't true of the airborne. From my point of view, they were absolutely magnificent fighters. One of the great strengths of the Vietnamese airborne was their noncommissioned-officer corps. They had NCOs that had been with the French colonial parachute battalions. Some of those guys had jumped into Dien Bien Phu. We never lost a single battle when I was with them. I saw a lot of really heroic acts, not just from the officers, but from the privates too.

You were mostly up against the NVA?
It was almost 100 percent NVA. They were coming across from Cambodia at that time. They were a disciplined force, not a ragtag bunch at all. What always amazed me about the NVA was that they never left any bodies behind unless there was overwhelming firepower and they had no possible way of getting their dead out. We had big battles where we would hit them with artillery, air strikes, and everything else we had. I knew we killed a bunch of them. We found lots of weapons, but we never found any bodies. That still blows my mind.

Did you believe in 1965 that we could have won the war?
I am absolutely convinced that we would have won had we bombed the north and mined Haiphong harbor. But, the U.S. strategy was a classic piecemeal commitment where we trickled in forces a little bit at a time. Washington believed that if we killed more of them than they killed of us, they'd give up and not want to fight anymore. We fought it locally. We never really fought the war strategically. We never took the war to the North.

Are you suggesting that we should have invaded North Vietnam with American troops?
We did, to a limited extent. Let's not forget the Son Tay [prison camp in North Vietnam] raid. When does an attack become a full-scale invasion? I don't think that we should have been providing sanctuaries that the enemy could escape to. We should have bombed more using B-52s and mined Haiphong harbor. We should have continued to escalate to include cross-border operations into North Vietnam and, if need be, into all of North Vietnam. Why? Because it would have brought the war to a conclusion. It was fruitless to continue to fight only in South Vietnam when the war was really being conducted by the people in Hanoi.

Had we taken the war to Hanoi, did you think then that China would intervene?

No, I didn't. I knew we didn't mine Haiphong harbor and bomb Hanoi for fear of upsetting the Chinese. That was always Washington's rationale. But remember, when the North Vietnamese backed away from the peace table, B-52s leveled Hanoi with bombs, and the North immediately returned to the peace table. Maybe I'm talking with 20/20 hindsight, and maybe it's my Desert Storm experience on top of everything else. We fought the North Vietnamese with one hand tied behind our back. For a long time, we couldn't cross the Cambodian border. Everybody was very sensitive about the Cambodian border because of China. During my first tour, after the NVA lost a tremendous battle at Duc Co, the enemy scrambled back across the Cambodian border to safety and we couldn't follow. We shouldn't have allowed the enemy sanctuaries. There should have been no sanctuaries. We didn't have a sanctuary, as I recall. Why should they?

From your position on the ground, were Westmoreland's search-and-destroy tactics effective against guerrilla forces?

Search-and-destroy tactics were not effective against guerrilla forces because they would almost never stand and fight. As you well know, they would quickly fade away and were very, very difficult to engage in decisive engagements. I think we should have had an entirely separate campaign against the guerrilla forces, rooting out and eliminating infrastructure and logistical support.

Was Westmoreland the right man for the job?

No. He was my division commander in the 101st Airborne and was commander of MACV during my first tour of Vietnam. I never felt that he was sincerely interested in anything I had to tell him. I had the distinct feeling that he was playing to the press and PR people who always seemed to be present anywhere that he went. I contrast that to Abrams, with whom I met on several occasions on my second tour and who was never accompanied by the press. Most of the time, the questions that Westmoreland asked were rather innocuous, and I never felt he expressed true concern for the well-being of my troops.

You were an Abrams fan?

Emphatically, yes. I served under him when I was a battalion commander. He always seemed very interested in what I had to say, asked my opinion about various subjects, and always seemed concerned about the well-being of my troops and how to fight the enemy. He was just the kind of "muddy boot" soldier for whom I had great respect. I admired him later on when he was the chief of staff of the Army, and he actually got up from his deathbed to support the Army before Congress. He was a great leader.

What were your thoughts in 1965 about McNamara?

My feelings were pretty much universal within the military. The fact that McNamara thought that he could run the war from Washington was idiotic. The fact that he was literally selecting targets to be bombed in North Vietnam without any regard to a campaign plan or how the bombings fit into a campaign plan was crazy. He stepped completely out of the box from the role and mission of the secretary of defense. I fault Westmoreland for not standing up to McNamara and reminding him that his job was in the policy business, not in the war-fighting business. There was a very clear line between the two.

Should the joint chiefs have resigned when McNamara refused to listen to them?

Harold K. Johnson said he should have. It could have made a huge difference, and it was not without precedent. General Jim Galvin quit over the doctrine of massive retaliation, and I think it made a difference that he resigned. There is no question about the fact that there's a political-military arena, and the higher you get on the ladder, the more political it becomes versus military. But, we should never forget that we are the military professionals. You can't let some hobbyists step in there and start doing their thing. There is also duty, honor, country. When do you start selling out honor for your career or your own political future? It doesn't win you any friends to take an unpopular position. God, this I know well. But I'm a firm believer that it's better to choose the harder right than the easier wrong.

You volunteered in 1969 to go back to Vietnam for a second tour?

I was a lieutenant colonel and wanted to command a battalion in combat. I had learned valuable lessons on my first tour under the leadership of Vietnamese professionals and wanted to put them to good use. I honestly believed that I could save American lives. But for five months I sat behind a desk at USARV headquarters in Long Binh working for [Maj. Gen.] George Mabry, who was chief of staff for the deputy commanding general, [Gen.] Frank Mildren. USARV was predominantly the logistics, personnel, and civil affairs headquarters for American forces in Vietnam. The tactical headquarters was being run by General Abrams at MACV in Saigon. I didn't know what Nixon's secret plan was to end the war, but it was clear to me that the blueprint involved the gradual withdrawal of U.S. forces from Vietnam. Vietnamization was the name of the game. USARV headquarters was a living example of how bad a military force can get when it is entrenched and stagnated on the ground. It had no viable perimeter and no defense whatsoever. The focus of the whole place was more on the social nightlife, the steam baths, and bars than on business. There was [a] lot of seedy stuff going on. It just wasn't professional at all.

You were finally given a combat battalion?

After five months of absolute frustration, I took command of the 1st Battalion of 6th Infantry, commonly known as the "worst of the sixth." It was a nightmare. My predecessor had quite literally punched his ticket. I learned later that he had spent only two days in the field with the troops. His operations officer, a guy by the name of Maj. Will Lee, was basically the battalion commander. It was a disgrace. When we had a change of command, my predecessor gave me a bottle of scotch and told me that I was going to need it. He said that I had just taken over the worst battalion in the United States Army. That was my debriefing with the former battalion commander. My brigade commander, a legendary combat infantryman at the battle of Pork Chop Hill during the Korean War, [Col.] Joe Clemons, visited me the very next day and walked my battalion's bunker line. It was probably the worst couple of hours of my entire life. The bunkers were completely caved in. The foxholes that were there weren't deep enough to cover up anybody. Claymore mines had no wires. Clemons gave me hell. I was embarrassed and angry at myself for not having walked the bunker line the day before. I told Clemons I would fix the problem, and I did.

Did your unit have a drug problem when you took command?

Yeah, but not to the extent that Oliver Stone pretends we had in his movies. I had a mortar base out in the middle of nowhere. There was no vegetation, only baked hard clay surrounded by barbed wire. If I couldn't handle my drug offenders through the military justice system, I sent them out there. Was that legal? Probably not, but it sure as hell cleared up my drug problem in a hurry. Offenders stayed there until the end of their tour and then went home. It was the way I could isolate my drug problem and keep it away from the rest of the troops. I don't want you to get the wrong idea. At the most, we had four or five drug users at any one time. I didn't have one of those scenes where everyone on the front line was stoned. The drug problems were mostly in the rear areas where guys were bored to death all day long and didn't have anything else to do. My troops pretty much policed themselves. They didn't want somebody in the foxhole next to them high on drugs.

Were American soldiers good fighters at that time?

No. American effort was drawing down; units were being shipped home. My battalion was grossly under strength in noncommissioned and professional officers. Most of my captains had made captain in two years. Most of my lieutenants were what I called commissioned PFCs. They were drafted and then had a choice of going to Officers' Candidate School and getting a commission or being sent to Vietnam as a private. They very quickly decided they wanted to go as an officer. So I had a terrible leadership vacuum. You talk about a leadership challenge. It didn't take the troops very long to figure out on night ambushes that if they didn't shoot at the enemy, the enemy wouldn't shoot at them. The Army had come apart at the seams. We had no professional leadership, and the troops knew what was going on back in the States. They were drafted and sent over to a war that wasn't being supported by the American people. I don't blame them. If I was a private drafted and knew that all these other guys back home were getting off and I wasn't, I don't think I would have been a very good fighter either. I'm sure many of my soldiers still hate my guts to this day. I was the biggest son-of-a-bitch in their minds because I made them wear steel helmets and flak jackets rather than go home in a casket.

How were you treated when you returned in 1970 to the United States?

It was terrible. Probably the one vivid memory I have more than any other was going to downtown Washington in uniform to buy my wife a gift. It was Christmastime. I felt hostility all around me. People stared at my uniform and turned up their noses. I just thought, "My God, here I am in the Nation's Capital wearing a uniform of the United States Army, and somehow I'm being made to feel that

I have to atone for something." It was an awful, awful feeling. But nobody ever spit on me. Had anybody spit on me, they would have paid a terrible price. I wasn't going to tolerate that.

Could we have won the war in 1970?

I think so. What lost the war for us—after we turned over our helicopters, artillery, and sophisticated equipment to the Vietnamese—was Congress cutting off the money. That cut off the supply of critical spare parts and ammunition that the South Vietnamese needed to employ what we had left behind for them. That was it. The war was over. That was an act of betrayal—an absolute act of betrayal. I can remember exactly where I was standing in the halls of the Pentagon when I heard the news that Congress had stopped the funding. It was treacherous and, I repeat, a clear act of betrayal. It was one of the blackest moments in the history of the United States of America because the day that happened, the South Vietnamese were doomed. China and Russia were still supporting North Vietnam, but we betrayed the South after giving them our word.

What lessons from Vietnam did you take with you to Desert Storm?

People ask me if Vietnam was all for nothing. I tell them no, because a whole generation of military officers came out of Vietnam saying, "Never again." That was my attitude from the outset of Desert Storm. I was determined not to make the same mistakes that we made in Vietnam. I made it very clear that if they chose to do it otherwise, they would do it without me. I was on my thirty-fifth year of service and getting ready to retire. I was totally against enemy body counts as a measure of success and against length of tours. Tours should be the same as in World War II. Troops were going to stay to the end. And we were going to commit the National Guard and Reserves, and get the whole country involved.

You were against body counts?

You're damn right. When the Pentagon told me during the Gulf War that they wanted to do body counts, I told them over my dead body. They'll have to fire me before we would have body counts in the Gulf War. When I was asked about how many Iraqis did we kill, the answer was "Beats the hell out of me; we don't know." I told the press that body counts in Vietnam were lies, a bureaucratic sham. Well, Westmoreland accused me of not having any honor for saying that. He said that if Schwarzkopf lied about enemy body counts in Vietnam, then obviously he was a dishonorable man or something like that. Ironically, Westmoreland had commissioned a study at the War College while he was Army chief of staff in 1970 to determine the cause behind the loss of integrity within the United States military. The conclusion of his own study was that the biggest contributor was the requirement for body counts in Vietnam.

Were the restrictions placed on the media in Desert Storm a lesson from Vietnam?

During the 1968 Tet Offensive, there were a total of eighty correspondents in South Vietnam. Of those eighty, many were not out with the troops; they were writing their stories from the bars in Saigon and Da Nang. In Desert Storm, we had 2,060 reporters to deal with. We basically had a management problem, so we instituted press pools. The press pool concept wasn't derived from Vietnam; it was from the debacle in the Grenada operation in which I participated. There were eighteen press pools consisting of ten members of the press corps out with various troop units at all times, or 180 reporters. This was a hundred more than the total number of reporters in Vietnam at Tet. In Desert Storm, the press had satellite communications to transmit immediately what they saw, which meant everything they sent was beamed right into Saddam Hussein's headquarters. We had to control that. This was more a management problem than censorship of the press. So we established guidelines about what could and couldn't be broadcast. It was a system that had been agreed upon by the press after Grenada. Some members of the press thought that they should have unlimited access to the battlefield at any time, anywhere. Obviously, that didn't work. Bob Simon was a good example. He took off into the desert by himself, got lost, and ended up in an Iraqi prison for the remainder of the war.

And the lessons learned in Vietnam about bureaucrats micromanaging the war from Washington?

Right. When McNamara was selecting targets in Vietnam from his office in Washington, [Lt. Gen.] Chuck Horner, my Air Force commander in Desert Storm, was one of the pilots who had to fly those missions into heavy antiaircraft artillery against targets that had been bombed three or four times. Chuck was rabid about Washington dictating tactics. I was exactly the same way. I was not going to have Washington dictate how to run military operations. We were very lucky that President George Bush had confidence in the American military. We were very fortunate that Dick Cheney understood that his role as secretary of defense was policy and that Colin Powell was in a position to have direct access to the president of the United States anytime that he needed it—so that we could get decisions immediately rather than have to go through a long, bureaucratic process. The chairman of the Joint Chiefs of Staff normally didn't have that. I insisted on having overwhelming force before we committed our troops. Remember piecemeal commitment in Vietnam? I didn't know how good the Iraqi forces were. They had just won a big war against Iran. The Iraqis had a hell of a lot of first-line Soviet equipment and airplanes and chemicals that they had used on the Iranians and their own people. Desert Storm wasn't going to be a trickle in, piecemeal commitment. We were going to go in there and get it over with as quickly as possible. And that was what happened.

Should the president and the secretary of defense have military experience?

It sure as hell made a difference with George Bush, who was a fighter pilot in World War II. He basically trusted the military, whereas McNamara and Lyndon Johnson didn't trust the military. I doubt if Richard Nixon trusted the military either. And, I personally wonder where Clinton's military advisers were during the operations in Kosovo. Yeah, it certainly makes a difference.

JAMES WEBB

Mark went to Canada. Goodrich went to Vietnam.
Everybody else went to grad school.

JAMES WEBB, *Fields of Fire*

I first talked with James Webb on the telephone and remarked that he was an anomaly among Naval Academy graduates; few had broken from the predictable military path and strayed far into the right side of their brains as he had. He laughed, assuring me that he indeed was abnormal in that regard. We then chatted about filmmaking. He was making arrangements to produce in Vietnam his novel, *Fields of Fire*, independent of the Hollywood system. He said the NVA agreed to play themselves.

He meets me at his office door wearing jeans and running shoes. Boyishly handsome at fifty-four years of age, he banters about how his men in "Nam" always wondered what the "old man" was going to do next to surprise the enemy. Keeping the enemy and his troops guessing had become an art form to him. There was something very present tense about his humor.

We sit down in the front room of his office complex overlooking the Iwo Jima Memorial at Arlington Cemetery. Behind him on a table is the original bronze sculpture of the Statue of the Three Servicemen at the Vietnam Veterans Memorial. Webb was the principal advocate for the addition of three soldiers to the original wall design. He says that the central figure is wearing his combat boots.

Although he was on active duty in the Marine Corps for only three years, he still looks like a Marine. But, unlike the usual "grunt," his very precise dialogue laced with "socialist meritocracy," "misplaced idealism," and "intellectual elites," reveals a gifted and bluntly independent mind that can wield the English language with the same ease with which he handled an M16 rifle in Vietnam. "In my mind, I am a writer. In my heart I am a soldier, and I always will be."

The son of an Air Force colonel, Webb was commissioned in the Marine Corps on graduation in 1968 from the U.S. Naval Academy at Annapolis. Shortly afterward he was sent to Vietnam, where he served as platoon and company commanders in the An Hoa Basin south of Da Nang. He left the Marines in 1972 to go to law school at Georgetown University in Washington. There, he was inspired to write *Fields of Fire*, considered by many to be one of the most realistic novels about the Vietnam War.

After graduating with a law degree in 1975, Webb worked for four years at the Committee on Veterans Affairs of the House of Representatives. He left government in 1981 to write his second novel, *A Sense of Honor*, set at the Naval Academy. His 1983 PBS coverage of the U.S. Marines in Beirut won him an Emmy Award. He returned to government in 1984 as first assistant secretary of defense for reserve affairs and, in 1987 was sworn in as the sixty-sixth Secretary of the Navy. He subsequently resigned in 1988 after refusing to agree to a reduction of the Navy's force structure during congressionally mandated budget cuts.

He described, in a Naval Institute interview, his conflict between a novelist's penchant to mingle with the people in the streets and high-level governmental work: "You're a prisoner when you're in government at that level. Even when I was Secretary of the Navy, I was locked up in some of the best hotels in the world. You could travel all the way to the Philippines, but you couldn't go see anything." He is quick to point out that he's returned to Vietnam on numerous occasions as a writer.

I flick on the recorder and lean back on the sofa. The smile on Webb's face vanishes; he's suddenly all business, a Marine.

You chose the Marines over going into the Navy upon graduating from Annapolis?

I had wanted to be a Marine since I was seventeen. As the war heated up, my dad tried to talk me out of it. He was at that time an Air Force colonel working on some sensitive programs in the Pentagon and had come to despise what McNamara was doing to the military in general and with the war specifically. He'd grab me when I came home on leave from the Academy and tell me I should sit this one out: "Go into the Navy, stay on the ship, and eat ice cream." He warned me that with the civilian overcontrol of the war and with the new satellite linkups, which he was working on, Lyndon Johnson would know I was wounded before my division commander did. Incidentally, he was wrong. It was Richard Nixon. But I had fallen in love with the traditions and esprit of the Marine Corps. I'd also grown up spending a lot of time outdoors. I loved to hunt. I loved to camp. I was a Golden Gloves boxer when I was a kid. I knew that whatever else I did in my life, I wanted to be an infantry guy— a Marine.

Did you volunteer for Vietnam?

I did volunteer, although in the Marine Corps it was a moot point, more of a gesture than a necessity. We all went to Vietnam in the Marine Corps, so there was no question about going. It also was the natural thing for me to do. I had received the right kind of training. I came from a family that had a strong military tradition. I was not political at that point, and I had a strong belief in the larger-scale reasons for our being in Vietnam.

Did you envision combat would be a rite of passage to manhood?

I didn't feel that I needed a war in order to be a man. I'd already had a lot of rites of passage, one of them as a boxer. There's nothing like stepping into a ring and staring across at some guy you haven't seen before when the sole purpose of being there is to beat each other's heads in. You get a pretty comfortable feeling about yourself after that. The Marine Corps training in and of itself tests you. By the time I got to Vietnam, I had already resolved a lot of these sorts of questions. I didn't feel that had there not been a war, I would have been less of a man. But given that there was, I definitely would have felt badly about myself if I hadn't gone. I know a number of people who didn't go who have confessed to me that they felt like they cheated by avoiding the draft.

Did you have any fears that you would come back in a body bag?

We were told in training that a Marine infantry lieutenant had better than an 80 percent chance of being killed or wounded in Vietnam, and my experience pretty well bore that out. Of the officers in my rifle company when I first got there, the Weapons Platoon commander was wounded, the 1st Platoon commander was killed, the 2d Platoon commander was wounded twice, I had 3d Platoon and was wounded twice, and our company commander was wounded. In addition, two of my original three squad leaders were killed and the third was shot through the stomach.

Why are some of us spared while others aren't? Is there some higher order that decides?

I remember that when things were going very badly during part of my tour, our artillery forward observer made the comment that either there is an absolute order here—God's plan—or there is absolute randomness. I really don't know. We had a tendency to give each other nicknames in my unit, and one of mine was "the lieutenant with the golden ass." There were so many times when I should have been dead that, after a while, I decided that there must have been a reason that I was not. And, certainly the fact that so many good people were not as fortunate as I was has been the motivation for a lot of things I have done with regard to preserving the dignity of those who fought.

When you were in training to go Vietnam, did you buy Washington's reasons for sending American troops there? Was it in America's national interest?

I need to give you a careful answer here. From my perspective today, having educated myself thoroughly on the war over the years since I returned, I feel very strongly that we were correct in attempting to help the South Vietnamese build a democracy, just as we were correct to help South Korea and West Germany prevent communist takeovers there. But, looking at that issue from the perspective of a twenty-two-year-old second lieutenant who was being sent to command a rifle platoon, it was so far above my pay grade that I had no time to think about it in intricate political detail. I spent eighteen hours a day trying to learn everything that I could to be the best rifle platoon commander that I could be. But I should say this—because I think it is important—in the macro sense, I trusted my national leaders. I don't regret that. I think that Lyndon Johnson did some very stupid things in terms of how he conducted the war, but there was no question in my mind about our being in Vietnam. The great tragedy of the period is that Johnson didn't ask Congress for an actual declaration of war. If he had succeeded, it would have created a totally different political climate, both domestically and internationally. And, if he had not been given a declaration of war by the Congress, it would not have been "Johnson's War" to lose.

You were assigned to a combat unit?

When I reached Da Nang, I was assigned to the 1st Battalion of the 5th Regiment, 1st Marine Division. From Da Nang I went to our regimental rear, a combat base in a place called the An Hoa Basin. We were the furthest regiment out, up against the mountains, where the North Vietnamese Army operated a division from what they called Base Area 112. They also had main force Viet Cong units operating every day, and, at that time, they were about 80 percent NVA soldiers. The An Hoa Basin also had many VC local units and had a very strong VC infrastructure in the villages. I was supposed to be five days in An Hoa, but my company commander found out that I had been my class honor graduate in basic school and said, "Get that guy out here." I joined my platoon on the move during an afternoon, took them out on a patrol that night, and walked into an NVA unit on my first patrol.

How long were you in the field?

I was in the bush for the first nine months of my tour. After I made first lieutenant, they made me commander of the same company in which I commanded a platoon.

Were your men good fighters?

My men were terrific. This was a very, very tough combat environment, and our country might never understand how good our troops really were. The Marine Corps lost three times as many combat dead in Vietnam as it did in Korea and took more total casualties than it did in all of World War II. At the same time, the communists now admit that they lost 1.4 million soldiers. Our company very rarely rotated out of the bush, even to the primitive base camp at An Hoa. I think the greatest surprise of my life was how capable these nineteen- and twenty-year-olds were and how uncomplaining they were under living conditions that were beyond belief. The troops used to make a wry distinction, "War is hell, but combat is a bitch." Where we operated, the fighting could be very up close and personal. It wasn't just the fighting, it was the entire environment in which we operated. Very few helicopters, no barbed wire, no tents, no hot meals, ring-worm, hookworms, shrimp fever, malaria, wormy water, making night moves constantly, all of this for months at a time. When I got to Vietnam, I weighed right around 170 pounds, with not an ounce of fat on me. When I was wounded the second time, I found that I weighed 138 pounds. That was typical. And these guys never complained.

What was your take on the NVA soldiers? And the Viet Cong?

The regular NVA units were highly disciplined. I respected them a great deal. The Viet Cong varied, but I would be the last person to demean the sacrifices of any soldier. And, on that point, I believe the South Vietnamese army and Marine Corps have been horribly defamed. They had some excellent units. After Nixon announced the Vietnamization program, I operated as a company commander with several ARVN units out in our area. The 51st ARVN Regiment was particularly good.

Much has been written about American soldiers using drugs. Did you observe a drug problem with your men?

The drugs issue varied from year to year and from unit to unit. In my company, there was very little drug use among the rifle platoons in the bush. They were highly disciplined, and they disciplined each other on this point. I knew there were recreational drug users when we rotated into the rear, but, quite frankly, I've always found this issue rather overblown. Drugs were a generational problem, not purely a military problem. I saw far more drugs at Georgetown Law School when I returned than I did in the Marine Corps. Where's the stigma for those folks, many of whom went on to prosecute drug offenders?

Did you enjoy combat?

I enjoyed the people that I was with, and I did enjoy parts of combat itself. There was a purity in the relationships out there that I don't think you can have in any other environment. I saw people at their very best and a few at their very worst. But, the whole idea of being out in the bush didn't bother me at all, and I felt very natural about the thinking part of combat. I loved to find ways to outthink the enemy and, after operating in the same area for a while, I found that I could do that on a regular basis. The biggest negative of being in a combat environment was the result of the very close relationships that I developed with my troops. When one of them was killed or wounded, I took it very hard. It was very emotional, and it never goes away. The "post–Tet 1969" period leading up to when Nixon went to Guam to meet with president Nguyen Van Thieu was the second worst period of the war after Tet '68. The communists made a huge push to run up our casualty figures as a way to pressure Nixon to withdraw American troops. This was the period made famous by "Hamburger Hill," and it was a very tough time in my company.

The other downside was seeing the villagers take a real beating. I instinctively liked the Vietnamese people. From the day I got to Vietnam, even in areas that were totally Viet Cong, I never developed a dislike for them like some Americans did. The hardest personal moment for me in Vietnam was when we couldn't get a medevac for a five-year-old kid who had received a concussion from a grenade thrown into a bunker. It was in the middle of a tactical operation, and medevacs for civilians were the lowest priority. I had to watch him slowly die—lying on an ammunition box right in front of me and staring at me the whole time. It just really numbed me out. Those sorts of things were hard, but, in the aggregate, I don't regret being in combat.

The sensitivity you describe is hardly what has been portrayed by the media as a stereotypical Marine.

I think the media—even to a certain extent today—have deliberately sought out the veterans who reinforce their own negative perceptions. And, quite often, the people who tell those stories are total phonies. For example, in 1981, *Time* magazine did a lengthy piece on Vietnam veterans. The two main writers were men in the Vietnam age group who did not serve. Except for myself, every single veteran they interviewed was bitter about the war—this at a time when the most accurate poll ever done on veteran attitudes indicated that 91 percent were glad they'd served their country, 74 percent enjoyed their time in the military, and 89 percent agreed that "our troops were asked to fight in a war in which the political leaders would not let them win." One of the guys they interviewed claimed that he'd been a two-tour infantryman and a prisoner of war and that, on one patrol, he'd shot a pregnant woman in the stomach and claimed two kills. As it turned out, he had never even been in Vietnam, a fact that *Time* never even corrected in subsequent editions. These kinds of stories have happened so often that they've become a litany. It's a slander of an entire generation of fighting men.

What was your feeling about the antiwar movement back home while you were out in the bush?

I was in Vietnam at a really odd time. 1969 was the second worst year of the war for American casualties, and yet there was a clear sense that something wasn't going right back home. Woodstock happened while I was in Vietnam, as did the moratorium. In truth, we didn't spend a whole lot of time thinking about it. Combat is the most apolitical environment I have ever been in. All we thought about was doing our job as well as we could do it, counting our days, and going home. But, I don't think any of us fully comprehended at the time that there was this cleavage between the people who went to Vietnam and the people who didn't go, and that the cleavage was largely based on social class. The antiwar movement back home was irrelevant to us in the bush.

But you must have had strong feelings about antiwar activists like Jane Fonda and the media?

I have some strong feelings about a lot of people who abused our system during that period, but I'm trying to answer your specific question. Those feelings were the result of what I learned after I came home, rather than what we were thinking when we were fighting the war. I believe Jane Fonda committed treason during her visit to North Vietnam. Not only did she oppose our involvement, but she actively encouraged the enemy by making speeches against America on radio Hanoi. But she wasn't alone. Many others were complicitous in terms of directly assisting the other side, and many of the antiwar movement's leaders directly coordinated their activities with Hanoi. Study, for instance, the period leading up to the march on the Pentagon in October 1967, which actually became the political setup for Hanoi's Tet 68 Offensive that, itself, began gearing up on the battlefield in November 1967. On the twentieth anniversary of the fall of Saigon, I was on CNN's *Crossfire* with George McGovern. Everybody wanted to talk about McNamara's mea culpa, supposedly as evidence that the strategy for the war was permanently flawed. My point was that McNamara was gone in 1967, and the war didn't end for eight more years, and that, if McNamara had presided over a poor strategy, we had plenty of time to correct his mistakes so that focusing on McNamara was a disservice to understanding the entire context of the war. Incidentally, my father, who, as I mentioned, was a career officer and worked at the Pentagon, despised Robert McNamara. I really never comprehended the depths of his feelings until I read *Dereliction of Duty* by H. R. McMaster, who showed the day-to-day stuff my dad had to put up with. Anyway, when we broke for a commercial, George McGovern turned to me and said, "What you don't understand is that I didn't want us to win that war." A lot of powerful people in this country felt that way and hid it behind rhetoric or through their attacks on the supposedly incompetent military. To single out Jane Fonda is to misread the depth of what was going on [on] the other side. As for the media inside Vietnam, except for a few brave souls like Peter Braestrup, they were sort of a joke. They didn't come out to where we were. Where we were was a pretty nasty place.

Did you have any revelations upon returning home about the way vets were treated?

It sort of hit me slowly. I found, by and large, that the people who stayed in the military had fewer emotional difficulties than the people who got out. In the military, there was a natural support base from others who'd gone, but the guys who were cut loose and sent home got atomized. The real hatred was from within our own age group. I believe that many of those who avoided Vietnam felt guilty about what they had done—or failed to do—and transposed that guilt by attacking the validity of the people who had gone. It was not the older generation against the younger generation, as some of the people in the antiwar movement wanted to put it. When I left the Marines in 1972, I went to Georgetown's law school. This was right after the Watergate break-in. I stayed there until the fall of Saigon in 1975. Those were three difficult years to be in Washington as a law school student. I think I met only 3 people out of a student body of about 1,800 who had been in combat in Vietnam. Those people who didn't go had become the experts on the war. They talked about it in legal terms as if it were an intellectual drill. The "Nuremberg precedents" were more real to them than the actuality of combat. I tried a few times to give context to what they were saying, but it was immediately dismissed as being anecdotal because I had actually been there. They had the big picture, and, from their perspective, all I saw was one little area. So I very quickly stopped talking about Vietnam. If any of these so-called experts had actually spent a few months in a grunt unit and had to deal with the moral complexities that nineteen-year-old kids had to confront every day out in the bush, their dialogue would have been totally different. It was so easy for them to sit back and pass judgment on something that they never experienced. So one day, while I was sitting in constitutional law class and watching them debate the War Powers Act, I started writing *Fields of Fire*. I wrote the last chapter first about a guy coming home from Vietnam. I wanted to put a human face on an American soldier for my law school classmates.

I sensed some real anger in you in that last chapter. Were you angry?

I have never felt anger toward people who simply didn't go, so long as they respected those who did. But I don't think I will ever get over the deliberate abuse of those self-serving members of our age group who persisted in demeaning the experience of the 2.7 million guys who went. I used to think that would be resolved with time—if we were patient and kept making our case in an affirmative way, that eventually the truth would prevail. But, the people who didn't go to Vietnam reached such positions of power in the media, film, academia, and publishing—all the places where opinion is filtered and the stories are told—that I'm not so sure anymore.

Vietnam was a sons of blue-collar workers' war.
There is a persistent presumption that this was a draftee's war, fought by the poor and the minorities, a comfortable allegation pushed by the better off in our society who didn't go. For many of the elites in the age group, saying simply that this was a minority's war, or a war fought by the poor, kind of let them off the hook. If only the lower end of society went, then what they did wasn't that unusual—but this was not true. The poor went. The minorities went. But, so did the middle class. Blacks were 13.1 percent of the age group, 12.6 percent of the military, and 12.2 percent of the casualties—and I'm proud of every one of them. But, I'm proud also of the middle-class whites who went, as well; 73 percent of those who died in Vietnam were volunteers, and 86 percent of those who died were white. The reality is that the elites were alone in not showing up. In terms of American history, Vietnam was the first major war in which this was so. I have spent a good part of my life assimilating this experience and trying to put it into context of what actually occurred and in the context of the stream of American history. In World War II, Harvard University lost 691 alumni. But in Vietnam, all the Harvard college classes from 1962 to 1972 lost only 12. What about these people who didn't go? Put yourself inside their minds at a time when 58,000 people of their own age group were going off and dying while they found a way out of serving. The only way to justify your refusal was to make Vietnam such a completely negative experience that it was honorable not to participate. It wasn't simply that they wanted to go to grad school, which is what most of them did, or that they could find a way around the corrupt draft system. It was that the war was supposedly so immoral and so genocidal that, as an act of conscience, they were going to take the high road and stay out of it. If you follow that logic, by definition, those who found a way out of serving committed an act of high morality by not participating in this "obscene" war. Then those who did participate

were either stupid or immoral. That is the reasoning behind why those who fought in Vietnam saw their experience so demeaned and perverted after they came back.

Did you envision when you were in Vietnam that you would someday be a writer?

I had no idea that I would ever write a book. I had no literary aspirations whatsoever. I didn't even keep a journal. It really wasn't until I got to law school that I started writing. It was like learning how to fight with my brain. I learned the power of marshaling facts and using them to shape an argument. After my first year of law school, when everyone was going off to law clerking, I hitched a military flight to Micronesia and came back and wrote a short book about how America should reconfigure its presence in the Pacific. It was during this period that I started having a passion for writing as opposed just to reading.

You said you were at Georgetown in 1975 when Saigon fell?

Yeah. It was a horrible moment for anyone who cared about what we had tried to do for the South Vietnamese people. I remember going to school that morning and seeing a group of law students actually celebrating. I wanted to throw up. It was amazing to me that they seemed so certain that the "pure flame of the revolution was going to burn," to use Francis Fitzgerald's phrase from *Fire in the Lake*. They thought that there would be a wonderful future for Vietnam under the communists. But most of them remained silent when the atrocities started in Cambodia; when a million of South Vietnam's best young leaders were marched off into the reeducation camps; when millions of others jumped into the sea, thus facing a 50 percent chance of dying rather than living under the system that had taken over their country; and when the Soviet Union set up a major military presence inside the country. I'm still waiting to hear from them on those issues.

When you were in Vietnam, did you feel that we could have won the war? What do you think now?

Having been back to Vietnam more than a dozen times and having traveled the entire length of the country, I have no doubt that we could have won the war. When I was a platoon commander and company commander, it was like being a boxer. When you're in a close fight, you really don't know if you're winning. You know how many times your opponent has hit you, but you really don't know how many times you've hit him. Out in the bush where we were, we had no context to measure against what we were doing, particularly on a national scale. That's the very nature of a war of attrition. Ho Chi Minh had said that he was willing to take ten times our casualties, and he did.

Kissinger said that we could have won had we gone into the sanctuaries earlier in the war.

He's right. Whatever people might think of Richard Nixon, if he'd conducted the war instead of Lyndon Johnson, at a time when American public opinion was still supporting the effort, it would have been a very different war. And of course the greatest sanctuary of all was North Vietnam. Do you realize that we never bombed Hanoi with B-52s until December 1972? When you go to Hanoi, the first thing a lot of their government people want to talk about is the impact of those days when the B-52s came. It got their attention. Instead of bombing with light-attack aircraft that gave them the illusion they were withstanding American military power and in the process strengthened their morale, it scared them and broke their morale.

Westmoreland said he did not invade the north with American troops for fear of China intervening.

I think that logic is not only wrong but backwards. Halberstam, in his book, *The Best and the Brightest*, makes a strong case that because of the [Joseph] McCarthy period, we lost our China experts and know-how to read Asia accurately. So we slid into Vietnam worrying about Chinese intervention. There was great concern about taking the war to North Vietnam because of what happened in Korea. I think I understand the Vietnamese now as well as any non-Vietnamese can understand them. This has taken thirty years of going back and forth. The last thing in the world the Vietnamese communists wanted was China inside Vietnam. They have always been afraid of China. Had we taken the gamble and violated the territory of North Vietnam with incursions of ground troops, just as they flooded South Vietnam with their ground troops, it would have scared Hanoi, not only because of our presence but because they would have been worried about the Chinese crossing the border into Vietnam. I think this was one of the tragic mistakes in terms of how we waged the war.

Did the United States have the wrong military leader in Westmoreland?

I don't pretend to be an expert on Westmoreland. We were fighting a civil war and a guerrilla war, and also a conventional war once the North Vietnamese started coming down. And we were doing it with constant political interference from Washington. I do believe that the Nixon policies with Abrams commanding—Vietnamization, as well as going into the sanctuaries in Cambodia and Laos—were militarily sound, although they were implemented at a time when, politically, the war had become unmanageable at home.

Should the Joint Chiefs have resigned en masse when Washington refused to heed their advice?

Having myself resigned as secretary of the Navy rather than walk a budget over to Congress that would have reduced the force structure of the Navy—which was one of the hardest things that I have ever done in my life—I would say that there comes a time when the issue is clear enough where you have to put the continuity of the institution you care about before your own tenure. What I have heard from many flag-level officers is that they never could find that clear, signaling issue, and, as a result, they thought that they could do more good from inside the administration than from outside it. But they still could have spoken out while their credibility was intact. That doesn't mean resigning. Gen. Bob [Robert H.] Barrow, commandant of the Marine Corps during the Carter administration, was very effective in doing this during some difficult times after the war. If a member of the Joint Chiefs had dared Lyndon Johnson to fire him, he would have been in a much more powerful position than by simply resigning. But they didn't do either, and few will do so today.

Was it right for Congress to cut off the money?

First of all, I think a lot of people don't understand how that happened. It was a direct consequence of Nixon's resignation. We had Democrats elected to Congress in 1974 who had run in solidly Republican districts purely as antiwar candidates. Tom Downey in New York was a classic example. I think he was twenty-six years old and still living at home with his mother. Their only issue was to end our involvement in Vietnam. I believe that cutting off the supplemental appropriation for the South Vietnamese was the most shameful act of our government in its entire history. Its impact was far greater than the funds, although they were needed badly. It was a signal to

South Vietnam that, after ten years of struggle, they were being thrown over the side, at the same time the Soviet Union and other Eastern bloc nations continued to support North Vietnam. People forget that many groups in this country continued to assist Hanoi even after American troops were withdrawn in January 1973. They weren't simply looking for an end to an American involvement, as so many of them like to say today. As McGovern mentioned, they wanted Hanoi to win. That money was going for beans, bullets, and Band-Aids to assist the South Vietnamese at a time when the North Vietnamese had received increased supplies from the Soviets and were getting ready to launch a major offensive. I have a lot of former ARVN friends who will tell you that they were down to two artillery rounds per day, once that final offensive began, because they'd run out. And as I mentioned, the symbolic impact of cutting off the funds fed the chaos in those final days.

You were secretary of the Navy. Should the president and the people he surrounds himself with have prior military experience?

I don't believe it's mandatory that any single individual in government have military service. But if there was a war going on and fifty-eight thousand people of their age were dying, I believe that someone who did not serve has an obligation to the public to explain why he didn't. That's not the same thing as saying that everyone should have gone to Vietnam. President Clinton has never said one word that admits that his judgment to avoid the draft was in error. But, ultimately, I believe there will be a judgment of history.

Why do you still carry this passion for Vietnam?

It's the most divisive issue in this country since the Civil War. It's an issue that hasn't been resolved. Early on, I felt that I had an obligation to the troops to achieve some dignity for what they had done in Vietnam. Now it's more than that. It's for our children and the succeeding generations, so that they might understand that this national effort, however flawed in its execution, involved the best intentions of our nation. And that the East Asian region did benefit greatly from our having taken a firm stand against communist aggression, which, at that time, was rampant, not only in Vietnam, Laos, and Cambodia, but in other parts of the region, such as the Philippines, Indonesia, and Malaysia.

WILLIAM WESTMORELAND

I was sharply conscious that I was a military man,
charged not with making policy but with executing it.
WILLIAM C. WESTMORELAND, *A Soldier Reports*

Mrs. Westmoreland answers the phone. I have known her since 1964 when I was medevaced in a helicopter to Saigon, and have held a special fondness for her ever since. Known affectionately as Kitsy, she was then a "Gray Lady" making daily hospital rounds to comfort wounded soldiers. She tells me that the general's memory is slipping, but that I may judge for myself if I want to include him in my book. Regardless, she says that he would be delighted to talk with me.

The general's voice comes on the phone. It is steady and still conveys authority. After some small talk, I mention that had politicians not micromanaged the war from Washington and allowed the military to unleash its full power without political restrictions, most assuredly we would have won.

"I'm not so sure I would say that," he responds.

This surprises me because he writes in *A Soldier Reports* about having his hands tied by civilians who had little knowledge of what it would take to win and that American forces never lost a single major engagement. Before I can follow up, he asks if I have been to Quito, Ecuador. He then proceeds to tell me about a special mission that he was sent on as a young second lieutenant bachelor just out of the Military Academy. He laughs as he recalls, with remarkable lucidity, people's names and places from sixty-three years ago.

At the end of the conversation, I ask if it would be convenient for me to visit him at his home in Charleston, South Carolina. He suggests that we talk first over the phone. I decide to make an exception to my insistence that all interviews be conducted face to face and agree to call the following Monday with the provision that I would travel to Charleston if the interview warrants it.

A 1936 graduate of West Point, William Childs Westmoreland, early in his career, had all the markings of becoming chief of staff of the Army. First captain of the corps of cadets, he fought in World War II against the Germans in North Africa and Sicily and landed with the D-Day offensive on Utah Beach in France. During the Korean War, he commanded the 187th Airborne Regimental Combat Team. In 1956, he was promoted to major general, which made him the youngest two-star general in the Army at the age of forty-two. Four years later, he was the second youngest superintendent of the United States Military Academy; only Gen. Douglas MacArthur, at age thirty-nine, had been younger. With the escalation of American military involvement in Southeast Asia, President Johnson tapped Westmoreland in 1964 to command MACV. For the next four years, he would head U.S. forces in Vietnam.

I can still recall the handsome, athletic figure of General Westmoreland standing ram-rod straight in starched fatigues, chin jutting out, next to my hospital bed in Saigon. I ask him my first questions and am quickly reminded of Mrs. Westmoreland's warning about the general's memory when he requests that I refer to his book for many of his answers. I choose to print only the first part of our conversation followed by extracts from his book that respond to talking points that are on my list to ask him.

General, could we have won the war?
The whole situation was a little more complex than that. There was great fear by the administration that, if we got too aggressive, we would bring the Chinese to the battlefield. The administration wanted no part of that because the Chinese had unlimited manpower and casualties meant nothing to them.

Did you believe that to be true?
It was difficult to put us in the role of the Chinese. The Chinese had unlimited manpower, of course, and we were along the North Vietnamese border. I was of the school of thought that if we got too aggressive, the Chinese would come to the battlefield as a matter of Oriental face, if nothing else. It was not in our national interest to get in a war with China.

You were against sending American forces into North Vietnam because of the threat of China intervening?
As commander of the forces on the battlefield, my concern for my troops was primary. I didn't want to be a party to any action that would encourage China to come to the battlefield.

So you believed that the Chinese would come to the battlefield if we provoked them?

I didn't know, but I thought it was a 50/50 proposition. It was quite conceivable that they would.

Did you subscribe to the domino mind-set that if we didn't stop the aggression in Vietnam, communism would spread throughout Southeast Asia?

I knew that was a school of thought, but I was not a party to it. As field commander, I was not involved in overall strategy, which was a function of Washington. I was quite aware what my military capabilities were and did not want to encourage the Chinese to come to the battlefield.

Did you ever consider resigning because of national policy being inconsistent with the situation on the ground?

No. As a field commander on the ground I was not in a better position to control national policy than the people in Washington. So, in no case did I try to inject myself into national strategy.

Did you feel that it was your position to tell Washington when you did not agree with their strategies?

No. As a field commander, my loyalty was to the commander in chief, who was the president of the United States. I would adhere to that.

Even if it was wrong?

Well, the thing is that the president of the United States was in a better position to know whether it was right or wrong than I was.

Did you feel that your communiqués from Vietnam were given the proper evaluation by Washington?

I have to pause and think about it. It's ancient history as far as I am concerned, but my recollection is that I didn't have any negative view of that at all. Have you read my book?

Yes, sir.

I think my views are well outlined in that book. As a matter of fact, I'm having trouble resurrecting my views at the time. But my book spelled my views out at the time.

In your book, you state that the media was irresponsible in its reporting to the American public about the Tet Offensive.
Well, I am having trouble reflecting on that also. Don't I cover that in my book?

Yes, sir, you do.
I guess what I am leading up to is that my book is authentic, and I am having a hard time recalling. This may sound strange to you, but being eighty-six years old, my recollection is hazy. I wrote the book thirty years ago, and I am not going to second-guess how I felt then. It's a fact of life.

★★★★★★★★★★★★

As requested by General Westmoreland, I have extracted his words from *A Soldier Reports* [Doubleday & Company, 1976], with page numbers, and have been careful not to take his stated opinions out of context.

On the media [509–510]:
"One problem was the youth and inexperience of many correspondents. Having little or no knowledge of military history, having seen no war, and, like most in the military, having no ability in the Vietnamese language, some reporters were ill-equipped for their assignments. Short deadlines contributed to inaccuracy and some freelance writers depended upon sensationalism to sell their wares. In general, journalism appears to nurture the pontifical judgment. . . . A second problem was what may be called a herd mentality among the reporters. Everybody tended to view everything through the same pair of glasses. If it came to be generally accepted by the press, for example, that Thieu was corrupt or that his regime lacked popular support, seldom did anybody among the press elect to challenge the prevailing view. A correspondent with long experience in Vietnam, Peter Braestrup, researched in detail the reporting by news media of the enemy's 1968 Tet Offensive. Braestrup wrote: Rarely has contemporary crisis journalism turned out in retrospect to have veered so wide from reality. . . . [557] Newsmen are supposed to report events, not influence or precipitate them. Like the young David Halberstam during his vendetta with Ngo Dinh Diem, many a newsman tried to usurp the diplomat's role of formulating foreign policy. What a change

from the proposition once widely accepted that criticism of American foreign policy stops at the water's edge."

On his mission upon taking command in 1964 of American forces [69]:
"To assist the government of [South] Vietnam and its armed forces to defeat externally directed and supported communist subversion and aggression and attain an independent South Vietnam functioning in a secure environment. Although the exact wording of that objective might change from time to time, it remained essentially the same throughout American involvement."

On Gen. Douglas MacArthur's advice to not use American troops in Vietnam [168]:
". . . I reflected frequently on my talk in January 1964 with General MacArthur in his apartment at the Waldorf before my departure for Vietnam. Hopeful that the South Vietnamese could carry the burden of combat themselves, General MacArthur nevertheless saw the possibility that foreign troops might be required, in which case, he said, we should try to get as many Oriental nations as possible to help, particularly the Republic of Korea, the Philippines, and Nationalist China. Critics of the war later said that MacArthur categorically ruled out using American troops on the Asian mainland, but they were misquoting him. He had been referring only to land-locked Laos; if using American troops was the only way to save South Vietnam, he believed it would have to be done. In the general's mind, there was 'no substitute for victory.'

On the issue of China and the Soviet Union intervening if the United States took the war north [500]:
"Influencing many of the major decisions was an almost paranoid fear of nuclear confrontation with the Soviet Union and a corresponding anxiety over active participation by Chinese Communist troops. On these matters the President's advisers took undue council of their fears, for much of the time the Chinese Communists were heavily involved in their own internal problems—including the machinations of the "Red Guards"—and later the two Communist countries were preoccupied with friction along their common border, where the Soviet Union massed a threatening number of troops."

On the possibility of defeating the North Vietnamese after the Tet Offensive [498–499]:

"Yet even with the handicap of graduated response, the war still could have been brought to a favorable end following defeat of the enemy's Tet Offensive in 1968. The United States had in South Vietnam at that time the finest military force—though not the largest—ever assembled. The build-up of troops and the logistical support base were slow in coming, but at last they were there ready for decisive action. Had the president [Johnson] allowed a change in strategy and taken advantage of the enemy's weakness to enable the command to carry out operations planned over the preceding two years in Laos and Cambodia and north of the DMZ, along with intensified bombing and the mining of Haiphong Harbor, the North Vietnamese doubtlessly would have broken. But that was not to be. Press and television had created an aura not of victory but of defeat, which, coupled with the vocal antiwar elements, profoundly influenced timid officials in Washington. It was like two boxers in a ring, one having the other on the ropes, close to knock-out, when the apparent winner's second inexplicably throws in the towel."

On the employment of nuclear weapons [411]:

"If Washington officials were so intent on sending a message to Hanoi, surely small tactical nuclear weapons would be a way to tell Hanoi something, just as two atomic bombs had spoken convincingly to Japanese officials during World War II and the threat of atomic bombs induced the North Koreans to accept meaningful negotiations during the Korean War. It could be that use of a few small tactical nuclear weapons in Vietnam—or even the threat of them—might have quickly brought the war there to an end. No one could say so with certainty, of course, but surely a detailed consideration of the possibility was warranted. Although I established a small secret group to study the subject, Washington so feared that some word of it might reach the press that I was told to desist. I felt at the time and even more so now that to fail to consider this alternative was a mistake."

On Washington micromanaging [143–144]:

"Interference from Washington seriously hampered the campaign. Washington had to approve all targets in North Vietnam, and even though the Joint Chiefs submitted long-range programs, the State Department constantly interfered with individual missions. This or that target was to be hit for this or that nebulous nonmilitary reason. Missions for which planning and rehearsals had long proceeded might be canceled at the last minute. President Johnson allegedly boasted on one occasion that "they can't even bomb an outhouse without my approval." Fortunately, as time passed, the interest of the self-appointed air marshals in Washington gradually lessened, and the airmen gained greater leeway."

On Washington's bureaucrats [144]:

"Washington's timidity was an outgrowth of the advice of well-intentioned but naïve officials and of its effect on a President so politically oriented that he tried to please everybody rather than bite the bullet and make the hard decisions. To President Johnson's credit, he later realized his error. He subsequently told me that his greatest mistake was not to have fired, with the exception of Dean Rusk, the holdovers from the Kennedy administration, which he called "the Kennedy gang," a group whose loyalty to him as President he questioned. . . . [145] Those officials and some White House and State Department advisers appeared to scorn professional military thinkers in a seeming belief that presumably superior Ivy League intellects could devise some political hocus-pocus or legerdemain to bring the enemy to terms without using force to destroy his war-making capability. . . . Such gimmicks as bombing pauses and crippling target restrictions told them [the North Vietnamese] not that we understood how to use force but that we were insecure, obsessed with a paranoid concern for criticism from a segment of American and international public opinion that ignored the fact that the United States was not out to conquer but to repel aggression."

On civilian control over the military [145]:

"However desirable the American system of civilian control of the military, it was a mistake to permit appointive civilian officials lacking military experience and knowledge of military history and oblivious to the lessons of communist diplomatic machinations to wield undue influence in the decision-making process. Over-all control of the military is one thing; shackling professional military men with restrictions in professional matters imposed by civilians who lack military understanding is another."

On taking orders from civilians [168]:

"I was sharply conscious that I was a military man, charged not with making policy but with executing it. Yet if the National Security

Council and the President deemed it in the interest of the United States to save South Vietnam from Communism, I bore the responsibility as the American military commander in Vietnam to advise from a military standpoint what had to be done to achieve that goal. Never in the Mission Council, chaired by the ambassador in Saigon, was there mention of pulling out and leaving the South Vietnamese to their fate. Like me, the others of the U.S. Mission were charged not with making policy or grand strategy but with executing it."

On McNamara and President Johnson [317–318]:

"Once the penchant of niggling officials in Washington for quibbling over B-52 bomb targets had passed, President Johnson and Secretary McNamara afforded me marked independence in how I ran the war within the borders of South Vietnam, and no commander could ever hope for greater support than I received from Admiral [Ulysses Grant, Jr.] Sharp at CINCPAC and from General [Earle G. ("Bus")] Wheeler and the other members of the Joint Chiefs. Yet a commander must recognize that political considerations will never allow independence. Politicians are imbued with French Premier Georges Clemenceau's dictum, however erroneously quoted, that "war is too important to be left to the generals." A commander must learn to live with frustration, interference, irritation, disappointment, and criticism, as long as he is sure they will not contribute to failure. I suffered my problems in Vietnam because I believed that success eventually would be ours despite political interference. I knew my forces would never be defeated."

On bombing North Vietnam [135]:

"The only way bombing the North could convince the North Vietnamese to desist was to hit surely, swiftly, and powerfully, not with everything in the American arsenal, for that would have been overkill, but with sufficient force to hurt and to demonstrate a clear, firm resolve. The strikes would have to be aimed from the first at vital targets, such as the limited but nonetheless important industrial facilities in the vicinity of Hanoi and Haiphong, and would have to include mining Haiphong Harbor. Washington's phobia that sudden heavy air strikes and mining the harbor would trigger Chinese Communist or Russian intervention was chimerical. Even had Washington adopted a strong bombing policy, I still doubt that the North Vietnamese would have relented. To force the North Vietnamese to desist, we had to do more than hurt their homeland; we had to demonstrate that they could not win in the South. . . ."

On the Tet Offensive [390–391]:

"Nobody in Saigon to my knowledge anticipated even remotely the psychological impact the offensive would have in the United States. Militarily, the offensive was foredoomed to failure, destined to be over everywhere, except in Saigon and Hue and at Khe Sanh, in a day or so. . . . The American people absorbed those psychological blows with little trauma. No one to my knowledge foresaw that, in terms of public opinion, press and television would transform what was undeniably a catastrophic military defeat for the enemy into a presumed debacle for Americans and South Vietnamese, an attitude that still lingers in the minds of many."

On ARVN fighting ability [118]:

". . . ARVN troops, when they came face to face with the enemy, more often than not gave as good as they got. When it came to life-and-death struggle on the field, the political turmoil had little effect on the rank and file. The effect instead was on the upper leadership—division and corps commanders—who were reluctant to take risks or act decisively, to move. If you did nothing, the government could hardly say you had done something wrong. . . . [305] The American news media contributed to a false image of the ARVN's performance. Serving an American public, the U.S. press and television understandably focused on American units, seldom covering ARVN operations unless something spectacular happened, such as heavy losses. . . . Following in the tradition of harshly critical American reporting established in the Diem days, few American reporters could find anything good to say about the ARVN. Limited messing and housing facilities with ARVN units discouraged newsmen from participating in ARVN operations, and so piqued by these newsmen's constant criticism were many South Vietnamese commanders that they did little to encourage their visits. One division commander refused to have an American reporter in his zone of operations. Many said better suffer in silence than try to change the unchangeable. One senior official said how presumptuous it was of some Americans to think the Vietnamese wanted them around forever when in fact it would be such a relief to be rid of the cynical criticism of the American press and congress."

On the inferior weapons provided ARVN forces [191–192]:

"I asked Secretary McNamara as a matter of urgency [in 1965] to equip all American forces with the M-16 [automatic rifle] and then also to equip the ARVN with it. Officials in the Department of Defense unfortunately disregarded the urgency of my request and failed to gear American industry to meet the need. Not until 1967 were there enough M-16s for all American troops, and only then was I able by degrees to begin equipping the ARVN. The ARVN thus long fought at a serious disadvantage against the enemy's automatic AK-47, armed as they were with World War II's semiautomatic M-1, whose kick when fired appeared to rock the small Vietnamese soldiers back on their heels. Armed with a light carbine, little more than a pea shooter when compared with the AK-47, the South Vietnamese militia was at an even worse disadvantage."

On body count as a measure of success [332]:

"Statistics were, admittedly, an imperfect gauge of progress, yet in the absence of conventional front lines, how else to measure it? Furthermore, Secretary McNamara and his Assistant Secretary of Defense for Systems Analysis, Alan Enthoven, constantly prodded for more and more statistics. . . . The most controversial of the statistics was the number of enemy killed, which was based on tally in the field and known as "body count." I abhorred the term. A WAC secretary in my Saigon office, Sergeant Betty Reed, told me years later that the only time during several years in my office she ever heard me swear was when somebody mentioned "body count.""

On resigning [318]:

"Only once did the possibility of resigning enter my mind, and that was not because of the question of success or failure. That happened early in 1968 when I saw the Joint Chiefs for a time leaning toward a parochial decision favoring one of the armed services in a matter that I saw as the field commander's prerogative and one that, if taken, would have been detrimental to my command."

GLOSSARY

AK47	Standard infantry weapon of the North Vietnamese and Viet Cong soldiers
AP	Associated Press
APC	Armored personnel carrier
ARVN	Army of the Republic of Vietnam
AWOL	Absent without leave
BAR	Browning automatic rifle
CIA	Central Intelligence Agency
CIB	Combat Infantryman Badge
CINC	Commander in Chief
CINCPAC	Commander in Chief, Pacific Command
Charlie	GI slang for Viet Cong and NVA soldier
Chopper	Helicopter
CNN	Cable News Network
COSVN	Central Office for South Vietnam
DMZ	Demilitarized zone
DOA	Department of Army
DOD	Department of Defense
FBI	Federal Bureau of Investigation
GI	U.S. Army soldier
GVN	Government of [South] Vietnam
HUAC	House Un-American Activities Committee
JCS	Joint Chiefs of Staff
KIA	Killed in action
MACV	Military Assistance Command, Vietnam
Medevac	Medically evacuate (usually by helicopter)
MIA	Missing in action
M16	Standard weapon of the U.S. soldier
NATO	North Atlantic Treaty Organization
NBC	National Broadcasting Company
NCO	Noncommissioned officer
NLF	National Liberation Front (Viet Cong)
NSC	National Security Council
Nuke	Nuclear weapon
NVA	North Vietnamese Army
NVN	North Vietnam
OSS	Office of Strategic Services (wartime intelligence agency of the U.S government and predecessor to the CIA)

PFC	Private First Class
POW	Prisoner of war
PTSD	Posttraumatic stress disorder
RA	Regular Army
RVN	Republic of Vietnam (South Vietnam)
R&R	Rest and recreation
SAC	Strategic Air Command
SAM	Surface-to-air missile
SDS	Students for a Democratic Society
SVN	South Vietnam
UPI	United Press International
USARV	U.S. Army, Vietnam
VC	Viet Cong
WAC	Woman's Army Corps
WWII	World War II

INDEX

Abrams, Creighton W. ("Abe"),
189, 207; Cambodian incursion
orders of, 15, 21; Kissinger on,
121; Schwarzkopf on, 205–206;
versus Westmoreland, 24
Allen, George, 61
Alsop, Joseph, 3, 63
American Guerilla (Hilsman), 95
American soldiers fighting in Vietnam: Hayden on, 78–79; McCaffrey on, 154–155; Schwarzkopf
on, 208; Webb on, 217. *See also*
military draft
Anderson, George W., 172
antiwar demonstrators/spokesper-
sons: on Cambodian incursion,
16, 21; Cambodian incursion
and, 135; Davison on morale
and, 21–22; Ellsberg and, 35–36;
Kissinger on, 122, 123; Lake
and, 132–133; McCaffrey on,
156–157; McCain on, 170; Nixon's strategy and, 32, 33–34,
113; North Vietnam and, 73;
Polgar on, 191; Webb on, 219–
221. *See also* Hayden, Tom;
Kerry, John
Aptheker, Herbert, 70
Army of the Republic of Vietnam
(ARVN): Davison on capabilities
of, 19; Halberstam on, 59–60; Le
on, 138, 141–142, 143; Westmoreland on, 235–236. *See also*
South Vietnam
Army Special Forces, 46

Arnett, Peter, 1–13, 55, 61; on
American efforts in Vietnam, 5,
9–10; antiwar nature of, 10; on
destruction of Ben Tre, 8–9; on
direct criticism of War, 9; on
domino theory, 6; on Ellsberg,
27; on Johnson analysis, 8; loses
objectivity in reporting, 10; on
McNamara, 6–7, 8; on My Lai
incident, 10; on Operation
Tailwind, 2–3; on reasons for
Vietnam conflict, 4–5; on reporting on Vietnam conflict, 5–6; on
returning to Vietnam, 11; on Saigon's last days, 11–13; on Vietnam conflict reporters, 3; on Vietnam conflict reporting, 4; war
assessment story by, 9; on Washington press, 7–8; on Westmoreland analysis, 6–7; on Westmoreland's viewpoint, 7
Asia experts, 101–102, 130, 182

Ball, George, 62, 182
Barrow, Robert H., 225
Ben Tre, Vietnam, 8–9
Berlin: airlift, 192; contingency
planning, 46
Bernstein, Carl, 41
Best and the Brightest, The (Hal-
berstam), 9, 56, 66, 170, 224
body counts, 100, 184, 209–210,
236
bombing, strategic, 32, 96–97
Braestrup, Peter, 221, 230

handling of war, 154; on winning
the war, 157, 158–159
McCaffrey, Jill, 153
McCaffrey, William J., 150,
151–152
McCain, John S., 165
McCain, John S., Jr. ("Jack"), 17,
20, 165
McCain, John S., III, 165–174; on
antiwar demonstrators, 170; on
close calls for, 167, 174; on domino theory, 171; on Joint Chiefs,
172–173; on McNamara, 172;
on military strategy in Vietnam,
170–171; normalizing relations
with Hanoi, 108; as POW, 166,
169, 174; shot down over Hanoi,
168–169; on Vietnam lessons,
172; volunteers for Vietnam,
167; on Washington's handling
of war, 168; on winning the war,
168
McCarthy, Eugene, 109
McCone, John, 102, 182
McGovern, George, 122, 220, 226
McMaster, H. R., 160, 175–185,
220; on acceptable casualties
level, 184; on causes of Vietnam
War, 175; interviews by, 177–
178; on Johnson's strategy, 183;
Joint Chiefs research by, 176–
177; on Kennedy's strategy,
182–183; LBJ administration
research by, 177, 178; on McNamara, 178–179, 181, 182; on military strategy, 183–184, 185;
multiarchival research technique
of, 177–178
McNamara, Robert S.: on America's Vietnam strategy, 6–7; on
body count, 236; Davison on,
18; Diem assassination and, 102;

Ellsberg on, 39; escalating war
and, 104; Galloway on, 175;
Haig and, 41, 42; Haig on, 47–
48; Halberstam on, 56–57, 60,
61–62; Hilsman and, 95, 96; Hilsman on, 98, 100–101, 105; Joint
Chiefs and, 180–181; Kennedy
and, 64, 97; Kerry on, 113–114;
Lake on, 130; McCaffrey on,
160; McCain on, 172; McMaster
on, 178–179, 179–180, 182,
185; McNaughton and, 29; on
National Guard and Reserves
activation, 17–18; nuclear weapons considerations of, 182; Pentagon Papers and, 27, 31; Schwarzkopf on, 206, 211; as Vietnam
War architect, 7; Vietnam War
reporters and, 7–8; Webb on,
220; Westmoreland on, 234; win-
ning-the-war claims, 18
McNaughton, John, 29, 184
media coverage: of ARVN, 141–
142; communists use of, 8;
Desert Storm, 210; Webb on,
220–221; Westmoreland on,
230–231
Merrill's Marauders (WWII), 95
Mildren, Frank, 207
Military Assistance Command,
Vietnam (MACV), 20–21
military draft: Davison on student
deferments, 22; Haig on student
deferments, 51–52; Hayden and,
69; Webb on, 222–223. See also
American soldiers fighting in Vietnam; professional military
military-industrial complex, 50, 65,
98, 182
Mitchell, John, 28, 37, 76
Morris, Roger, 135
Munro, Ed, 83